How did the concept of judicial review
get involved in Marbury

- Made courts

~~James Madison~~ is considered an federalist

~~Marbury~~ Antifederalist

How does ~~Jefferson~~ feel about

Hamilton — wanted a strong national bank
                        there fore he is
                            a federalist

Jefferson — Antifederalist — Jefferson thought the
courts had to much power, believed that
~~powers~~ should rest in the government.

When reading, look for
① The different ~~between~~ public/private law
② pressure groups
③ * for

A Conflict of Rights

Also by Melvin I. Urofsky

Big Steel and the Wilson Administration (1969)

A Mind of One Piece: Brandeis and American Reform (1970)

American Zionism from Herzl to the Holocaust (1975)

We Are One! American Jewry and Israel (1978)

Louis D. Brandeis and the Progressive Tradition (1980)

A Voice That Spoke for Justice: The Life and Times of Stephen S. Wise (1981)

Two Hundred Years of Mr. Jefferson's Idea: Religious Liberty in America (1986)

A March of Liberty: A Constitutional History of the United States (1987)

The Continuity of Change: The Supreme Court and Individual Liberties (1990)

Edited by Melvin I. Urofsky

Why Teachers Strike: Teachers' Rights and Community Control (1970)

Perspectives on Urban America (1973)

Letters of Louis D. Brandeis (5 vols., 1971–1978) (with David W. Levy)

Essays on American Zionism (1979)

Turn to the South: Essays on Southern Jewish History (1979)
   (with Nathan Kaganoff)

The Supreme Court, the Bill of Rights, and the Law (1986)

The Douglas Papers (1987) (with Philip E. Urofsky)

*From Confederation to Constitution: Documents on the Constitution
   and Ratification* (1988)

Documents of American Constitutional and Legal History (1989)

"Half-Son, Half-Brother": Letters of Louis D. Brandeis to Felix Frankfurter
   (1990) (with David W. Levy)

A Conflict
of Rights

The Supreme Court
and Affirmative Action

Melvin I. Urofsky

CHARLES SCRIBNER'S SONS
New York

COLLIER MACMILLAN CANADA
Toronto

MAXWELL MACMILLAN INTERNATIONAL
New York   Oxford   Singapore   Sydney

Charles Scribner's Sons
Macmillan Publishing Company
866 Third Avenue, New York, NY 10022

Collier Macmillan Canada, Inc.
1200 Eglinton Avenue East, Suite 200
Don Mills, Ontario M3C 3N1

Library of Congress Cataloging-in-Publication Data
Urofsky, Melvin I.
    A conflict of rights : the Supreme Court and affirmative action /
  Melvin Urofsky.
        p.   cm.
    Includes bibliographical references and index.
    ISBN 0-684-19069-9
    1. Johnson, Paul, 1925—Trials, litigation, etc.   2. Santa Clara
  County Transportation Agency—Trials, litigation, etc.
    3. Discrimination in employment—Law and legislation—United States.
    4. Affirmative action programs—Law and legislation—United States.
    5. Affirmative action programs—California—Santa Clara County.
    I. Title.
    KF228.J64U76   1991
    342.73'0873—dc20
    [347.302873]   90-39646   CIP

Macmillan books are available at special discounts for bulk purchases for sales
promotions, premiums, fund-raising, or educational use. For details, contact:

    Special Sales Director
    Macmillan Publishing Company
    866 Third Avenue
    New York, NY 10022

10 9 8 7 6 5 4 3 2 1

Printed in the United States of America

For
A. HARRY PASSOW on his special birthday
and for
SHIRLEY S. PASSOW for being so special

Contents

Preface
and Acknowledgments

There is an old story of two feuding peasants in a small Eastern European village who finally appealed to the rabbi to resolve their dispute. The first peasant went in and with great emotion told the rabbi his side of the story. The rabbi sat carefully, and then said, "You are right!"

Then the second peasant came in, and with equal fervor and conviction presented his case. The rabbi looked very thoughtful, and then said, "My son, you are right!"

The rabbi's wife, who had been sitting quietly in the corner while both men made their appeal, could hardly restrain herself until the second peasant left the room. "What have you done?" she cried. "You told both of them they were right! How could you do that?"

The rabbi scratched his head for a second, and then turned to his wife. "And you, my dear," he said, "you are also right!"

As one looks at the social and legal aspects of affirmative action in general and of the *Johnson* case in particular, one often feels like this poor rabbi, wanting to shout "You are both right!" Except for extremists, most people recognize that affirmative action and the social and economic conditions that are behind it are very complex and not amenable to simple or easy answers. It is not a question of good versus evil, an obviously "correct" policy as opposed to one obviously "wrong," and certainly not a story of "good guys" and "bad guys." The story that follows, stories actually, of Paul Johnson and Diane Joyce, of Steve Woodside and Connie Brooks, of Michael Baratz and Kristy Sermersheim, of William Brennan and Antonin Scalia, are not stories of heroes and villains.

Shortly after the Court handed down its decision in the *Johnson* case, I told a friend that I thought it would make a good case study. It involved not only a difficult question of law and an even harder problem in social policy; here one could see how great issues and cases affected common people, men and women who go to work every day, and whose lives, whether they want it or not, are affected by policies over which they have little control.

Because Santa Clara County saw that it had no women in a skilled-craft category in its Transportation Agency, it instituted an affirmative action plan to remedy what it saw as a problem, and also to foreclose potential lawsuits. Diane Joyce and Paul Johnson both applied for one of the jobs in that category, a road dispatcher. Joyce believed she qualified but would be frozen out by the old-boy network in the agency, so she appealed to the affirmative action officer, and eventually got the job. Paul Johnson thought he had earned the position, and had been discriminated against. Joyce did not see herself as a feminist heroine; she was a widow who needed to earn more money for her family. Johnson did not see himself as a David battling the bureaucratic Goliaths, but as a person who had had something stolen from him that he wanted back. So he did what many Americans do every day of the year—they appeal to the law for redress. Sometimes it works for them, and sometimes not.

Interestingly, when I interviewed Paul Johnson and Diane Joyce in the summer of 1989, both of them said they wanted fairness, they wanted equal opportunity, they wanted to be judged on their own merits. They came at these ideals from different angles, but in an ideal world one would not find the two of them very far apart. They are pretty much old-fashioned Americans who believe fervently in their country and in its promise of equality for all under the law.

Ultimately it was their human stories, and not the broader issue of affirmative action, that drew me to write this book. In teaching constitutional history, I try to remind my students—and myself— that while "great" cases may enunciate important legal principles, they start with people, men and women who for one reason or another believe they have not been treated rightly, and appeal to the law for help.

Brown v. *Board of Education* pronounces the great principle that segregation in public schools is constitutionally wrong; it starts with a little girl in the Kansas City school system, Linda Brown.

Gideon v. *Wainwright* assures each American that if faced with a criminal prosecution, he or she will have access to an attorney regardless of finances. That noble idea is written into the Bill of Rights, but it is a reality and not just a platitude because of a rather unlikely hero, the scruffy Clarence Earl Gideon.

Whether *Johnson* v. *Transportation Agency, Santa Clara County* ever takes its place among the "great" cases or not, it dealt with an important issue, and we can understand that issue better if we can place it in a human context. That is what I have tried to do in the pages that follow.

There are many people who helped make my idea of a book on the *Johnson* case into a reality. My editor at Scribners, Edward T. Chase, was immediately enthusiastic about the idea, and as I learned, Ned's enthusiasms are an irresistible force. Other folk at Scribners who helped turn the manuscript into a real book included Ned's assistant, Hamilton Cain, and designer Erich Hobbing; Barbara Campo and Ann Bartunek did the copyediting the way any author loves, with a maximum of competence and a minimum of unnecessary queries. As always, I could count on my agent, Audrey A. Wolf, for friendship and sanity. I also derived great pride and pleasure in having my son Robert I. Urofsky as research assistant throughout the project.

A summer fellowship from the National Endowment for the Humanities provided time for research and writing, while a Littleton–Griswold grant from the American Historical Association helped to underwrite travel costs. I am grateful for their support.

I owe a special debt of thanks to Justice William J. Brennan, Jr., who generously permitted me to examine his files on the *Johnson* case.

What made this case different, at least to me, were the people involved, and their stories are at the heart of this book. I want to thank Michael Baratz, Constance Brooks, Charles Fried, James Dawson, David Rosenfeld, Kristine Sermersheim, Suzanne Wilson, and Steven Woodside for taking time out of their busy schedules to talk to me about their roles in the case.

The two key interviews were, of course, with Paul Johnson and Diane Joyce; both invited me into their homes and spent several hours answering innumerable questions. I made only one promise to each of them: that I would try to tell the story fairly. When they read this book, I hope their judgment will be that I kept my word.

This book is dedicated to my aunt and uncle, who have played so important a part in our lives. When my wife and I first embarked on our respective careers, Harry and Shirley provided not only role models but understanding and support for what we were trying to do. They are a tough act to follow.

A Conflict
of Rights

1

Diane Joyce
Makes a Phone Call

Paul Johnson always believed that if you set goals and worked hard, you could achieve them. He had set a goal—the dispatcher's job in the Santa Clara County highway department—and he had worked hard, and soon, his boss told him, the job would be his. Johnson had taken the examination for the position in the spring of 1980, and placed second among the seven finalists. Under the county rules, the supervisor could choose any one of the top seven, and in a second interview, conducted by the department supervisors, they had made clear that Paul was their choice. He had been filling in on the job, he was popular with the other workers, and he knew the business; once the paperwork had been taken care of, he would have the dispatcher's mike on a regular basis, with the title and the $480-a-week salary.[1]

Diane Joyce had also been one of the seven finalists; like Paul Johnson, she also believed that if you worked hard and did the work well, then you ought to be rewarded for your efforts. But as a widow with young children, she found that the best-paying jobs always went to men, and she did not consider that fair. As a clerk in the dispatcher's office, Joyce realized that she could do the job, and that it paid a lot more than she would ever make as a clerical worker. To get to be dispatcher, though, she had to have experience on a road crew, a job no woman had ever held before. Joyce forced the road department to hire her, worked on road crews for four years, and took the dispatcher's test at the same time as Paul John-

1

son. Then she began to hear rumors of a done deal, that the supervisors had already chosen their man, and that she had never had a fair shot at the job. The more she thought about it, the madder she got, until one morning she pulled off on the side of a road, dropped a dime in the telephone, and called the county's affirmative action officer, Helena Lee.

"I'm Diane Joyce," she said. "I'm number four on a list for road dispatcher. No woman has ever held this position before. Are you interested?"

Helena Lee took her name, asked how she could reach her, and said she would be back in touch.[2]

Santa Clara County stretches from the southern tip of San Francisco Bay down through one of California's lushest valleys, divided from the Pacific Ocean on the west by the Santa Cruz mountain range. In 1777, Spanish priests raised a cross in a laurel thicket near the Guadalupe River and named it Mission Santa Clara; that same year, settlers built their first home nearby in the Pueblo of San Jose. When California became a state in 1850, Santa Clara served as the first capital, and the region prospered as French settlers planted vineyards in New Almedon. Grain fields gave way to orchards and population grew slowly; at the end of World War II, Santa Clara County had about 290,000 people, most of them engaged in some form of agricultural work. County government was small and simple, and the roads met the needs of the local farmers.[3]

With a Mediterranean climate, scenic location, and general prosperity, Santa Clara seemed a wonderful place to live and work. Before long, a lot of people had that idea. The presence of Stanford University at Palo Alto, in the northern part of the county, attracted aerospace and electronics firms, and the sleepy agricultural area soon had another name, Silicon Valley. The 2,600 high-technology companies now in the county produce more than 22 percent of American-made electronic computers. County population reached 1.4 million by 1988, with San Jose, the county seat, ranked as the fourteenth largest city in the United States. Companies in and around San Jose produced more than $24.7 billion worth of goods in 1987, the fifth highest in the nation. The comfortable agricultural area had now become a prosperous commercial community, with the highest median family income of any metropolitan area in California; two out of every five households earned $50,000 or more a year.[4]

As the county grew so did county government and the road and transportation system, and much of the political style derived from the highly educated and sophisticated newcomers who flocked to Silicon Valley. As Suzanne Wilson, a member of the Board of Supervisors, noted: "You have to look at who came to this valley in the 1950s—engineers. Who did they bring with them but the kind of women that engineers marry—probably college-educated, but also women who were willing to pick up and move, women who had the same sense of adventure and need to expand their horizons."[5]

An "IBM wife" herself, Wilson says that the mix of farmers, blue-collar workers and educated professionals has created the unique political mix in the county. The people in general are conservative, especially on fiscal matters, but are quite progressive, even liberal, on social issues. A self-described "liberal feminist," Wilson has been elected for three terms from the most conservative district in the county.

But liberal or conservative, the county residents have gotten used to women in politics, women who "are very outspoken and aggressive in their needs." In 1989 women held three of the five seats on the county Board of Supervisors, and a woman county executive supervised daily affairs; the San Jose City Council had eight women among the eleven members. Perhaps the high percentage of women in local government accounted for the county's early endorsement of a voluntary affirmative action plan.

Although affirmative action is normally considered tied to the civil rights movement, blacks constitute only 3.4 percent of Santa Clara County; the two largest minority groups are Hispanics (17.5 percent) and Asians (7.7 percent).[6] From the start, county officials involved with drafting the affirmative action plan, as well as union and citizen groups, had assumed it would apply to women as well as to minorities. Steven Woodside, who would later defend the plan before the Supreme Court, worked on it as a junior county counsel in 1973, and recalled how at the time there had been a lot of discussion in the county about nontraditional jobs for women, job-sharing, and other means of creating opportunities for women.[7] Over the next several years, however, application of the plan appears to have been uneven. Some agency heads made a determined effort to bring in women and minorities; in other departments, the plan might as well have not existed.

The Transportation Agency, like other county units, had its own affirmative action officer in its personnel office, but at least in the highway section[8] things had not changed for a long time. As a number of people described it, the road unit had a "good ole boy" network almost impenetrable to outsiders. Union leader Michael Baratz claimed:

> It's families, all connected, and it's very political. . . . You had to be in the family to get a job, and you found cousins and daughters and sons, and they're all working there. . . . The bottom line is, these guys were racist and sexist. They didn't want women, and they had no intention of ever hiring a woman or a minority person. I'm not saying they were mean-spirited racists. It's just they wanted "one of the boys," somebody they could curse and spit with.[9]

Paul Johnson was, in the best sense of the term, one of the boys, despite the efforts of some people to paint him as a bigoted ogre. His attorney, James Dawson, perhaps caught this best when he described Johnson as the sort of man you would like to have as a neighbor—quiet, industrious, and decent.[10] He had been born in 1925 to Kansas farmers who barely eked out a living. His mother was pregnant with her fifth son when his father died of pneumonia. Unable to hold the family together, she parceled Paul, just eight, and the other boys out to various relatives.

He grew up in Gladewater, Texas, and in World War II joined the navy and served on a submarine. After the war Johnson worked as a roustabout, a roughneck, in the oilfields until he married Betty Elliot, with whom he would have three sons. In 1948 they moved to San Jose, and Paul got a job with Pacific Coast & Aggregate, a construction firm that later became part of Lone Star Industries.[11] He worked for the company seventeen years as a dispatcher and supervisor. In the mid-sixties the company transferred him to their Oakland facility, at a higher salary and with the potential for promotion. The Johnsons by this time owned their home in San Jose, and did not want to uproot their three sons from the local schools. For a few months Paul commuted more than four hours a day, a situation that he and his family found very stressful, so he looked around closer to home. With the building boom in Santa Clara County, the Public Works Department, as it was then known, gladly hired a man familiar with road construction.

Johnson began as a Road Yard Clerk II in the East Yard in 1967, with responsibility for requisitioning and purchasing materials for county road construction and maintenance, including road surfacing materials, signs, and concrete culverts. In emergencies, he had the task of finding whatever equipment and supplies might be needed and making sure they got to the site.[12] Paul occupied an office adjacent to the East Yard dispatcher, and would occasionally fill in if the regular dispatcher took a break or was out sick or on vacation.

In 1979 the county reclassified all the clerical positions and, as part of a general reorganization, downgraded Johnson's position and reduced the salary. Realizing that he had no chance for advancement unless he changed jobs, Johnson requested reassignment as a Road Maintenance Worker II. The road maintenance category had several levels, and could also lead to other higher-paying jobs, such as dispatcher.[13] In fact, Johnson had already taken the dispatcher's test once, in 1974, just to see how well he could do, and had qualified. Another person, Ron Neal, had been appointed, and had been in the job for five years before being promoted to road foreman.

So in 1979 the dispatcher's job came open again, and this time Paul Johnson felt confident he would be the next dispatcher. "I had almost twenty years' experience . . . and I knew there was no one else taking the test that was anywhere near qualified as I was." For one thing, he had in effect been the acting dispatcher ever since Neal had been promoted; personnel rules allowed people to "work out of class" temporarily until openings could be filled through the regular hiring procedures. "Usually, if you're doing the job, you automatically get it." Johnson also believed that "99 percent" of his coworkers and his supervisors supported him.[14]

When Johnson had applied for the dispatcher's job in 1974, the procedures had called for a written test. This time candidates sat for an oral board, where people from outside the department would question them on their knowledge and demeanor, asking questions such as "If you were faced with this type of problem, what would you do?" Twelve applicants originally applied; seven of them scored over seventy to qualify for the position. Under the county personnel policies, a "rule of seven" applied; the hiring supervisor could choose any one of the seven people in the final pool. The Transportation Agency, however, also had a second, informal oral interview with departmental supervisors. Johnson scored a seventy-five on the first board, although that was not the highest score. After the second board, Bert Di Basilio, the general superintendent, told Johnson that its members had strongly endorsed him, and that the job would soon be his; a few days later he found out otherwise.

Paul Johnson fit in easily to the camaraderie of the road yard; Diane Joyce did not. Born in Chicago in 1937, the only child of union stalwarts, she learned early on that she had to stand up for her rights; she also learned that in a male-dominated world, life would not always be fair. After a brief stint at the University of Illinois, she took a test for a computer programmer trainee and scored well, but was told that the company only hired men for those jobs. Another lesson she learned was that when she did stand up for her rights, not everyone would cheer.

Married at eighteen and eventually the mother of four children, Joyce went to work as a bookkeeper in 1958 when her husband, Donald, a factory hand, was laid off during the recession. When he did find a job, he told her to quit, and she refused. Donald stormed into an attorney's office, only to learn that employment did not constitute grounds for a divorce. He eventually accepted the situation, and Joyce continued to work. She had seven years' seniority as an account clerk at the Triner Scale Company when the firm hired a man to do part of her job, and paid him thirty-five dollars a week more. When she asked why, they told her that she had a husband to support her. A year later, in 1969, Donald Joyce died, and Diane decided to move to California. "I wasn't afraid to go out there on my own," she recalled. "I had a trade, and I knew everybody in California needed a bookkeeper."[15]

She rented a house in Santa Clara and got a clerical job with the county's education office, at $506 a month. In early 1972 Joyce heard of a vacancy for a senior account clerk in the Transportation Agency which paid fifty dollars more a month, a lot of money for a widow with small children. Although the hiring supervisors told her matter-of-factly that they preferred a man, the job had recently been downgraded, and only women applied; Diane got the job. For a few months, she kept quiet, but she saw that women had most of the clerical jobs, while men had the better-paying road jobs. Joyce also watched what the dispatcher did, and said to herself, "I can do that, it's not that hard, and he makes $5,000 a year more than I do." When the dispatcher's job came open in 1974, she applied, only to be told that she needed road-crew experience.

Joyce calls the requirement for road-crew experience an "artificial barrier." Paul Johnson had no road-crew experience, yet the county accepted his application and never said a word about road work. As for the job itself, both Joyce and Johnson admit that a good part of the work is clerical, and that the most important part is knowing about what sort of equipment and materials are needed for different jobs. She began to pick up the information, and before long she, too, filled in when the dispatcher at her yard went on break. Unlike Paul Johnson, however, she never got assigned to work as a dispatcher "out of class."[16]

Whether it was an artificial barrier or not, Joyce realized that she would have to get the road-crew experience if she ever hoped to become a dispatcher. As she filled out an application at her desk, her supervisor came in.

"What are you doing?" he asked.

"Applying for a road-maintenance man."

"Don't you realize that you're taking a man's job away?" he shouted at her.

Diane had been listening to this all her life, and had finally had enough.

7

"No, I'm not," she replied, "because a man can sit right here where I'm sitting."[17]

She took evening courses on road maintenance and light equipment, and scored an eighty-seven on the test, coming in third. The county had ten vacancies, and Joyce got one of them. For the next four years she worked on road crews, doing everything from flagging traffic to shoveling hot tar. Although she says that she "had a ball" and the men on the gangs treated her well, she also tells stories of constant harassment from some of her coworkers as well as her supervisors.[18]

Joyce had learned from her parents that strong unions can protect their members from management persecution. She joined Local 715 of the Service Employees' International Union and quickly became a leading figure in union activities. Her coworkers, even if they resented her presence on the road crews, recognized her intelligence, and elected her shop steward. "I got to do the dishes," Joyce explained. "I think they saw I was intelligent. I think they saw I knew the rules, and I think they saw I could do a good job. And they being basically a very lazy bunch, I was a natural."[19]

She certainly knew the rules, and realized that if a harassing practice violated the union's contract, she could file a grievance and be protected from overt retaliation. One time her supervisor reprimanded her in writing for an alleged safety violation, even though normally a first or minor violation triggered only an informal verbal counseling. Joyce then learned that there had been six accidents in which people had been injured in the previous six months because of unsafe practices, and not one of the *men* had even been given a verbal warning.

When Joyce complained to the supervisor, he got a big grin on his face, and said, "What are you going to do about it?"

"I'm going to grieve it," she replied.

"Aha, you can't," he gloated. "You can't grieve safety."

"Watch me," she shot back.

Joyce had helped negotiate the last union contract, and while a worker could not grieve a safety reprimand, she could grieve harassment. When she got her case to the hearing stage, the personnel officer asked her what she wanted.

"Simple: either all six of those guys who got hurt because of safety violations get written reprimands, or tear mine up."

The hearing officer looked at the supervisor, who recognized that writing *post hoc* reprimands would make him look bad; he resentfully agreed to tear up Diane Joyce's.[20]

Joyce's role as a union shop steward endeared her to union officials, one reason they came to her defense later on in the case. But it did not endear her to the supervisors, nor to the men in the yards who opposed the union, such as Paul Johnson. Although road workers had been among the founders of the county employees' union, many of them either did not want any union at all, or perceived SEIU as a "women's union," and wanted to be associated with the Teamsters or the Operating Engineers.

Johnson, according to one union official, was the acknowledged leader of a cadre of antiunion stalwarts. He once came to a union meeting in the yard with a sandwich board saying "I Hate Local 715." The union's contract with the county gave it the right to have bulletin boards in all county offices, where news of union activities could be posted. Paul Johnson, with at least the tacit endorsement of his supervisor, put up his own bulletin board, and there he would tack up newspaper clippings of union leaders getting arrested or accounts of union funds embezzled.[21]

Looking back now, Diane Joyce cannot believe how naïve she was at the time not to recognize that the yard bosses had already chosen Paul Johnson. She began to hear stories that Johnson had been selected, but "I didn't want to believe them." Then she got a card informing her that she had qualified for the dispatcher's post, and that she should call Bert Di Basilio, the general superintendent, to arrange for an interview with the informal board. She called Di Basilio to tell him that she wanted the job; then, according to the procedures, he was to let her know within three days when the interview would take place.

Ten days passed, and Joyce still had not heard anything, so on a Friday afternoon she drove over to the East Yard where Di Basilio had his office. She told him that she hoped the interview would not be set up for the following Tuesday, since she had a four-hour disaster-preparedness class all that morning, part of her responsibilities as safety steward for the West Yard. Di Basilio told her he did not know when it would be. The following Monday when she got back to the yard after work on the roads, she found a note that the interview would be the following morning at ten o'clock, right in the middle of her class. As Joyce laconically noted, "It's hard for me to believe that's just coincidental." That "coincidence," together with the rumors she had been hearing that Paul Johnson already had the job sewed up, led her to take action and call the affirmative action officer.

Following her interview with the superintendents, nothing happened. "I don't hear anything for three weeks," Joyce later recalled. "Not a word. Nobody calls me back, but there's no announcement [that Johnson got the job]. So I knew something was up. . . . And I thought, the longer it takes, the better off I'll be." But even during these three weeks, she did not believe she would actually get the job. The affirmative action office, as Joyce well knew, did not have any power to make appointments.[22] In fact, unbeknownst to her, the affirmative action people had begun looking into her case right after she had called them, and in a very effective manner.

Normally, the responsibility for hiring a dispatcher would rest with the supervisor for road operations, a man named Ron Shields, who not only thought well of Paul Johnson but had already had several run-ins with Diane Joyce. Once Shields made his decision, it required only routine approval from James Graebner, the director of the Transportation Agency. Before Shields could get that approval, the county affirmative action office notified Victor Morton, the Transportation Agency's affirmative action coordinator, about Diane Joyce's telephone call, and he immediately went to see Graebner. As Graebner later testified at the trial, Morton

just walked into the office one day and said, "Hey, this is a promotional opportunity, and you need to know about it." Mr. Morton was less interested in the particular individual; he felt that this was an opportunity for us to take a step toward meeting our affirmative action goals, and because there was only one person on the list who was one of the protected groups, he felt that this afforded us an opportunity to meet those goals through the appointment of that member of a protected group.[23]

Graebner did not consider the appointment a major issue; in fact, had it not been for Morton suggesting that choosing Diane Joyce would help implement the affirmative action plan, he would never have involved himself in a routine, low-level appointment. Once Morton assured him that both Joyce and Johnson had qualified for the job, he did not even bother calling for their files. Under the rule of seven, any of the seven qualified candidates could be named. Graebner had no problems with the idea of affirmative action, nor with appointing a woman to a job never before held by a female.[24] And as he quite openly admitted, Joyce's sex had not only been a positive factor; it had been the main factor leading to her selection.[25]

Despite arguments from Shields that Johnson ought to get the job, Graebner stuck to his decision, and Bert Di Basilio had to tell Paul Johnson. He called Johnson into his office and said, "I've got some bad news for you. You did not get the job."

An astonished Johnson exclaimed, "You must be kidding!"

"No," said Di Basilio. "Diane Joyce was appointed. You had already been appointed, and affirmative action got it reversed."

Di Basilio assured Johnson that he had done everything that he could have in his behalf, but that the matter was out of his hands.[26]

Paul Johnson "felt like tearing something up." He knew Diane Joyce, and believed then and still believes that he had the better qualifications for the job. "But she wanted a middle-level position right off, without having to work for it like I did. I would never ask for preferential treatment, and that's what she was doing."[27]

Johnson determined to fight right from the start, but because the system had always worked for him before, he would give it one more chance and go through the channels. He spoke with supervisors Allen Jones and Ron Shields, and they more or less repeated what Di Basilio had said, that he had been their choice, he had been named dispatcher, and then Graebner had given the job to Joyce. Johnson then called Graebner's office for an appointment. Graebner's secretary asked what he wanted to discuss, and when Johnson told her "the dispatcher's job," she told him he would have to see Victor Morton first. She then transferred the call to the affirmative action coordinator, who told Johnson he could meet with him that afternoon.

"If it was in any way close," Johnson later said, "I wouldn't have had any problem." Di Basilio, Jones, and Shields, men who had been his bosses and whose judgment he respected, had told him that it had not been close, that he had far better qualifications than Diane Joyce. At this point, still believing in the system, Paul Johnson wanted someone to tell him that there had been a rational reason why he had not gotten the job.[28]

Victor Morton did not give him that reason. Johnson met Morton and his assistant, and asked Morton if he could explain how he could make an appointment like that, or even recommend it.

"Well," Morton said, "your qualifications are very similar."

Johnson immediately challenged that, and asked Morton to show him how the records justified such a conclusion. Morton did not have any records with him, and an exasperated Johnson nearly exploded. "Well, what do you think I wanted to talk to you about?"

In an effort to calm Johnson down, Morton tried to explain that he did not control the appointment process, but merely had made a recommendation to the agency head. He had done so because, in accordance with the affirmative action plan, they wanted to put a woman in a position that no woman had ever held before.

When Johnson met with Graebner a little while later, the Transportation Agency chief told him essentially the same thing—he considered both applicants evenly matched, but he wanted to use the opportunity to put a woman into the position. Johnson angrily asked if Graebner intended to ignore the merit system and "just throw it out the damn window." Graebner did not comment, and Johnson went home to think about his next step.

Betty Johnson felt as outraged as her husband. Paul had worked hard, he had demonstrated his competence, he had played by the rules—and now they had unfairly changed the rules. When she told her brother-in-law, Otis Ray, about Paul's problem, Ray told her that he knew someone on the San Jose police force who had been denied a promotion because of affirmative action, and had successfully sued in court. Ray recommended contacting the lawyers who had handled the policeman's case, Wiley, Blunt & McBride, one of the first firms in the Santa Clara area to handle labor law. Paul called their office, and the switchboard put him through to one of the junior associates, James Dawson.[29]

Dawson had worked for Legal Services after law school, and had gradually come to specialize in employment-discrimination cases. Johnson came in to see him and explained the situation. Affirmative action had stopped his appointment, Johnson claimed, and this violated the county's rules for nonrepresented employees.[30] Could anything be done?

Dawson said, "I don't know; let's write a letter." Acting on behalf of Johnson, Dawson wrote to Jim Graebner, asking for an opportunity to discuss Paul Johnson's complaint prior to invoking the county grievance procedure. Graebner did not respond. Acting through Dawson, Johnson next filed a claim with the Equal Employment Opportunity Commission.

All of this, it should be noted, took place in the three weeks following Diane Joyce's telephone call in the spring of 1980. Bert Di Basilio finally called her in to Room 8 at the West Yard, a room normally reserved for disciplinary meetings, and said, "Well, you got it."

"Great," Joyce responded. "What did I get?"

"The East Yard road dispatchership. You and your friends got you the dispatcher's job."

Joyce, who up until now had not really believed she would get the position, suddenly realized what Di Basilio had said, and exclaimed, "Fantastic!"

Di Basilio did not think it so fantastic. "You got it through affirmative action, even though you were not qualified."

"What do you mean, not qualified?" she shot back. "I was number four on the certification list. I'm certified to the department. That makes me qualified."

"Well, not as qualified as Paul Johnson," and he told her about the rankings.[31]

As Diane Joyce prepared to take over the dispatcher's job in East Yard in June 1980, the local EEOC office invited the county to meet with Jim Dawson in an effort to resolve Paul Johnson's complaint. The county ignored this letter as well, and EEOC now had a choice of what to do next. One option would be to follow regular administrative procedures and send out "requests for information." The aggrieved party in a complicated case may often prefer this route, since it is a cheap method of discovery—that is, of getting information from the employer's records that can be used in building the case. But Dawson believed he had a solid, straightforward case, and that the county had delayed long enough. He wanted to get into court and force Santa Clara County to do right by Paul Johnson.

So Dawson invoked another option, and secured a "right to sue" letter from the EEOC. Such a letter implies no guilt, but indicates that there is a potential violation of the law amenable to suit in federal court. Without the "right to sue" letter, Paul Johnson could not go forward. With it, Jim Dawson filed papers in the U.S. District Court for the Northern District of California, alleging that the county's action had violated Title VII of the 1964 Civil Rights Act, 42 U.S.C. §2000e, which prohibits discrimination on the basis of gender.[32]

The court had a crowded docket, and Paul Johnson would have to wait almost two years before Judge William A. Ingram would hear the case. During that time, Diane Joyce ran the dispatcher's desk at East Yard, the same yard where Paul Johnson worked as a member of the road crew. During those two years his resentment of her and of affirmative action did not abate at all.

2

The Debate
over Affirmative Action

No aspect of the modern civil rights movement has generated so much heat and so little agreement as affirmative action. Its advocates claim that setting goals for the admission of minorities and women into colleges, training programs, and employment will eventually move these groups out of second-class status and give them true equality in American life. To its opponents, quotas that favor one group must inevitably discriminate against another, and lead to the hiring of lesser-qualified minorities and women at the expense of better-qualified white males, who themselves are not guilty of discrimination. The debate has raised many questions about whether affirmative action in fact works, and if it does, who benefits and at whose expense.

Following the Civil War, Congress passed a number of laws designed to put former slaves on a rough par with white people. The Fourteenth Amendment made the freedmen citizens, and prohibited states from enforcing any law which abridged the privileges and immunities of any citizen, deprived him of life, liberty, or property without due process of law, or denied him the equal protection of the laws. It also gave Congress the power to enforce these provisions, and in 1875 the Republican majority in Congress, aware that Reconstruction would soon end, passed a civil rights act to secure by law some semblance of equality for black Americans.

15

It is doubtful if many white Americans really endorsed the idea of equality for the freedmen. Gideon Welles, who had been Secretary of the Navy in Lincoln's Cabinet, captured the prevailing sentiment when he wrote in 1871: "Thank God slavery is abolished, but the Negro is not, and never can be the equal of the White. He is of an inferior race and must always remain so."[1] The Supreme Court agreed, and in 1883 emasculated the civil rights act and diluted much of the protection of the Fourteenth Amendment. Justice Joseph Bradley interpreted the enforcement provisions of the amendment as strictly remedial; Congress had the power to remedy a discriminatory state law, but could not take affirmative steps to protect blacks from other forms of prejudice.[2]

As a result of this decision, the federal government took no action to combat racism in this country until the Second World War, when it became embarrassing to claim we were fighting racism abroad while tolerating it at home. Black resentment became more vocal, and to forestall threatened civil rights demonstrations, including a march on Washington, President Franklin D. Roosevelt issued an Executive Order on June 25, 1941, directing that Negroes be accepted into job-training programs in defense plants. The order also forbade discrimination by employers holding defense contracts, and set up a Fair Employment Practices Commission to investigate charges of racial discrimination.[3] When Congress proved unwilling after the war to enact fair employment legislation, both Harry Truman and Dwight Eisenhower continued Roosevelt's policy through Executive Order.

Following the Supreme Court decision in *Brown* v. *Board of Education* in 1954, pressure mounted on both Congress and the Executive to take some positive steps on behalf of civil rights. John F. Kennedy entered the White House in January 1961 amid high hopes from blacks that he would provide the moral leadership that had been so painfully absent during the Eisenhower years. Roy Wilkins of the NAACP called for immediate action to promote employment opportunities for Negroes, and the new President responded with Executive Order 10925, creating the Presidential Commission on Equal Employment Opportunity, and mandating federal contractors to take "affirmative action" to ensure that there be no discrimination by "race, creed, color, or national origin." For the first time, the government ordered its contractors not only to avoid discrimination, but to take positive steps to redress the effects of societal discrimination.

Kennedy realized that an Executive Order could only go so far, and that real progress in civil rights required congressional action. In 1963 he secured passage of the Equal Pay Act, which prohibited employers from paying women less than men for the same work. He also proposed sweeping civil rights legislation, which southerners managed to bottle up in committee. After Kennedy's assassination, however, Lyndon Johnson called for the passage of the civil rights bill as a memorial to the slain President, and he skillfully guided an expanded version of the Kennedy proposal through both houses of Congress, broke a southern filibuster, and signed the Civil Rights Act into law on July 2, 1964. Title VII of the act banned employment discrimination based on "race, color, sex, or national origin," and created a permanent Equal Employment Opportunity Commission to enforce its provisions.[4] The act extended for the first time the obligation not to discriminate to private employers, labor unions, and governmental agencies.

Despite the sweeping language of the act, very little progress occurred, and within a short time Johnson realized that merely banning current discrimination was not enough; something had to be done for blacks to overcome the lingering effects of decades of systematic exclusion from jobs and education. In a speech at Howard University, Johnson explained why the country needed to adopt affirmative action: "You do not take a person who for years has been hobbled by chains, and liberate him, bring him up to the starting line of a race, and then say, 'You are free to compete with all the others,' and still justly believe that you have been completely fair. Thus, it is not enough just to open the gates of opportunity; all our citizens must have the ability to walk through those gates."[5]

In Executive Order 11246, issued on September 24, 1965, Johnson required federal contractors to take affirmative action to recruit, hire, and promote more minorities. Two years later, in Executive Order 11375, Johnson added women to the groups covered by previous antidiscrimination orders.

17

Johnson's vision, however, soon bogged down in the Great Society bureaucracy. Affirmative action, according to some critics, became an umbrella term for a vast hodgepodge of remedial programs, ranging from efforts to place more women on university faculties to hiring more blacks in the construction industry. Over a dozen federal agencies shared responsibility for enforcing two dozen equal-opportunity laws or Executive Orders; these agencies overlapped in some areas and left huge gaps in others. In an effort to plug all loopholes, zealous bureaucrats drew up seemingly endless forms and regulations, whose net effect, if any, no one seemed to know.[6]

When Richard Nixon took office in 1969, he faced on the one hand a growing backlash by blue-collar whites against civil rights, and on the other the realization that many of the economic problems associated with welfare and big cities stemmed from the job discrimination confronting black Americans. Compliance with Title VII still remained voluntary, and most American businesses had chosen to wait and see what they would be required to do rather than initiate any programs on their own.[7] Nixon, with prompting from domestic affairs adviser Daniel Patrick Moynihan, accepted the idea that blacks had to be brought into the economic mainstream or they would never escape the chains of poverty and discrimination that had bound them since the chains of slavery had been struck off.

The President called in Art Fletcher, the Assistant Secretary of Labor and a black himself, and told him to find a way to enforce the hiring provisions of Title VII, a way that would withstand court challenge. Fletcher did, and in 1971 Nixon unveiled the so-called Philadelphia plan, a model for bringing minorities into segregated trades. In Philadelphia federal contractors would have to meet specific numerical goals in hiring minorities, with the long-term goal equaling the percentage of that minority in the available labor force. The Nixon plan, issued as the Office of Federal Contract Compliance (OFCC) Revised Order No. 4, strengthened the two Johnson orders by requiring annual affirmative action plans from major contractors, and including hiring goals and timetables. According to Fletcher, the Nixon Administration ordered what Congress had not: numerical goals and enforcement.

In the next eighteen months Fletcher toured the country urging blacks to take advantage of the new order. "I went to wherever I could get a platform," he later recalled, "to make sure that everyone understood that this standard required that you be prepared to make a contribution. . . . It is not a futile effort anymore. The door is open."[8]

Fletcher provided a walking case in point of what it had been like for blacks in the 1950s. He had graduated from college in 1950, played professional football for a few years, and then could not get a job. He went back to his native Kansas, and could not even get hired as an assistant coach in high school. People told him, "You are ready, but we are not." So Fletcher worked as an iceman, ran a janitorial service, and played trumpet on weekends to support his wife and five children. When he moved to California in 1956, Republican Party leaders welcomed him into their ranks, and appointed him to some legislative advisory groups. Nonetheless, as Fletcher later told a reporter, it took him fifteen years to find a job that required his college degree. By then he had moved to the State of Washington and had become the first black to run for statewide office. Although Fletcher lost the bid for the lieutenant governorship in 1968, he caught the attention of national party leaders, and Nixon named him to the Labor Department in his new administration. In 1990 George Bush would name Fletcher to the U.S. Civil Rights Commission.

The plan Fletcher designed, with its innovation of goals and timetables, soon caught the attention of frustrated federal judges looking for ways to force recalcitrant public employers to integrate their work force. A good case in point is Alabama, whose more than seventy state agencies employed only a handful of blacks above the menial level. In January 1972 the NAACP sued the Alabama state police, which did not have a single black among troopers, officers, or even support personnel. Federal Judge Frank M. Johnson, Jr., imposed a rule that one black trooper had to be hired for every new white person hired, until 25 percent of the force consisted of blacks. Twelve years later, the state had the most thoroughly integrated state-police force in the country.[9]

The Nixon order also proved the turning point for private employers. Businesses do not deal well with vague generalities, but they do respond to specifics. As one article put it, "Businessmen like to hire by the numbers."[10] They now had something specific to work with, and hundreds, indeed thousands of firms began the often painful process of self-examination, of looking at their past hiring practices and recognizing that they had, consciously or not, excluded minorities from employment and promotion. In little more than a decade, affirmative action became a way of life for many large corporations. Once embarked on the program, primarily through fear of losing lucrative federal contracts, corporations began discovering, or at least rationalizing, other reasons for their policies. Marion Sandler of Golden West Financial explained that "the whole country is moving away from being white, Anglo, and Protestant to polyglot," especially in places like California and Texas where Golden West did business. "You have to recognize what's happening and be part of it."[11] John M. Stafford, head of the Pillsbury Company, shared this sentiment. "It has become clear to us that an aggressive affirmative action program makes a lot of sense."[12]

A 1983 survey of fifty major federal contractors conducted for the Center for National Policy Review indicated that all had accepted affirmative action as "an integral part of today's corporate personnel-management philosophy and practice."[13] B. Lawrence Branch, the director of equal employment for the Merck Company, admitted that the pharmaceutical firm would not have initiated an affirmative action plan without the government's prodding, but now "we don't need the government involved in this—affirmative action is a way of life here."[14]

One should not suppose that all American businesses endorsed the philosophy behind affirmative action or that, on the other hand, they went along only out of fear of losing government contracts. In fact, the threat of federal retaliation has always been more potential than actual.[15] As Alan Farnham noted, a quarter century after the Civil Rights Act: "The mortar binding CEOs to affirmative action—a compound of social conscience, fear, and self-interest—appears strong. Some CEOs believe fervently that the programs are the best way of righting past wrongs. Others half-heartedly endorse them because, like eating oatmeal, it's the right thing to do. Still others fear the penalties for backsliding."[16]

*   *   *

That thousands of firms initiated affirmative action programs is indisputable; how much these programs helped minorities and women is greatly disputed. It is impossible to get accurate figures because in many instances blacks and other minorities might have been hired even in the absence of an affirmative action plan. The best numbers come from those firms or agencies that had admittedly discriminated in the past, and where blacks or women entered the job force only because of affirmative action. There is no question that these plans helped some talented individuals who might not otherwise have gotten a chance. Art Fletcher claims that one-third of black Americans used the civil rights acts and Presidential orders "to position themselves in middle-class America. One-third of black America has made it within the last twenty years—the life of this document, affirmative action." The only ones who did not make it, he charges, are those who did not try.[17]

Not everyone agrees. Thomas Sowell, a senior fellow at the Hoover Institution, argues that affirmative action has not helped those who need help most, those with little education, training, or job experience; rather, it has benefited the top 10 percent poised to move into the middle class in any event. Affirmative action "may help a black professor get an endowed chair, but it is counterproductive for the black teenager trying to get a job."[18] Other critics, including sociologist Nathan Glazer and Douglas Glasgow, author of *The Underclass*, have indicted affirmative action for failing to help the mass of poor blacks.[19]

One can certainly find success stories. Earl Jenkins, a black, is now a national marketing manager for AT&T, overseeing one hundred people and an annual budget of $25 million, and believes that without affirmative action he would never have had the opportunity to demonstrate his ability. AT&T recruited Jenkins in 1975 under a consent decree with the Equal Employment Opportunity Commission. In 1969 blacks made up 6.7 percent of the nearly 600,000 employees in the Bell System, mostly black women working as operators, but only 2.4 percent of black employees held management positions, compared to 12 percent of whites. Less than 1 percent of the blacks held professional jobs, compared to 8 percent

21

of the whites.* In 1971 the EEOC charged AT&T and its affiliates with discrimination against blacks and women, and the consent decree signed four years later became the catalyst for rapid change within the giant telephone system. By 1979 blacks and other minorities made up 14.4 percent of the Bell System's managers, 18.7 percent of its outside craftsmen, and 23.3 percent of its sales workers.[20] The talent had been there all along; employers had not looked for it.

Similar stories can be told about minority experiences in other firms and industries, and how affirmative action opened up doors previously closed to blacks and women. Coal mining, for example, had traditionally been a male industry, and there were no women miners in 1973. The EEOC targeted the coal industry as one of several whose hiring policies flagrantly violated the letter and the spirit of the Presidential orders. By the end of 1980, 3,295 women had become coal miners, 8.7 percent of the total work force. Similarly, the number of women in shipbuilding increased dramatically when the Maritime Administration required contractors to establish goals and timetables. Although many shipyard owners had claimed woman had no interest in shipbuilding, they found that as more women were hired, more applied.[21] The Wilson Meat Company of Cedar Rapids, Iowa, proudly declared that it has the only woman hog buyer in the country, but admitted that a few years earlier it would never have even considered a female for that job.[22] The Office of Federal Contract Compliance believed that in certain "hard-core" industries such as construction, "unless specific affirmative action steps are prescribed, employment opportunities will not reach the female work force of this country."[23] Several studies support the claim that affirmative action does provide minorities and women with equal employment opportunity.[24] Perhaps the most visibly successful affirmative action programs are those of the armed services, which in a relatively short period of time brought in large numbers of women and minorities not only to the army, navy, and air force, but to the respective service academies as well.

*By way of comparison to the total work force, in 1988 there were 182,628,000 Americans aged eighteen and over, the group that statistically comprises the work force. Of these, 78.6 percent were white, 11.2 percent black, 7.1 percent Hispanic, and 3.1 percent "other," a group that includes Asians, Native Americans, and other small minorities, such as Aleuts. By gender, the population is 51.2 percent female and 48.8 percent male.

After the city of Indianapolis instituted hiring goals in 1976, black representation on its police force rose to 14 percent. Barry Goldstein of the NAACP Legal Defense Fund noted that in 1970 there were about 23,000 black police officers in the country; in 1979 there were 43,000; in that same decade, the number of black electricians rose from 15,000 to more than 37,000. For him, numbers such as these proved that affirmative action worked.[25]

Critics of affirmative action have their own numbers to show that the programs have not worked that well, and have not helped more than a small number of people. Thus, for example, in 1970 31.5 million women held jobs, and they earned on the whole only 59.2 percent of men's salaries. In 1985 the number of working women had grown to 51.1 million, and the salary gap had closed somewhat to 65 percent.[26] A breakdown of those numbers, however, indicated that white women entering the job market in 1980 were actually further behind the wages of comparable white men than they had been in 1970, despite the alleged success of affirmative action.[27] A 1985 study by the National Research Council reported that sex segregation in employment had remained fairly stable since 1900. Despite some changes after 1975, the segregation index still remained at 60, which meant that 30 percent of workers would have to move into job categories dominated by the opposite sex just to even the numbers out. Moreover, in its study, the council found that overall, women still only earned 60 percent as much as men.[28]

The debate, however, is not over numbers; it is over social philosophy, and what the nation as a whole should do in its efforts to eradicate race and gender discrimination.

In its bluntest form, the argument for affirmative action is this: Past discrimination in the job market has placed minorities and women at a disadvantage that will never, left to itself, go away. Minorities and women will always be in an inferior position unless steps are taken to pull them up. This requires some temporary discrimination against white males, but it is necessary for the sake of social justice and progress. As McGeorge Bundy acknowledged:

> The reason is simple; it is also painful: the gaps in economic, educational, and cultural advantage between racial minorities and the

white majority are still so wide that *there is no racially neutral process of choice that will produce more than a handful of minority students in our competitive colleges and professional schools.* . . . Precisely because it is not yet "racially neutral" to be black in America, a racially neutral standard will not lead to equal opportunity for blacks.[29]

In other words, to compensate for past injustice, there must be a form of reverse discrimination now. One economist described the position of blacks and other minorities as comparable to a caboose on a train. "No matter how fast the train goes, the caboose will never catch up with the engine unless special arrangements are made to change its position." Minorities and women will always be at the tail end of the economy, and even in good times will always trail after white men—unless affirmative action provides them with greater opportunities.[30]

Ralph F. Davidson, the chairman of the board of Time Inc., despaired for the future of the country unless something could be done to break "the treadmill of underemployment and joblessness, of opportunities forever beyond reach." Affirmative action, he believed, constituted one of the few "proved and practical means" to help people stand on their own feet.[31] Only by giving minorities this chance, according to columnist Charles Krauthammer, would the country ever have a chance of fully integrating blacks into American life.[32]

Another argument put forward in defense of affirmative action is that the country cannot afford to waste the talents of people who would, because of their race, gender, or national origin, be prevented from realizing their potential. "How am I," asked HEW Secretary Joseph A. Califano, "ever going to find first-class black doctors, first-class black lawyers, first-class black scientists, first-class women scientists, if these people don't have the chance to get into the best [schools] in the country?"[33] These professionals will also serve the needs of their respective communities, which at present are underserved in terms of medical and legal services. Minority doctors, according to one study, are more likely to care for poor and minority patients and practice in ghetto areas than white doctors.[34]

Educators have claimed that affirmative action is needed not only for the benefit of minorities and women, but also to provide the schools, and their white students, the benefit of a student population reflective of the outside society. The dean of Columbia College, Robert Pollack, described affirmative action as justice, not charity:

> I despair at how vulnerable our affirmative action policies are to the short-term politics of the day. To lose sight of the distinction between charity and justice is to promulgate injustice in the name of fiscal responsibility, and to condemn our white classmates and colleagues to intellectual ghettos of their own making. . . .
>
> Each year we seek out black and Latin candidates for admission to the College. We show underrepresented minority candidates and their families the ins and outs of life in this diverse but still largely white institution. . . . The impetus of all our recruiting programs is the same: to bring to the College the most diverse possible group of students with high intelligence and character.[35]

This last phrase, "students with high intelligence and character," involves another argument for affirmative action, that it is not a lowering of standards, but an opportunity to involve skilled and talented people who would otherwise be excluded from attending certain schools or securing certain jobs. McGeorge Bundy denied that anyone wanted to admit unqualified students; rather, "there are qualified minorities, and they need a boost."[36] Some recent studies, however, show that many colleges have in fact deliberately lowered admission standards for certain groups in order to increase their percentage of minority students.[37]

The issue of whether persons benefited by affirmative action have the necessary qualifications, be they for a job or admission to college, ties in closely to whether one views affirmative action programs as setting out *goals* or *quotas*. Advocates argue that setting goals is acceptable; we all set goals in our lives, businesses set goals for sales and production, and nations can also set goals toward which to strive. To try to shape one's work force or student body so that it roughly corresponds to the general population is a worthy goal, and discriminates against no one. To set a specific number of blacks or women or Hispanics, however, is a quota, and critics charge that quotas do discriminate against nonfavored groups, and that often an unqualified person is hired or admitted so that the quotas can be filled.

Reams of paper have been written on the distinction between "goals" and "quotas."[38] Eugene Rostow, when asked how the two differed, said that one meets goals in affirmative action plans by recruiting women, blacks, and other minorities "where there simply has been no history of hiring such people."[39] The editors of *Commonweal* spoke of casting a "wide net" in which "job training efforts and serious attempts at remedial education can well be seen as indications of good intentions that make imposition of a quota system unnecessary."[40]

In other words, one opens the door wider, and invites—indeed seeks out—people who previously have either been turned away or led to believe they would be unwelcome to apply. Then, by the natural distribution of talent and ability, those chosen will include women and minorities. As a result, the overall pool potential of students or employees expands to include more qualified people, and those chosen will, as a group, have a higher level of ability.

The problem is, as critics claim and some friends admit, it does not work this way. Setting goals and timetables at some point fades into setting quotas. It is all too easy to go from saying, "We should have 10 percent blacks or 50 percent women, and that is the goal we should work toward by active recruitment and training," to saying, "The next thirty people we hire must be black or female so we meet our quota." As then Attorney General Edward H. Levi charged in 1975, affirmative action programs established goals which were "said with great profoundness not to be the setting of quotas. But it is the setting of quotas . . . [even though] we will call quotas goals."[41] And goals do discriminate, because in order to fill the quota, one will hire people if they are female or black or belong to another minority, even if they are less qualified than available white males.

To some advocates of affirmative action, quotas are acceptable. Arthur Fleming, then chairman of the U.S. Commission on Civil Rights, asserted in a 1981 report that sometimes "quotas are needed to make equal opportunity a reality for members of historically excluded groups."[42] Merely opening the doors wider will do no good, runs the argument, because the same prejudice that barred minorities from getting these jobs also worked to provide them with inferior education and training. John Fischer, former dean of Columbia Teachers College, said of a typical black child, "On the day he enters kindergarten, he carries a burden no white child can ever know."[43] Telling an unqualified person who carries such a burden that he or she is free to apply to good schools or for good jobs is a charade. What has to be done is to take members of previously excluded groups, and treat them preferentially until such time as they can compete for jobs or places in colleges and medical schools.[44]

The issue here, according to Daniel Maguire, is not fairness or equality, but justice. It is true that quotas are unfair and treat people unequally, but we as a society accept certain inequalities because we perceive them as just. "A school that was established to allow unequal and special education for the gifted would not be resented. The handicapped have a right to unequal, extra help from the state." Minorities who have been discriminated against have the right to expect not only compensatory programs, but some preference as well.[45] Charles Krauthammer makes a similar argument: "While color blindness may be a value, remedying centuries of discrimination through (temporary) race consciousness is a higher value"— namely, justice. Moreover, the rapid integration of blacks into American society "is an overriding national goal," and quotas are a means to that goal.[46] That integration, according to affirmative action advocates, will mean not only a more economically productive work force, but less poverty among minorities and a reduction in crime and other social problems that stalk the nation's ghettos.

But what about the white males who will pay the price for these preferential programs, white males who, like Paul Johnson, have never even been accused of personal discrimination? Mayor William Hudnut of Indianapolis, where police and fire departments ran extensive affirmative action programs, said that he did not think that white males suffered greatly, since they still got 80 percent of the jobs in those agencies.[47] According to Ira Glasser, head of the American Civil Liberties Union, white males have enjoyed unfair advantages over blacks, women, and minorities for many years.

"Fairness," he argues, "requires ending discrimination, not perpetuating it, and that includes ending the advantages that whites enjoyed."[48]

Key to the question of alleged discrimination against white males is how one views an individual's responsibility for social injustice. Does everyone bear the blame for past racial injustice, prejudice against women, or exclusion of minorities from schools and jobs? Why should a white person whose grandparents came to this country long after slavery had ended have to pay a price for the iniquities inflicted upon blacks by their white masters years earlier?

The "just citizen," answers Daniel Maguire, cannot be at peace while social injustice exists. Even if he is guilty of no personal offense, "he owes a debt to legal justice by the very nature of social personhood. Here the guilt is the guilt of omission, the guilt of not having done enough, of not caring enough. . . . In the matter of American racism, the white who would claim to be without such guilt is, in the phrase and spirit of the Apostle John, 'a liar.' "[49]

Paul Spickard faced a personal test of his commitment to this Christian view of justice. Spickard, a white male, had degrees from Harvard and Berkeley in Asian history, but was twice turned down for jobs because colleges wanted a minority person. "Isn't all this unfair?" he asked. Yes, he concluded, but:

> My family came over on the *Mayflower* and made money in the slave trade. Doctors, lawyers, judges, and comfortable business people go back several generations in my clan. . . . I am standing on the shoulders of my ancestors and their discriminatory behavior.
>
> Contrast my experience with that of a Chicano friend, whose immigrant father had a fourth-grade education and ran a grocery store. Without affirmative action and the social commitment it symbolizes, my friend might not have gone to Amherst, nor to Stanford Law School. . . . Our society would be poorer for the loss of his skills. . . .
>
> Affirmative action may not always be fair. But I'm willing to take second best if overall fairness is achieved. After all, for biblical Christians, fairness—often translated in our Bibles as "justice" or "righteousness"—is a fundamental principle by which God calls us

to live. And affirmative action is an appropriate program aimed at achieving the godly goal of putting others' welfare before my own.[50]

All arguments in favor of affirmative action boil down to the fact that women, blacks, and other minorities have historically suffered discrimination and have been precluded from various educational and economic opportunities. In order for society to eliminate the lasting vestiges of that discrimination, and to realize the potential contributions of all its citizens, it has to take certain steps to allow these groups access to good schools and good jobs. Whether one talks of goals or quotas, the aim is the same: admit more members of the excluded groups into schools; hire them into jobs and job training programs. If, in the past, the majority used a person's race or gender or national origin against him or her in a discriminatory manner, it is now fair to take those same considerations into account, and use them to the person's benefit.

For critics of affirmative action, race-conscious or gender-conscious programs which benefit minorities are as bad as the discrimination against these groups. Where advocates claim that the programs work, critics say they do not. Moral arguments for are met by equally moral arguments against. While defenders assert that affirmative action will eventually lead to an America in which minorities and women take their rightful and equal place, critics foresee an even more race- and gender-conscious society.

The nub of the moral argument is that while women, blacks, and other minorities have been discriminated against as *groups*, quotas[51] that benefit these groups disadvantage *individual* white males. Not all white males pay the price of society's desire to compensate victims of past discrimination, only those in targeted jobs or schools. The political philosopher Sidney Hook agreed that society had in the past immorally discriminated against minorities—blacks, Asians, Jews, women, and others.

But it is illiberal and unjust to redress the effects of past discrimination by punishing innocent parties in the present whose ancestors had no part in imposing the patterns of discrimination in the past. If society in the past has been guilty of discrimination, then the

29

costs of reparations should be borne by society as a whole to the extent that there can ever be adequate reparation rather than by innocent persons in the present.[52]

The system, as *The New Republic* admitted, cannot be designed so that only "oppressors" are excluded, even if society could identify such people. "The fate of young men and women is at stake, and they are classified according to their racial or ethnic identity, not according to their moral conduct."[53]

Not only is the price paid for by individuals, but most of these individuals come from marginal white groups. Affirmative action rarely affects upper-class white males; they have been well educated, and usually have no trouble getting into good colleges, graduate schools, or beginning managerial or professional positions. Rather, marginal candidates, those who have not been as well educated, who themselves may come from poor or disadvantaged backgrounds, are the ones bumped to make room for women and minorities. The result is that the bottom groups will not be pushed up to an equality with all others, but merely pushed ahead of the "next-to-last" group, primarily white ethnic Americans. And that, according to critics, is "grossly unfair" and "simply shifts injustice one notch up the social hierarchy leaving the basic inequalities of American society untouched."[54]

If the program worked, critics maintain, then there might be grounds for supporting it as an avowed national policy, recognizing that for certain groups to benefit, others will have to suffer. Life is unfair, and we have many national policies that benefit one group at the expense of others. But, they claim, affirmative action does not work. Thomas Sowell, one of the most forceful critics of affirmative action, charges that its track record in helping to alleviate social ills is even poorer than busing. While various programs helped some of the "more fortunate" blacks and women, "the truly disadvantaged—those with little education or job experience, or from broken families—have fallen even further behind during the era of affirmative action."[55]

In fact, Sowell claims, the real gains among blacks in high-level occupations began not with affirmative action or even with the passage of the Civil Rights Act in 1964, but are part of a "historic, ongoing process created by one of the great social transformations of a people." "Don't make things worse," he pleads. The progress of American blacks since emancipation has been "remarkable," but "massive intervention" on their behalf has had "massive counter-productive effects," most notably a swelling white backlash that threatens to unleash new waves of racism.[56]

Sowell does not claim that all racial or sexual discrimination has ended in the United States, but George Gilder, a conservative writer for *The National Review*, does argue along those lines. Affirmative action, he declares, should be stopped not just because it is unconstitutional or unfair to poor white males, "but because discrimination has already been effectively abolished in this country." Since *Brown*, a "relentless and thoroughly successful" campaign against the old prejudices has made it impossible to label modern America as oppressive and discriminatory, with gaps in income between truly comparable blacks and whites "nearly closed."

As for women, Gilder believes that their problems are caused not by gender discrimination, but by conditions which can never be changed. Most of the differences in pay are due to the *fact* that women between the ages of twenty-five and fifty-nine are eleven times more likely than men to leave work voluntarily, and the average woman spends only eight months on a job, compared to nearly three years for the average man. Lower pay for equal work, he further maintains, "is an effect not of discrimination but of locational preference"; women are less mobile than men, because they must live where their husbands work, and therefore cannot be as choosy in finding well-paying jobs.[57]

Few people would take such a sanguine view of contemporary American racial or gender conditions, but a number of critics worry that imposing quotas to benefit particular groups could undermine the real progress that has been made. Where, for example, would one draw the line as to what groups should be protected? One finds in a leading news magazine such stories as "Short People—Are They Being Discriminated Against?"[58] and "Fat People's Fight Against Job Bias."[59] A white female office worker, fired after she was caught fornicating on business premises during working hours,

filed a discrimination charge against her employer, as did a Carib-
bean-born stewardess who claimed that her airline discriminated
against her because she flaunted her voodoo equipment on the job.
A young man fascinated by an expensive dress in a boutique window complained of discrimination because the shopkeeper would
not let him try it on. All three suits were dismissed, but not before
the various state enforcement agencies had held hearings.[60]

Many civil rights advocates fear that a quota system could generate a backlash that would undo all the progress of recent years.
Throughout the seventies and into the eighties, a variety of public
opinion polls indicated public support for affirmative action when
it involved compensatory programs, such as additional job training
for minorities, but overwhelming opposition to quotas.[61] When *The
New York Times* editorially endorsed the quota system that had kept
Allan Bakke out of medical school, the letters in response ran at a
fifteen-to-one ratio against the paper's stand, and this from a predominantly liberal readership.[62] A decade later, some observers
believed they saw overt evidence of that backlash in the growing
number of racial incidents on college campuses, and the growth of
racist "skinhead" groups. "Whether rightly or wrongly," wrote Gerald Kreyche, "the underlying mood of many white males is that
they perceive themselves as bearing the brunt of so many of society's
burdens that they don't want to take any more."[63] As a sign of what
they considered unfairness, six white police officers in New York
asked that their racial classification be changed to black or Hispanic
so they could qualify for promotion under a racial quota system.[64]

The counsel for the Senate Subcommittee on the Constitution
has publicly worried that as affirmative action quotas become more
institutionalized, the country will have to officially categorize its
citizens by race. The Minority Business Enterprise program, in
which Congress mandated that 10 percent of public-works funds
go to minority-owned firms, defined such companies as those owned
by "Negroes, Spanish-speaking, Orientals, Indians, Eskimos, and
Aleuts."[65]

That quotas could lead to such classification is certainly one of
the complaints that Jewish groups, long allies of blacks in the civil
rights struggle, have raised and which has put such a strain on that

alliance.[66] Jews remember that in Europe the infamous *numerus clausus* kept them out of universities and the professions, and that even in the United States, many colleges and medical schools had Jewish quotas which crippled rather than helped bright young men and women. Morris Abram, former head of the American Jewish Committee, charged that quotas create an "ethnic spoils system" that pits one group against another, and will inevitably result in an "institutionalized division of the pie of opportunity by bureaucratic decisions as to the group disadvantaged and the numbers of each group to be benefited."[67] In a passionate and moving essay, legal scholar Alexander Bickel wrote:

> A racial quota derogates the human dignity and individuality of all to whom it is applied; it is invidious in principle as well as in practice. Moreover, it can easily be turned against those it purports to help. The history of the racial quota is a history of subjugation, not beneficence. Its evil lies not in its name, but in its effects; a quota is a divider of society, a creator of castes, and it is all the worse for its racial base, especially in a society desperately striving for an equality that will make race irrelevant.[68]

As for past injustices, most critics of affirmative action do not deny that blacks, women, and other groups have been discriminated against, but that it is illogical and unfair to compensate present members of these groups for ills suffered by their ancestors, at the expense of other, and innocent, groups today. It simply does not follow, charged Carl Cohen, either "in morals or in law, that individual blacks, or Orientals, or Jews who were not damaged are entitled now to special favor in the name of group redress." In a blunter tone, EEOC Commissioner Fred Alvarez declared: "When somebody tells me they ought to get something because they're Irish and saw signs in Boston that said IRISH NEED NOT APPLY . . . or because their ancestors were in slavery, I say 'So what?' "[69]

Another fear, especially among educators, is that colleges and universities will be forced to accept unqualified students, and in order to do so will have to lower their overall standards. In California, for example, a state report noted that only 3.6 percent of the state's black public high school graduates and 4.9 percent of the Hispanic graduates would have been eligible under regular admission standards for the elite Berkeley campus of the University of California, compared to 13.2 percent of all graduating seniors. As a result, more than half of the black first-time freshmen and almost that high a ratio of Hispanics were "special admissions" students. To gain admission, applicants in targeted "protected" classes had to graduate from high school with a GPA of at least 3.3, *or* earn a GPA of 2.79–3.29 and have sufficiently high test scores, *or* score at least 1100 on the College Board's Scholastic Aptitude Test. In contrast, white or Asian students needed a GPA of 3.7 or better for admission.[70] The result, as Andrew Hacker notes, is that although the Berkeley and UCLA campuses, the showpieces of the California system, have a more diverse student body, the schools do not necessarily have as well-qualified a group of students.[71]

In a society where education is perhaps the key to economic and social mobility, access to educational opportunity is obviously crucial for minorities.[72] Yet the very groups that have sought such access have also been the least prepared. It is not a question of blacks being intellectually inferior; they and other minorities have suffered from poor schooling, a legacy of society's pervasive discrimination against them. When some public college systems instituted an "open admissions" policy, blacks poured into those schools, and in many instances failed out almost as quickly, while driving away faculty and qualified white students. Even when colleges did provide remedial services, many minority students rejected this help as patronizing.[73]

Even in the elite schools, as Thomas Sowell charges, "the drive to get a good-looking 'body count' of black students leads the top colleges and universities to go way beyond the pool of black students who meet their normal admission standards." This may ease the conscience of white administrators, but unfortunately "many black students discover too late that the 'opportunity' to go to a big-name school turns out to be a trap."[74]

The larger question to some educators, however, is whether colleges and universities are the appropriate agencies to undertake the task of remedying decades of societal discrimination. The purpose of a university is to advance knowledge, and to benefit society by training the best and brightest of the new generation in the arts, humanities, sciences, and the professions. Advocates of affirmative action argue that maintaining high academic standards will mean too few educated minority members, and this will hurt the country in the long run. But so, too, will the failure to educate the nation's very brightest if resources are diverted to compensatory programs. The university, John Bunzel reminds us, "is not the Department of Health and Human Services, and should not be mistaken as an adjunct agency of the federal government in the important business of political and social reform."[75]

By the early 1980s, most large employers had adopted some form of affirmative action program; they had the staff and an employee pool large enough to manipulate in order to meet government requirements. Complaints increased, however, from small firms who tried to comply with federal regulations that, in their context, made no sense. Jim Supica, Jr., a building contractor in Lenexa, Kansas, claimed that federal rules had created a nightmare for his small bridge-building company. He employed fifteen men, three of them black, but the government cited the firm for not meeting the numerical goals of 12.7 percent minority-group members and 6.9 percent women in one job category, truck drivers. Supica, however, only employs two truck drivers, both white males who, as he pointed out, could sue him for reverse discrimination if he fired them to hire a black or a woman. Other small firms also complained about the inordinate amount of paperwork required by the government.[76]

In his 1980 campaign for the Presidency, Ronald Reagan constantly attacked the government for interfering too much in the private sector, and he also made it clear that he opposed employment quotas in any form. Shortly after the election, Senator Orrin G. Hatch, scheduled to be chairman of the Senate Labor and Human Resources Committee, let it be known that his committee would pressure the Labor Department's Office of Federal Contract Compliance Programs to take a softer approach on affirmative action goals. If the OFCCP failed to take the hint, Hatch promised to introduce legislation forcing it to do so. The senator could count on help from one of the new President's closest advisers, Edwin Meese, who strongly opposed quotas.[77]

In its first term, the Reagan Administration sent mixed signals on affirmative action. In 1983, for example, Executive Order 12432 required federal agencies to increase their "goals" for employment of minority-owned subcontractors by at least 10 percent, at the same time that high officials in the government denounced all such "quotas" as illegal. Reagan did, however, reconstitute the U.S. Commission on Civil Rights, and the new majority firmly opposed any use of numerical quotas. At the same time, the Civil Rights Division of the Justice Department, led by William Bradford Reynolds, openly attacked affirmative action programs. Mary Frances Berry, a holdover member of the Civil Rights Commission, charged that the commission had "become a twin of the Civil Rights Division of the Justice Department, and the bank of justice, as Martin Luther King used to say, is now bankrupt. . . . I despair for women and minorities in this country."[78] In response to some complaints from former staff members that the commission no longer accepted its reports, Morris Abram, the Reagan-appointed vice-chairman, responded that the facts put forward by the staff were irrelevant. "The decision to support or abhor racial tests for jobs in America should not be based on empirical data. Of course quotas work. They give jobs to those preferred and deny jobs to the victims of the new discrimination."[79]

The attack on federal affirmative action programs took on a more strident tone in Reagan's second term, when Meese became Attorney General. In his first press conference at the Justice Department, Meese approved affirmative action plans that sought to widen recruiting and training programs, but expressed his implacable opposition to quotas.[80] The Justice Department shortly thereafter sent out letters to fifty city governments that had signed consent decrees establishing hiring plans for women and minorities, informing them that it believed such plans unconstitutional. The strong reaction to this policy seemed to indicate that both public and private sector officials stood diametrically opposed to the administration's policy.

The National Association of Manufacturers' Equal Employment

Opportunity Committee, alerted to Meese's plan, opposed any proposal that would weaken federal requirements, and passed a ringing endorsement of affirmative action as a national social policy. In Omaha, Los Angeles, Cincinnati, and elsewhere, city officials declared that they would not back away from a program that had proven successful. As John Myers, deputy solicitor for Philadelphia, explained: "It was the right thing to do when we [did it], and it's still the right thing to do."[81]

The stubborn Meese kept up his attack on any plans that included hiring goals, but the public uproar alerted Reagan's more astute political advisers to leave the issue alone. Labor Secretary William Brock publicly defended affirmative action and his department's enforcement of federal policy, and managed to stymie Meese's efforts to have Reagan repeal the Executive Orders establishing the program.[82] When the President and the Attorney General left office in January 1989, they left a legacy of eight years of indifference to civil rights, but the various federal regulations concerning affirmative action remained intact.

Not all the voices in the debate are strident; occasionally one finds a still, small voice of reason. Hyman Bookbinder of the American Jewish Committee reflected the concerns of many Jews over the growing split with the black community over affirmative action. The Jewish community, he declared, would continue to support a whole range of affirmative action goals, including the "prudent" use of goals and timetables, but would oppose "rigid, inflexible, preferential quotas." But the goals-quota debate, he asserted, diverted attention from other aspects of the fight for equal opportunity:

> If tomorrow morning, by some inexplicable miracle, every American citizen and every American company or institution were suddenly entirely free of any prejudice and were determined forever to end discrimination, it would take a long time before our labor force would reflect the mix of our general population. Too many would remain unprepared for the new opportunities.
>
> It is equally true that if tomorrow morning, by some inexplicable

miracle, every American subgroup—blacks, Hispanics, women, etc.—had the same range of qualified individuals for the whole range of employment opportunities, it would similarly take a long time before our labor force would reflect the mix of our general population. Too many Americans and American institutions, unfortunately, would still be unprepared to abandon their prejudices and habits.[83]

The struggle for equal opportunity has to be pursued in both arenas, eradicating prejudice on the one hand, and providing better education and job training on the other. Too great a concern with institutional prejudice, leading to quotas, he concluded, has diverted the nation from dealing with the goals of creating more opportunity for its citizens.

The debate over affirmative action, while too often generating more heat than light, has nonetheless forced Americans to ask some hard questions. Admitting that women, blacks, and other minorities suffered and still suffer discrimination at the hands of a white-male-dominated society, what is fair? Should the government impose a policy that benefits women and minorities at the expense of white males? Is race-conscious and gender-conscious affirmative action the proper policy to achieve a truly race-blind and gender-blind society? Can women and minorities ever achieve true equal opportunity in education and employment without such programs? Does affirmative action work to benefit large numbers of women and minorities, or does it help only the few who would succeed in any event? Is a practice that discriminates against one group, even to compensate victims of past discrimination, the right policy for a democratic society pledged to the equal protection of the laws for all its citizens?

Such questions are at the heart of the debate, and as Alexis de Tocqueville noted long ago, in the United States all public issues eventually become legal questions. Even as political leaders tried to define what affirmative action meant, the courts pondered whether and how the Constitution allowed such programs.

3

The Law
and Affirmative Action

As Judge Ingram prepared to hear Paul Johnson's suit, he had a certain body of legal precedent to guide him. By the spring of 1982, the Supreme Court had decided several cases dealing with affirmative action, and had also considered questions regarding discrimination against women. It had not, as yet, heard any cases directly involving women and affirmative action, but these two paths of law had converged in some areas. In general, the law as expounded by the High Court condemned discrimination in employment based on immutable characteristics such as race or gender, and approved, albeit sometimes guardedly, efforts to remedy the effects of past discrimination. But just as affirmative action had proved socially divisive, it also caused deep splits on the bench.

In the 1960s and 1970s, Congress passed a number of measures designed to attack racial discrimination in general, and in employment in particular. The most notable remains Title VII of the 1964 Civil Rights Act, but in the following years Congress passed several other measures aimed at eliminating discrimination in employment. In the Equal Employment Opportunity Act of 1972, Congress statutorily confirmed several lower-court decisions that had interpreted Title VII to mean that affirmative steps could be taken by the courts to remedy discrimination. The 1972 law also expanded the coverage of Title VII by including state and local government employees, as well as those in federal executive agencies, in its protection.[1]

In the next few years Congress addressed other forms of employment discrimination. Title IX of the Higher Education Act of 1972 forbade sex discrimination in educational institutions receiving federal funds. The Vocational Rehabilitation Act of 1973 required federal contractors to provide employment opportunities for disabled and other veterans of the Vietnam War. The Age Discrimination Act of 1975, as well as several state and local fiscal assistance acts, spread the umbrella of congressional protection even further, now taking in race, gender, religion, age, and disability. Moreover, by 1982 most of the fifty states also had some form of antidiscrimination statutes, some of which went even further than federal law in covering such categories as prior arrest records or marital status. A number of municipalities also passed local ordinances targeted at specific types of discrimination.[2]

With all these laws on federal, state, and local statute books, case law began to expand. The Supreme Court had heard cases involving employment discrimination as early as the Second World War, and had tentatively started to limn a legal notion of fair employment. In a 1944 case, it had ruled that trade unions governed by the Railway Labor Act owed black and other minority union members a duty to represent them "without hostile discrimination, fairly, impartially, and in good faith."[3] The case had limited applicability, because it affected only those unions operating under federal law. Otherwise, discrimination in the private job market did not then seem amenable to Court remedy.

Between 1948 and 1961, however, the Court decided a number of civil rights cases which cast doubt on the previous immunity of private discrimination against the reach of the equal-protection clause. It struck down judicial enforcement of racially based restrictive covenants,[4] and following the school desegregation cases, determined that when governmental activity intertwined with private discrimination, then the latter constituted a form of state activity proscribed by the Fourteenth Amendment.[5]

Despite all the civil rights cases it had decided up to 1965, the Court had not really established any firm doctrinal guidelines by which to evaluate the problems that Title VII would generate. The law itself talked more to broad objectives than to specifics. For example, while it prohibited employment discrimination, it did not define what constituted proof of that discrimination. Beyond the obvious, such as "whites only" or "men only," what constituted a discriminatory practice? Did the law reach the effects of past practices, even if those practices had been abolished prior to the new law? What did the law intend if an existing, and bona fide, seniority system encouraged some discriminatory practices? What conduct sufficed to show "intentional" discrimination? What if employment tests tended to disfavor certain groups? Above all, what remedies could the courts order if they found discrimination? According to Robert Belton, the courts faced these issues in three "generations" of cases. The first involved procedural issues, such as whether a plaintiff could sue in federal court before going to the EEOC; the second generation centered on definitions of what constituted unlawful discrimination; and the third dealt with appropriate judicial remedies.[6]

While it is beyond the scope of this book to trace out the entire judicial development of Title VII and employment discrimination,[7] a few cases need to be discussed because their rulings affected the progress of Paul Johnson's suit as it made its way through the courts.

One of the earliest cases, *Griggs* v. *Duke Power Company* (1971),[8] involved the question of how one determined if, in fact, discrimination existed. The Duke Power Company required new applicants for jobs as well as those employees seeking transfer or promotion to have a high school diploma and to take a standardized general intelligence test. Given the inferior education that most blacks had received in North Carolina, the tests tended to keep them confined to the least skilled and lowest-paid ranks within the company. Several blacks filed a class-action suit charging that the tests had no relevance to job skills and, in fact, existed solely to perpetuate job segregation within the company.

In speaking for an 8–0 Court, Chief Justice Burger found that the tests, while neutral on their face (that is, the same tests were administered to both black and white applicants), nonetheless had a "disparate impact" in that they resulted in job discrimination.

41

Congress had intended, Burger said, to prohibit not only overt discrimination but also those practices which perpetuated discrimination. "If an employment practice which operates to exclude Negroes cannot be shown to be related to job performance, the practice is prohibited." Legitimate tests that related to job skills would be permitted under Title VII, but the employer had to establish that relationship.[9] In 1976, the Court did sustain tests administered by the District of Columbia Police Department, even though these tests tended to screen out more black than white applicants. The Police Department proved that the skills measured by the tests had a direct relationship to the skills it required of its police officers.[10]

Aside from the question of testing, the Griggs case provided civil rights advocates with what seemed a sure-fire tool to prove the existence of job discrimination, the disparate-impact theory.[11] Plaintiffs could establish the discriminatory nature of a particular practice, such as an irrelevant test, by statistics demonstrating the racial imbalance resulting from that practice. In a 1977 case, Justice Stewart declared that statistics by themselves could prove the existence of employment discrimination.[12] Moreover, they did not have to prove that the employer had a discriminatory motive; only that the practice, whatever the reason, discriminated against blacks or other minorities.[13] Disparate-impact analysis also gave employers, such as Santa Clara County, indications of where there might be problems in their work force, so they could design programs to address those imbalances.

Employers, however, could often identify a problem far more easily than they could design remedies, since a number of conditions affected the employment profile. A high-tech firm, for example, would need well-educated workers, and past patterns of segregated and inferior schooling might have resulted in very few blacks having the necessary schooling. A firm located in a university town in the 1960s could often count upon a pool of graduate student wives, themselves highly educated but willing to work for very low wages out of economic necessity, and as a result distorting the employment picture. How much did cultural patterns, status considerations, availability of transportation, a seniority system, a union contract —none of which specifically intended to discriminate—affect employment patterns in a prejudicial manner? To overcome these and other conditions, as well as to remedy the effects of past discrimination, Executive Orders and congressional statutes called for affirmative action, a concept noble in purpose but fraught with legal problems.

Early cases involving affirmative action rose under the various Executive Orders promulgated by Presidents Kennedy, Johnson, and Nixon. In *Farmer* v. *Philadelphia Electric Co.* (1963), the first case of record under the 1961 Executive Order, a federal district court sidestepped the entire question of discrimination by ruling that the plaintiff could not sue, since he had not availed himself of the administrative procedures established by the Executive Order.[14] Other early cases also tended to focus on procedural technicalities rather than on constitutional issues.[15] The Supreme Court, no doubt aware of the legal land mines in affirmative action, tried to evade the issue as long as possible, and denied certiorari in several appeals of these early decisions. Eventually, however, the High Court had to confront the legal and constitutional questions raised by affirmative action, and it chose to begin this examination not in the context of employment programs, but in preferential admissions plans for schools.

In the various desegregation cases following *Brown*, the Court had ruled that any racial classification faced strict scrutiny—the highest level of judicial review. Nonetheless, the Court confirmed a number of race-conscious voluntary school integration plans without imposing strict scrutiny, supposedly because these plans helped rather than discriminated against blacks.[16]

A number of colleges and graduate schools, sensitized to the fact that conscious or unconscious policies had previously barred minorities from higher education, instituted preferential admissions programs, often without any specific findings that they themselves had discriminated. White students, denied admissions for allegedly less qualified blacks, launched a number of Title VII challenges against these programs in the early 1970s. In the first case to reach the Supreme Court, a bare majority of the justices chose to avoid the issue.

In 1971, Marco DeFunis challenged a preferential admissions program at the University of Washington Law School, on the grounds that he had been denied admission in favor of a less-qualified black. While the case was in litigation, the university allowed DeFunis to attend the law school, and by the time it reached the Supreme Court in 1974, DeFunis was about to graduate. As a result, five of the justices joined in a *per curiam* decision dismissing the suit as moot. Of the four who voted against the dismissal, only William O. Douglas wrote an opinion that actually dealt with the merits of the case, and the man who arguably may have been the most liberal justice to sit on the Court in this century strongly condemned racial considerations in admissions programs, even for benign purposes: "A DeFunis who is white is entitled to no advantage by virtue of that fact; nor is he subject to any disability, no matter what his race or color. Whatever his race, he had a constitutional right to have his application considered on its individual merits in a racially neutral manner."[17]

The Court had sidestepped the issue temporarily, but it would not go away. In *DeFunis* "the bomb failed to go off";[18] four years later it exploded in *Bakke*, next to abortion the most controversial decision of the 1970s.[19] Allan Bakke, a thirty-seven-year-old white male, had been denied admission to the University of California Medical School at Davis. He contended that the school's special admissions program, which reserved sixteen slots in a class of one hundred for disadvantaged minority students, operated to deprive him of his rights under the California constitution, Title VI of the 1964 Civil Rights Act,[20] and the equal-protection clause of the Fourteenth Amendment. Unlike DeFunis, Bakke had not been allowed to register, and so the Court could not hide behind a mootness issue. Did a program that consciously favored minorities and as a result discriminated against whites, be it in education or in employment, violate federal law and the Constitution? Specifically, the Court had to answer two questions: Could race be a legitimate factor in admissions decisions (and by implication in other public and private programs)? If so, did this particular program operate in a way to violate either Title VII or the equal-protection clause?

Civil rights advocates as well as opponents of affirmative action watched the progress of the Bakke case carefully.[21] Benjamin Hooks of the NAACP warned that if the Court ruled in favor of Bakke, "everything that has happened in the last twenty years will be rolled back."[22] Conservative John H. Bunzel hoped the Court would find for Bakke, because affirmative action undermined basic premises of American society. "In a country of many minority groups," he asked, "is it possible to discriminate in favor of a minority without discriminating against another minority (let alone the majority)?"[23] Few people approached the degree of alarm that McGeorge Bundy did in warning that if the Court did not support the Davis plan, it would be turning its back on blacks and others seeking to escape the legacy of discrimination. The Bakke case, he declared, has "an importance not exceeded by any single case from the past, not the Brown case of 1954, and not the Dartmouth College case itself, in which the independence of the chartered private college was first upheld."[24]

The nine justices filed six separate opinions, with no majority agreeing on any one point. Four of the justices—Brennan, White, Marshall, and Blackmun—believed that neither the Civil Rights Act nor the Fourteenth Amendment invalidated affirmative action programs, and therefore Bakke should not be admitted. Four others—Burger, Stewart, Rehnquist, and Stevens—adopted a straightforward statutory interpretation: the law said no racial discrimination, the Davis program had excluded Bakke because of his race, and he should be admitted.

Lewis Powell attempted to break the deadlock in an opinion that received full endorsement from none of his brethren. In his opinion he ruled that race could be a factor in admissions programs (the Brennan group supported him on this point), but that the Davis program had used race incorrectly, thus discriminating against Bakke, who should now be admitted (the Burger group joined this part of the opinion).

Powell had evidently struck this balance early in the Court's deliberations, but had been unable to win over any of his colleagues, a sign, if any were needed after *DeFunis*, that affirmative action would be a divisive issue within the Court. The decision would be widely attacked by both proponents and opponents of affirmative action, but whatever its legal merits, it seemed an astute political compromise, designed to buy time in which the Court could sort out some of the troubling issues raised by affirmative action.[25]

Meg Greenfield, writing in *Newsweek*, had in fact predicted that the Court would find a way to "blur the edges of the controversy" while at the same time reaffirming the important values on both sides of the question. "You say that is fudging the issue?" she asked. "Fine. It ought to be fudged."[26] That would allow employers to continue to work on solutions to the problems caused by past discrimination, but with greater care that the solution related directly to problems it had caused. One of the defects in the Davis program had been that the relatively new medical school did not have a record of discrimination against blacks and other minorities, but had undertaken to address a larger societal problem. Affirmative action plans could continue, but the *Bakke* decision left many questions in the air that the Court would have to address in the near future.

The Court answered at least some of these questions fairly quickly. In the very next term, it examined an affirmative action plan voluntarily adopted by a private employer, and its decision in *United Steelworkers of America* v. *Weber* would be its definitive statement for the next several years.[27] In 1974, the United Steelworkers and the Kaiser Aluminum and Chemical Company signed a collective bargaining agreement that included an affirmative action plan. At the time, practically no blacks held the higher-paying skilled-craft positions, and the union and the company agreed that Kaiser would establish an in-plant training program and reserve 50 percent of the slots in these programs for blacks. The goal would be for blacks eventually to hold a percentage of the skilled-craft positions equivalent to the percentage of blacks in the local labor force. One of the criteria for selection into the training programs would be seniority in the plant.

At the Kaiser plant in Gramercy, Louisiana, management set up a training program that accepted thirteen people, seven black and six white. The most senior black worker chosen had less seniority than several white workers who had not been accepted. One of them, Brian Weber, filed a class-action suit charging discrimination under Title VII. Both the district court and the Court of Appeals for the Fifth Circuit ruled that the plan violated the Civil Rights Act in that it granted preference based solely on race.

The Supreme Court, speaking through Justice Brennan in a 5–2 decision,[28] reversed the lower courts and ruled that Title VII did not prohibit race-conscious affirmative action plans. Brennan, probably in order to sustain his majority, emphasized the narrowness of the decision. The Kaiser plan did not involve either the state or the federal government, and thus did not trigger any constitutional considerations.[29] The only question the Court would answer, then, was whether Title VII actually forbade "private employers and unions from voluntarily agreeing upon bona fide affirmative action plans." Title VII, of course, applied to whites as well as blacks, and its purpose had been to prevent any discrimination based on race.[30]

A literal meaning of Title VII would prohibit any affirmative action plan, but an examination of the statutory history showed clearly that Congress had intended the law to deal with discrimination against Negroes, and that it had not intended to foreclose voluntary programs to remedy the effects of past bias. In fact, the very wording of the statute, as well as statements in the accompanying House and Senate reports, supported the view that Congress wanted the bill to spur employers and unions to examine their own practices, and take voluntary steps not only to remove discriminatory practices but to work toward full equality. "It would be ironic indeed," Brennan noted, "if a law triggered by a Nation's concern over centuries of racial injustice and intended to improve the lot of those who had 'been excluded from the American dream for so long' (remarks of Sen. Humphrey) constituted the first legislative prohibition of all voluntary, private, race-conscious efforts to abolish traditional patterns of racial segregation and hierarchy."[31] But, Brennan concluded, Title VII did not automatically legitimate any plan merely because it claimed the title of affirmative action.

> The plan does not unnecessarily trammel the interests of the white employees. The plan does not require the discharge of white workers and their replacement with new black hires. Nor does the plan

create an absolute bar to the advancement of white employees; half of those trained in the program will be white. Moreover, the plan is a temporary measure; it is not intended to maintain racial balance, but simply to eliminate a manifest racial imbalance. Preferential selection at the Gramercy plant will end as soon as the percentage of black skilled craftworkers in the Gramercy plant approximates the percentage of blacks in the local labor force.

Here we have what came to be the *Weber* criteria, the standards by which affirmative action plans would be judged for the next several years:

- The interests of whites would, to some extent, be restricted, but not to an unnecessary degree, and no white worker could be fired to make room for a black.
- The plan would have to be temporary, with either a fixed end date or a specific goal that would terminate the program.
- The plan could not be used to maintain a fixed percentage of minority workers, but only to eliminate obvious disparities.

The Chief Justice filed a relatively brief dissent that in essence said he would be glad to vote for such a plan if he were a member of Congress, a body charged with making public policy. The majority had, in his opinion, transgressed the line separating judicial from legislative responsibility, and in its interpretation of what Title VII meant had engaged in legislative amendment, distorting the original meaning of the words.

Justice Rehnquist proved far less restrained in his impassioned dissent, comparing the majority's reading of the plain words of Title VII to George Orwell's *Nineteen Eighty-four*. The Court had been consistent, at least until this day, in holding that Title VII prohibited *all* racial discrimination in employment, and "were Congress to act today specifically to prohibit the type of racial discrimination suffered by Weber, it would be hard-pressed to draft language better tailored to the task than that found in §703(d) of Title VII." Now, like Orwell's characters, the majority said that the words meant exactly the opposite of what they had meant only a short time earlier.

The differences between the Brennan and Rehnquist opinions continued the split in *Bakke*, between the liberal wing of the Court, which believed race-conscious programs permissible to remedy past injustice, and the conservative bloc, which held that to achieve a society free of racial injustice, any and all discrimination based on race, be it directed against blacks or whites, had to be prohibited. Here the Court did no more than mirror the philosophical split in the larger society, and despite the fact that only two members of the Court dissented, only five of the justices—a bare majority—upheld the Kaiser plan. A shift of one or two votes, or one or two new appointees, and the Court might reverse *Weber*.

The very next term, an even more fractured Court upheld congressionally mandated set-aside programs. Affirmative action programs could take a variety of forms, such as preferential admissions to schools (*Bakke*) or job-training programs (*Weber*). In 1977, Congress took notice of extensive discrimination against minority contractors in the construction industry, and in the Public Works Employment Act of that year required that 10 percent of federal funds supplied for local public works projects had to be spent with businesses owned and controlled by members of identified minority groups.[32]

The lead opinion came from the Chief Justice, joined only by White and Powell, in *Fullilove* v. *Klutznik* (1980).[33] Burger noted that Congress had found extensive evidence of racial bias in the construction industry, and that sufficed as the predicate by which Congress could act under its remedial authority in section five of the Fourteenth Amendment as well as its larger authority under the commerce clause. But if Congress had the power, had it chosen a legitimate means, namely the use of racial and ethnic criteria? Relying on various decisions in the school desegregation cases, Burger held that in appropriate circumstances, race-conscious remedies passed constitutional muster. Applying a variation of the *Weber* criteria, the Chief Justice reiterated the broad remedial power assigned to Congress and ruled that the set-aside program came within this power.

So stood employment law in terms of affirmative action as Paul Johnson made his way to the courthouse in the spring of 1982. But in addition to statutes and case law regarding racial discrimination, the 1970s had also seen the rise of the women's movement, and corresponding efforts to modify the law as it affected women's rights in American society.

Women confronted a legal and social system that for centuries had placed them in a position subordinate to men. Until fairly recently state laws prevented them from owning property in their own name, voting or serving on juries, or even suing in tort or contract; when married, they found themselves totally at the mercy of their husbands. Marriage made man and woman into one, and that one, as far as the law was concerned, was a man.

During the progressive era reformers attempted to ameliorate the condition of women workers by enacting protective legislation establishing maximum hours and minimum wages. Later feminists condemned these laws—supported at the time by both male and female reformers—as but another example of male domination,[34] and no doubt they do reflect the predominant male view of women in need of special care. For the most part, judges had tended to view all gender based classification as designed for women's benefit or protection, and applied a simple rational basis test in the few instances when confronted with equal-protection challenges.

The Supreme Court, for example, had no trouble sustaining state statutes which denied women the right to practice law, for as Justice Joseph Bradley wrote in *Bradwell* v. *Illinois*:

Man is, or should be, women's protector and defender. The natural and proper timidity which belongs to the female sex evidently unfits it for many of the occupations of civil life. The constitution of the family organization, which is founded in the divine ordinance, as well as in the nature of things, indicates the domestic sphere as that which properly belongs to the domain and functions of womanhood. The harmony, not to say identity, of interests and views which belong, or should belong, to the family institution is repugnant to the idea of a woman adopting a distinct and independent career from that of her husband. . . . The paramount destiny and mission of women are to fulfill the noble and benign offices of wife and mother. That is the law of the Creator.[35]

In 1948, the Court upheld a Michigan law that prohibited a woman from obtaining a bartender's license unless "the wife or daughter of the male owner." Justice Frankfurter, speaking for a 6–3 majority, declared that the Michigan legislature had acted rationally, and the Court would not second-guess its belief that "the oversight [of a woman's virtue] assured through ownership of a bar by a barmaid's husband or father minimizes hazards that may confront a barmaid without such protecting oversight."[36]

For all that the Warren Court did in awakening America to the problems of racial discrimination, it did nothing regarding bias against women. As late as 1961, the Court upheld a Florida regulation preventing a woman voter's name from automatically being placed on a jury list, as would a man's; Justice Frankfurter found the state's assumption that a woman's place is in the home to be unexceptional.[37]

Although some reformers have attempted to draw an analogy between legal discrimination faced by blacks and by women, the two are different. Professor, later Judge, Ruth Bader Ginsburg, who played a prominent role as advocate in a number of leading women's rights cases, pointed out that the generators of race and sex prejudice are not identical: "Women are found in every neighborhood, in every economic class. They live in intimate association with men who, under traditional arrangements, held a control rein over them. Also of critical significance, the law's special treatment of women was long considered 'preferential.' Classification by sex was thought by gallant men to operate benignly in women's favor—to place women on a pedestal."[38]

Interestingly, the allegedly conservative Burger Court[39] began and sustained the legal revolution in women's rights. In 1971, a unanimous Court struck down an Idaho statute granting preference to men over women in the appointment of administrators of estates.[40] The Court did not even begin to explore the ramifications of gender classification, but applied a traditional equal-protection analysis that emphasized procedural arbitrariness. Nonetheless, legal scholars as well as feminists believed that a new day had dawned, and began to push the Court to declare gender a suspect classification, and this subject to the same strict scrutiny accorded racial classifications.[41]

The Court came as close as it ever would two years later in *Frontiero* v. *Richardson*,[42] in which the justices struck down a federal law permitting male members of the armed forces to receive automatically a dependency allowance for their wives, but requiring servicewomen to prove that they supported their husbands. Justice Brennan elaborated a powerful argument for treating gender as a suspect classification, but won the support of only three other members of the Court—Douglas, White, and Marshall—one shy of the needed majority. Justice Powell, joined by Chief Justice Burger and Justice Blackmun, concurred in the result, but refused to go as far as Brennan in declaring gender suspect. Only Justice Rehnquist dissented, on grounds that since sex was not a suspect classification, the law could be sustained on a rational basis test.

Over the next few years the Burger Court struck down several statutes that discriminated on the basis of sex, without achieving a consensus on the doctrine that justified such results.[43] In 1976, however, the Court seemed to have found the rationale it had been seeking, a level of "intermediate scrutiny" more demanding than the simple rational-basis test, yet not as stringent as the strict scrutiny applied to racial classifications. To withstand an equal-protection challenge, Justice Brennan explained, "classification by gender must serve important governmental objectives and must be substantially related to achievement of those objectives."[44] Henceforth intermediate scrutiny would be the standard by which any gender distinction, benign or invidious, would be judged.[45]

One wonders why the Court never took the logical next step in developing a law which would ideally be as blind to gender as it would be toward race. The whole idea of equal protection is that the law applies to all persons in the same manner, that accidents of birth—such as race or gender—do not put a person at a disadvantage before the law. Title VII, the statutory basis for equal opportunity in employment, makes no distinction between race and gender; it shall be illegal to discriminate because of an individual's race, color, religion, sex, or national origin. It is true that the Fourteenth Amendment had originally been intended to prevent racial discrimination, but the wording of the equal-protection clause says that no state shall "deny to any *person* within its jurisdiction the equal protection of the laws."

Would the fact that the Court viewed gender discrimination as somehow more acceptable, at least in its less virulent forms, mean that affirmative action plans designed to redress the effects of past discrimination against women would face a higher hurdle in the courts? Following *Bakke*, at least some commentators believed that would in fact be the case. Race-discrimination law had always been the paradigm for all discrimination law, but the courts had rarely had any trouble in defining racial discrimination. Moreover, as previously noted, racial classification had been assumed, at least since World War II, to be malign and discriminatory; gender classification, on the other hand, had been assumed, at least until the 1970s, to be benign, and thus male judges often had difficulty in defining gender discrimination.[46]

If the Court, which had been dealing with racial discrimination for more than thirty years, had so much difficulty with affirmative action based on race, how would it be able, without comparable analytical tools, to deal with affirmative action for gender? Justice Powell had been able to define specific instances in which affirmative action would be an acceptable remedy for past racial discrimination—intentional discrimination, facially neutral rules which serve as a pretext for discrimination, and neutral rules which perpetuate past intentional discrimination. But, feminists asked, what about the type of discrimination women had faced resulting from cultural assumptions about gender differences and stereotypical attitudes about sex roles? Women rarely faced signs that said "No women need apply" or "Males only." They did not go to public schools segregated by gender, or have to drink from separate water fountains. Rather, their opportunities had been subtly but nonetheless effectively restricted by what society considered "appropriate" for women. Under Powell's *Bakke* analysis, "sex-conscious remedies designed to eliminate this kind of discrimination would be prohibited."[47]

By the late seventies no one could question that the status of women before the law had changed, but how far it had changed remained debatable. The courts no longer blindly deferred to legislative enactments that assumed a woman's place should be in the home; at the same time, the courts had refused to make gender a suspect category akin to race. In some cases judges showed a remarkable sensitivity to the subtleties of gender discrimination;[48] in others, the courts approved so-called benign programs that allegedly discriminated in favor of women.[49] "The female of the species," Justice Stewart told a group of Harvard students, "has the best of both worlds. She can attack laws that unreasonably discriminate against her while preserving those that favor her."[50]

The only problem seemed to be that not everyone agreed on what laws unreasonably discriminated against women and which ones worked to their benefit. One solution would be to treat all forms of gender discrimination as wrong, the same way one viewed racial bias, and subject supposedly benign programs, such as affirmative action, to the same set of factual predicates for women and blacks. A few cases decided toward the end of the decade hinted that even if the High Court refused to adopt strict scrutiny in theory, the justices had erected fairly high walls to distinctions based on sex.

In the *Manhart* case,[51] the majority rejected statistical evidence that women on the whole lived longer than men as a justification for charging women higher premiums for a retirement system that paid equal benefits to men and women. Justice Stevens acknowledged "that as a class, women live longer than men," but Title VII barred discrimination against any *individual*, and "the basic policy of the statute requires that we focus on fairness to individuals rather than fairness to classes." Two years later, the Court struck down a Missouri statute that set up differing requirements for widows and widowers to claim death benefits under the state's workmen's compensation law. In his opinion for an 8–1 Court, Justice White reiterated that gender classifications had to serve important governmental objectives, a confirmation that at the very least the Court still adhered to the notion of intermediate scrutiny.[52]

This, then, was the law Judge Ingram had to work with as he gaveled his court to order. The equal-protection clause as well as Title VII prohibited outright discrimination based simply on race or gender, even though, although not always, the classification operated in a benign manner. In regard to affirmative action, the decisions in *Bakke* and *Weber* indicated that if certain conditions had been met, both public and private employers could institute plans to remedy the effects of past discrimination. Aside from broad statements of policy, however, Judge Ingram really had very little case law on which to rely; Paul Johnson's suit would be one of many that would help shape employment discrimination law in the 1980s.

4

"A Simple Title VII Case"

When case number 81–1218, "Paul E. Johnson, Plaintiff, vs. Transportation Agency, Santa Clara County, California, Defendant," opened in Judge William A. Ingram's courtroom on Friday morning, May 7, 1982, only Diane Joyce felt any apprehension about either the trial or its outcome. Johnson and his attorney, James Dawson, believed they had an open-and-shut case of discrimination under Title VII; the county, represented by its deputy counsel, Steven Woodside, felt equally confident that it had acted within its lawful discretion. But Diane Joyce, the cause of all this, worried that something would go wrong. In the weeks preceding the trial she had called the union's executive director, Michael Baratz, several times to tell him that she did not think the county was taking this case very seriously. Baratz tried to reassure her that there would be no problem. He considered Johnson's suit "bizarre and ridiculous," and seven years later still thought the whole thing "cut and dried. . . According to the county procedures, she took a test, she qualified, they could pick anybody they want on the list, and they picked her."[1]

But Baratz liked Diane Joyce, and valued her work for the union, so he asked one of the stewards, Kristy Sermersheim, to see if Joyce had any reason to be worried, and if so, whether the union should intervene. Sermersheim called Ann Ravel, who had been assigned the responsibility of initial preparation of the county's defense.

Ravel assured her that "there's no problem. They have such a stupid case they will never even go to trial."[2]

Well, Sermersheim said, that's good, but the union stood ready to join in if necessary. "We are real worried about this."

"Kristy, they are such fools," Ravel responded. "In the deposition the boss has said, 'I hate Diane Joyce, and I hate women stewards.' You don't have to worry. This will never go to trial."

Sermersheim reported this conversation to her boss, Michael Baratz, and also called Diane Joyce to reassure her, to tell her that "Ann Ravel says this is easy and there will be no problem." So the union relaxed, and later both Baratz and Sermersheim were surprised to learn that the case had gone to trial.[3]

In fact, no one on the county's side seemed to worry. Suzanne Wilson, a member of the Board of Supervisors, recalled that Selby Brown, Jr., the county counsel, had informed the board of the suit, but they all saw it as a routine matter, "a low-level case," nothing to get very concerned about.[4] In the county's legal department, nothing about the case seemed to warrant special concern. After a briefing on the facts, Brown decided to leave the matter in the hands of two of his deputies, Steven Woodside and Ann Ravel, both of whom had had previous experience with employment discrimination cases, including a few that went on appeal to the Ninth Circuit.

Only a handful of the tens of thousands of lawsuits decided in America each year wind up as cases before the Supreme Court, and even those later recognized as "landmark" decisions hardly ever appear as such at the trial stage.[5] Yet in retrospect there appears to have been an unusually relaxed atmosphere among the attorneys preparing this case. The county engaged in practically no discovery, but relied almost entirely on the argument that under acceptable personnel procedures the hiring official could choose any of the seven candidates who qualified for the position; if the affirmative action plan tipped the balance in favor of Diane Joyce, that did not violate any principle of law.

Jim Dawson thought he had a straight summary judgment[6] under Title VII and the ruling in the *Weber* decision. The county had discriminated against his client on the basis of gender, prohibited by Title VII, and the affirmative action plan did not meet, at least in his eyes, the criteria set forth in *Weber*. He did a little pretrial discovery, to make sure that the facts as Johnson had reported them could be verified. His major decision had already been taken, in whether to go the state or the federal route.

In terms of employment law, the California code at that time had even stronger prohibitions against discrimination than did federal law, and since all of the parties involved were California residents or entities, he could have lodged his initial complaint with the California Department of Fair Employment and Housing. Dawson went to the Equal Opportunity Employment Commission because he considered the federal agency better equipped to handle complaints, and because Paul Johnson wanted a fairly rapid determination, which he got. Once they had the EEOC right-to-sue letter in March 1981, they still could have gone into either state or federal court. At that time state and federal courts in California shared concurrent jurisdiction. State courts could determine suits either on state or federal theories of law, and the federal courts could do the same. The decisive factor was time, and with a backlog of cases causing extensive delays in state courts, Dawson had decided to file his suit in federal court.

Other lawyers later criticized Dawson for relying solely on statutory law, and not invoking the constitutional argument of equal protection.[7] Dawson admits that with twenty-twenty hindsight, he probably should have invoked equal protection, but at the time "I thought we had a slam-dunker under *Weber*, which is Title VII." Moreover, his prior experience with employment discrimination cases led him to believe that most judges looked at Title VII in much the same way, but had widely disparate views on how constitutional equal-protection theory applied in the job market. Constance Brooks, who later argued Johnson's case before the Supreme Court, defended Dawson's decision as absolutely proper lawyering. A lawyer's job is to win the client's case in the fastest, cheapest way possible, not to develop elaborate constitutional theories.[8] Steve Woodside agreed. "He didn't think, and I certainly didn't think, that it was going to go anywhere beyond [the trial stage].

Maybe an appeal, but you don't sit there thinking this case is going to go to the Supreme Court and raise every issue to cover yourself."

Moreover, Paul Johnson did not want anything more than to have the court give him the job he believed he had earned fair and square. As a result, Dawson framed his strategy on an individual basis, not as an attack on affirmative action. We wanted to say, he explained, that affirmative action is all well and good, "but you have to use some care and precision when you're applying it, and that did not happen here. This was a back-door job with someone who had some power with the county." Had his client wanted to launch a full frontal assault on affirmative action, Dawson would have employed different tactics. "We would have filed a constitutional claim, we would have filed state statutory claims of various types, and I suspect we would have associated someone else who could have carried the brunt of that additional cost."[9] Instead, Dawson had what he considered a much simpler burden to bear—to show that the county's affirmative action plan as it had applied to his client violated the 1964 Civil Rights Act prohibition against discrimination.

Because both sides believed that the law and the facts clearly supported their positions, they waived a jury trial and chose to have the judge decide the merits. Both Dawson and Woodside thought highly of William A. Ingram, whom they described as a gentleman and as a judge who knew the law and presided over trials fairly but firmly. The fifty-eight-year-old Ingram had moved to San Francisco from Kentucky after graduating from law school, and after a few years moved south to San Jose. He had been a deputy district attorney and then a successful lawyer before going on to the California Superior Court in 1971. Woodside had, in fact, upon graduation from law school clerked for Ingram in the state court,[10] and had nothing but praise for him. In the 1970s the bar conducted an annual poll on judges, and local attorneys had consistently ranked Ingram number one in terms of fairness and ability.

President Ford had named Ingram to the federal bench in 1976, and once there, he lobbied for several years to get a division of the Northern District located in San Jose, so local lawyers, litigants, and witnesses would not have to make the trek to San Francisco.

He ultimately secured a separate court for Santa Clara and three neighboring counties, and at the time of Paul Johnson's suit, construction had begun on a new federal court building. In the meantime, Judge Ingram heard cases in a temporary courtroom in a trailer.

Dawson also lauded Ingram as fair: "He is probably not a result-oriented liberal judge by anyone's stretch of the imagination." Dawson had earlier tried two Title VII cases before Ingram, and even though he had lost both of them, believed the judge had acted fairly. In the case of Paul Johnson, Dawson believed Ingram would look at the facts and apply the law fairly. Both sides, then, felt secure in their cases and content with the judge who would hear their pleas when the clerk called the court to order and asked opposing counsel to identify themselves.

After Judge Ingram gaveled the court to order, the plaintiff's attorney, James Dawson, opened the proceedings with a straightforward statement of his client's case—that a promotion Paul Johnson had earned had been denied solely on the basis of gender, a violation of Title VII of the Civil Rights Act. Johnson "does not challenge the existence of the affirmative action plan, this one in particular, or affirmative action plans in general, but simply challenges the way [this plan] was used in this context."[11] For sex or race or national origin to be used as an employment or promotion criterion, Dawson argued, "it has to be a remedial action, it has to be based on something other than general societal discrimination." The county did not have such a record of discrimination, and could only support a claim by categorizing the road dispatcher's job as a skilled-craft position. In fact, road dispatching required only clerical ability, and women already held 75 percent of the department's clerical and office positions.

Dawson took about ten minutes to sketch out his case, and when he had finished, the judge asked him what relief his client wanted.

"The plaintiff, your honor, requests that he be appointed to the position of road dispatcher, retroactively to June of 1980, that he be afforded differential in pay between his present position and that of road dispatcher, that the court issue an injunction stating that the plaintiff will not be discriminated against again in connection with his sex. Plaintiff [also] requests costs of suit and reasonable attorney's fees."

Steven Woodside then presented the county's defense, namely that Paul Johnson was not better qualified than Diane Joyce, and unless he could prove that he had been passed over for someone of lesser qualification, he had not borne the burden of proof required for a Title VII discrimination case. The facts showed that both Joyce and Johnson had about the same qualifications, and that the hiring supervisor had discretion to choose from among those who qualified in the top pool. Under the county's affirmative action plan, the fact that not a single woman held any of the road department's 238 skilled-craft jobs constituted a legitimate consideration in the eyes of the hiring authority.

Woodside recognized that he could not just come out and say that the county had adopted an affirmative action plan because it had deliberately discriminated against women and minorities in the past, since that would open the county to all sorts of Title VII lawsuits. Previous decisions in the Supreme Court had recognized this dilemma, and had held that an employer did not have to admit to prior discrimination in order to implement an affirmative action plan. Woodside did admit that the county was in "a very vulnerable position in terms of Title VII, as a matter of defending history, given the very few women who have ever held a position of responsibility in road maintenance."

The county felt it had a much stronger case in regard to the question of whether the road dispatcher should be classified as a skilled or a clerical position. Because it had been classified as skilled long before the case arose, there could be no charge that the county had manipulated the classification for affirmative action purposes, and the numerical disparity—one woman out of 238—seemed to support the county's claim. But Woodside had a fallback strategy. The plaintiff would have the burden of proving that the dispatcher's job had been misclassified, and if he could, if Dawson could show that it ought to be considered as clerical, then the county would argue that as a clerical worker, Diane Joyce had far better qualifications than Paul Johnson.[12]

With the brief opening statements complete, Dawson called his first witness, James H. Graebner, director of the Transportation Agency, and the man who had chosen Diane Joyce over Paul Johnson. From later reports, it appears that Dawson had not intended Graebner to go first, that he planned to use his other witnesses to show that Johnson had the better qualifications, and then had been passed over solely on the grounds of gender discrimination. But Graebner was getting married that weekend and did not want to delay his honeymoon if the trial ran more than one day, so he asked if he could testify first. Dawson agreed, but this did not give Woodside a chance to go over Graebner's testimony with him, and alert him to potential traps.[13] As it turned out, Graebner's version of what happened seemed to support every one of Paul Johnson's assertions.

The Transportation Agency director acknowledged that he normally would not have been involved in the hiring process for a job at this level; that the road operations people wanted Paul Johnson; and that the affirmative action director, Victor Morton, had come to him to urge the appointment of the woman candidate.

Q. Mr. Morton felt that Diane Joyce should be appointed?

A. Mr. Morton was less interested in the particular individual; he felt that this was an opportunity for us to take a step toward meeting our affirmative action goals, and because there was only one person on the list who was one of the protected groups, he felt that this afforded us an opportunity to meet those goals through the appointment of that member of a protected group.

This brought Dawson almost immediately to the questions that he most wanted to ask.

Q. Mr. Graebner, did you have any basis to distinguish as to whether or not one or the other was more qualified than the other?

A. No. They both appeared, and my conversations with people tended to corroborate, that they were both capable of performing the work. . . .

Q. Did you take Ms. Joyce's sex into account in making the decision?

62

A. Yes.

Q. Was that a positive factor for Ms. Joyce?

A. In terms of affirmative action, yes. . . .

Q. If Diane Joyce had not been on the eligible list, in your mind, would Mr. Johnson have been appointed?

A. Quite possibly. I see no reason why he wouldn't have been.

Dawson later noted that he thought Graebner "hadn't looked at this stuff in years,"[14] and for much of his examination, Dawson had to prompt the witness on how the agency's personnel policies and affirmative action plan worked. He spent a long time, unsuccessfully, trying to get the director to concede that the dispatcher's position did not require extensive skills and should, in fact, have been classified as a clerical position.

He had more luck in getting Graebner to concede that the county's affirmative action plan left an enormous amount of discretion to the hiring authority, and that no clear guidelines existed as to how much race or gender should be taken into account when hiring or promoting people.

On his cross-examination of the witness, Steven Woodside tried to undo some of the damage, and he asked Graebner a number of questions to elicit statements that he had sufficient information that Joyce was as well qualified as Johnson for the job. Graebner, while certainly trying to be helpful, just did not know a lot about her, only that she appeared to have performed her previous job duties satisfactorily. She had been chosen, quite clearly, because the affirmative action officer had said they should appoint a woman. Realizing that further testimony might prove even more damaging, Woodside cut it short.

Reflecting back on the case, Woodside agreed that Graebner's evidence had been critical. An administrator more experienced with affirmative action and the problems it can generate might have privately decided to hire a person because of gender or race, but would publicly have said, "I think she's well qualified for the job, and I've considered the other candidates, and my decision is Diane Joyce. Period." But Norman Graebner normally would not have even been involved with appointments at this level, and when confronted by Paul Johnson, "he owns up to his thought process and tells him absolutely honestly" why he had chosen Joyce. And, Woodside noted, Judge Ingram believed him, and questioned why gender should have been considered at all.[15]

Following Graebner, Dawson called Diane Joyce to the stand, and identified her as "the individual who was appointed to the position of road dispatcher." When asked if she thought herself more qualified than Paul Johnson at the time of the appointment, she looked Dawson in the eye and said, simply, "Yes."

Dawson carefully led Joyce through a recitation of her work experience in the highway agency, and the type of skills one needed for dispatcher, trying to demonstrate that the job did not require any skills beyond clerical ability. In the middle of her testimony, Judge Ingram decided that he had heard enough for the morning, and recessed the trial at twelve-thirty for lunch. An hour later, Diane Joyce went back on the stand to face more questions.

Dawson now switched tactics, to try to elicit from her why she thought the process had been unfair, why she had decided to go to affirmative action. He kept emphasizing that she had not scored as highly as Paul Johnson on either of the two boards, but Diane Joyce proved a cool witness.

Q. When you walked into the second interview, Ms. Joyce, did you feel at that point that it was going to be unfair?

A. Yes.

Q. Was that because you were a woman?

A. Yes. . . .

Q. Did you think the first oral interview was fair?

A. Yes.

Q. Do you think it was fair because there was a woman on the interview board?

A. Yes.

Q. Do you think it would have been less fair had there not been a woman on the interview board?

A. Yes. . . .

Q. Why, in your opinion, did a woman being on the board make it more fair than if a woman hadn't been on the board?

A. I believe it prevents collusion; keep[s] each other honest.

Q. Simply because she's a woman.

A. Yes.

Just as Woodside had recognized that further testimony from Graebner would not help his case, so Dawson decided that he would be better off getting Diane Joyce off the stand. Steven Woodside, however, wanted to demonstrate something first. Where Dawson had tried to show that she had not been as qualified as Paul Johnson, Woodside now led her through a series of questions designed to show not only that she had extensive experience on the roads, but also that she had faced discrimination as the only woman on the crews.

Diane Joyce gladly obliged him. She told the court how, when she had first applied for a job with the transportation agency, the supervisor had told her they wanted a man, but since no men had applied they would have to settle for a woman. She also told stories of how she had been singled out and reprimanded for actions that, if done by a man, would have gone unnoticed.

On reexamination, Dawson decided to follow up on these stories, on her active role as a union shop steward, and the fact that she often filed complaints against the agency for actions she believed discriminatory.

Q. How many grievances have you filed on your own behalf since you have been employed by the Transportation Agency?

A. Regarding sex?

Q. Regarding anything. Let's start with that.

A. Five, ten.

Q. How many of those have been resolved to your satisfaction?

A. Ten.

Q. They all have, is that correct?

A. Yes.

Dawson did not push this line of questioning too far, since he did not want to depict Joyce as a victim. Rather, he wanted to show that because of her tendency to file complaints and her backing from the union, the county had promoted her over a more qualified applicant because it had been afraid she would sue if she did not get the job. In contrast to the "troublemaker," he next called his client, Paul Johnson, to the stand.

Johnson's suit alleged that, because of his gender, he had been passed over for the promotion which he had earned, and that he was the victim of discrimination. Dawson wanted the court to see his client as a hard-working, decent man, one who had always played by the rules, and to see how the county had cheated him out of what he should rightfully have received—the dispatcher's post. Under Dawson's prompting, Johnson told his story, how he had worked hard in order to get the promotion, and then his amazement when Bert Di Basilio had told him that he had "already been appointed, and affirmative action got it reversed." He could not believe this, he told the court, and so he went through channels trying to get someone to explain what had happened. He had met with the affirmative action people, who told him that they thought "it was a good opportunity to put a woman in the position." He had then met with the director, Mr. Graebner, who had told him essentially the same thing.

Q. Mr. Johnson, did you feel that in May of 1980, at that time, that you were more qualified to do the job than Diane Joyce?

A. No doubt in my mind.

Q. What's the basis of your opinion?

A. Well, first off, performing the job, I guess, approximately ten months full-time, or fill-in time, plus possibly over approximately thirteen years, I probably worked as a dispatcher between two and a half and three years. . . .

Q. During the period of time that you functioned as a road dispatcher, did any of your superiors ever complain in connection with your job performance?

A. None whatsoever.

Q. Have you ever had any negative reviews in connection with your job performance with the county?

A. No.

Q. Have you ever had any counseling by a superior in connection with your job performance?

A. None.

Q. Have you ever filed a grievance against the county for anything?

A. No.

When Dawson finished with his client, Steven Woodside made a somewhat halfhearted attempt to explore Johnson's past experience, to see if it could be made to compare unfavorably with that of Diane Joyce. But while Johnson had not had some of the experience she had had on the road crews, there could be no denying the fact that he had worked in the job, and had done so quite satisfactorily. In a few minutes the county counsel decided that this further questioning would probably hurt his case more than help it, and he excused the witness. When Johnson stepped down from the stand, Judge Ingram recessed the court until 10:00 A.M. the following Wednesday.

In examining the testimony of that first day, the reader would be hard put to determine if either side had an advantage. James Graebner had testified that yes, he had chosen Diane Joyce for the simple fact that she was a woman, and he wanted to help meet affirmative action goals. Joyce had told about her experiences, and the discrimination she had faced, and how she had fought to overcome them, while Paul Johnson, in his own quiet way, had made a strong case that merit should be rewarded. If everyone seemed to agree on the key fact—that Johnson had been passed over so a woman could be appointed—this by itself did not necessarily violate the law. Affirmative action often means that white males who may not have personally been guilty of discriminatory activity will have to pay the costs of society's efforts to redress past injustice. Both Congress and the Supreme Court had said that, under certain circumstances, this would be acceptable as a matter of social policy. In his questioning, Dawson had tried to show that the circumstances of this case made a decision based solely on gender inappropriate; in response, Woodside had suggested that because Diane Joyce had been as well qualified as Paul Johnson, gender had been a legitimate consideration in light of the absence of women in the Transportation Agency's skilled labor force. So far Judge Ingram had asked practically no questions, and neither side had any indication, at the end of that first day, of whether they were winning or losing.

When the trial resumed on May 12, Dawson intended to put four more witnesses on the stand, continuing his strategy of establishing that his client had been chosen because of his superior credentials, and then had been deprived of the job by out-and-out discrimination. The county had only one witness, James Baldanzi, a road superintendent in the West Yard. Baldanzi felt sick that day, and Dawson agreed to let Woodside call him first, before continuing his own presentation.

Baldanzi had been a member of one of the interview panels, and in his testimony he indicated that he did not know a lot about Diane Joyce. Woodside, however, pressed his memory, and brought out a deposition he had made in which he had called Diane Joyce "a rebel-rousing, skirt-wearing person." Yes, he did recall that statement. Could he explain it? "Well, Ms. Joyce was quite affiliated with the union," Baldanzi said, "that did not have full representation of the county in them days, and she more or less had the people going all different ways. I called it a rebel-rouser. This is my own personal opinion."

He denied, however, that he had let her union membership affect his judgment as a member of the panel; he had looked for someone with good experience for the dispatcher position.

Q. And who was that?

A. The gentleman that I came up with was Mr. Paul Johnson, I believe was the number-one candidate.

Q. Is it correct to say that there were a number of candidates who were qualified to do the job?

A. I believe you could say that everybody was qualified or they wouldn't have been on the interview.

Although he had been unable to get Baldanzi to say outright that he would never have chosen Joyce over Johnson, Woodside had left the impression that Baldanzi and Johnson had been part of the old-boy network in the highway system, a network that would never have permitted a "rebel-rousing, skirt-wearing person" to breach their ranks.

On his cross-examination, Dawson tried to remove that impression, and show that whatever his personal feelings, Baldanzi had been fair in his role as a member of the panel. Did he socialize with Paul Johnson? No. Did they work near each other? No, they worked in different facilities. How often did they see each other on the job? About once every four months. Did he ever discuss the dispatcher's opening with Paul Johnson? No. Did he ever discuss Ms. Joyce with the other two members of the panel outside of the interview? No, he had not. Had he had any preconceived ideas as to who should get the job? No, he had gone in with an open mind. Had the panel been unanimous in its selection of Mr. Johnson? Yes, it had.

An eager Steven Woodside began his redirect examination. He recalled Baldanzi's testimony that Diane Joyce's union activity had not influenced his judgment. But what about his deposition, in which he had said that her union activity conflicted with the requirements of road dispatcher because "she manipulates people"? Well, maybe he had said that, but he was not sure what he had meant at the time. Woodside pressed on.

Q. Did you also, in your deposition, make a comment that "she's not a lady"?

A. That's true. I made that statement.

Q. Can you explain what you meant by that statement?

A. Well, I've worked with Ms. Joyce in the past in the West Yard, and I have never heard a lady use the type of language that Ms. Joyce uses. And her actions at times, my personal feelings were that she did not act as a lady, as I know a lady to be.

Q. When you say type of language, you're talking about rough language?

A. I'm talking about, yes, I'm talking about a lot of very vulgar-type profanity.

Q. Would you say that that is the language that's used on the roads with some frequency?

A. It is amongst men, yes.

Q. Did you feel that your perception of her as not a lady influenced you in any manner in the making of your recommendation?

A. No, sir. It did not.

Woodside excused Baldanzi, and Dawson wisely decided to forgo any further questioning, instead moving on to his remaining witnesses.

First came Clyde Davis, a road superintendent for the county, who had been a member of the second panel. Dawson led him through a fairly detailed account of how the panel had operated, what questions had been asked, whether notes had been made, and the fact that the panelists had not discussed the interviews until after the last applicant had been seen.

> *Q.* Do you remember discussing Diane Joyce after the interview with the other interviewers?
> *A.* No more than we did any other applicant, no.
> *Q.* Do you remember making mention of her gender after the interview?
> *A.* No. Her gender was apparent.
> *Q.* Do you remember making mention of her union activities after the interview?
> *A.* No. That was apparent also. It's a well-known fact.

Davis had, earlier in his career, held a dispatcher position, although it had not been called that at the time, so he could speak of its requirements with some familiarity, and he, too, described it as primarily clerical in function. Moreover, he had served on several other review panels, so he could assure the court that this one had been carried out in exactly the same way as the others. And when the panel had compared notes at the end, "the consensus was Mr. Johnson was number one unanimously. . . . A clear-cut favorite."

Davis had been a strong witness for Johnson, cool, calm, professional, and he bolstered Dawson's strategy of showing Paul Johnson as the best-qualified candidate of the seven. Woodside tried to shake that image by linking Davis to Baldanzi as part of the old-boy crowd.

> *Q.* You indicated, in response to questions as to her gender, that her gender was apparent. Can you explain that?

70

A. Yes, she's a female.

Q. Was that in any way unusual, or did that strike you as being a factor in your decision-making?

A. Not in the least.

Q. Not in the least. What about her union activity?

A. That affected me not in the least.

Q. Mr. Baldanzi testified just a moment ago that he perceived Ms. Joyce as using rough or vulgar language. Do you have the same perception?

A. I do not.

Q. You do not? Can you characterize the type of language that she uses from day to day in the course of her work?

A. In my opinion, she uses normal language from day to day.

Woodside spent a few more minutes trying to show up some discrepancies in Davis's testimony, and then gave up.

Dawson next called Humbert Anthony Di Basilio, whom Diane Joyce had painted in her testimony as the man who had set the process up in Paul Johnson's favor, and who had been infuriated when she had gotten the post. Dawson questioned Di Basilio closely on his role in filling a vacancy, and determined that he had had nothing to do with it until the creation of the second interview panel. As for its makeup, he had had only five men from which to choose three, so there had been very little discretion. As to charges that he had not been helpful to Diane Joyce in either informing her of the interview time or scheduling it to help her meet her other obligations, Di Basilio said he could not remember. Nor could he remember whether he had ever discussed Paul Johnson with the members of the second panel. But he did know that in the twenty-six years he had been with the roads the recommendations of review panels, especially strong recommendations, such as in this case, had rarely been overridden. And he also knew that Mr. Graebner never bothered with appointments at this level of the organization, and that the affirmative action office had never interfered in any other promotion.

Di Basilio had said several times that he had considered Paul Johnson the most qualified of the candidates, and he had heartily endorsed the panel's selection. Woodside spent some time sparring with Di Basilio to try to show bias, and that Johnson's selection had been preplanned, but to no avail.

After lunch, Dawson called his next witness, Myra Beals, who had been a personnel officer in the Transportation Agency in 1980 and responsible for implementation of the affirmative action plan. She proved a reluctant witness, and Dawson had to remind her constantly of what she had said in her earlier deposition about the county wanting women and other underrepresented groups to have greater opportunities, especially in the road system. She conceded that she had helped to put together written comments on Johnson and Joyce for the memorandum that would be used to confirm Joyce's hiring.

An essential part of any rationalization for an affirmative action program is that it addresses and remedies past discriminatory practices. Woodside had been intimating throughout his questioning that women had been discriminated against in the road division. If Dawson could show that there had been little impediment to hiring women, whatever the numerical discrepancies might be, he could bolster his case considerably. He asked Myra Beals if, during her more than seven years working for the Transportation Agency, she had been aware of any practices specifically discriminatory against women.

Well, she remembered a few cases that came to her on complaints, and the fact that statistics pointed to continued underrepresentation of women and other minorities in certain EEOC categories, but she could not point to evidence of particular discriminatory practices.

Q. Do you remember the percentage of women in the Transportation Agency as a whole increasing during that period of time [when you were affirmative action coordinator]?

A. I can't say. I don't remember.

Q. So you can't say if the percentage of women increased in the Transportation Agency as a whole between 1980 and the present, either?

A. No. I can't. . . .

Q. Did you ever look into why there were so few women in the road maintenance division?

A. As a specific topic, no, I can't recall doing that.

Dawson then turned to the question of goals in the county plan, and over the next several minutes elicited some of the most damaging testimony of the entire trial against the county plan. In the fall of 1978, the total county work force had been 22.4 percent women, and in its affirmative action plan, Santa Clara County had set an overall goal of 36.4 percent. That goal had been standard across every EEOC category, regardless of the current percentage of women already in that area, and without reference to the number of women in the available work force in the area who could qualify for those jobs.[16] The plan, moreover, had no end date, and could go on indefinitely.

In certain areas, such as clerical and office help, which were predominantly staffed by women, the plan would not apply because the goals had been met. But if a white male applied for any of those positions, even if white males were underrepresented in that category, there would be no application of the plan because white males did not fall into any of the protected groups. Moreover, when pressed about whether there had been meetings to train county officials in implementing the plan, she could remember only one such meeting. All in all, Dawson succeeded in eliciting from an ardent defender of affirmative action rather damning admissions that the plan had rigid goals, no terminal date, and that there seemed to have been little if any training provided for its implementation.

Woodside could do little to repair that damage, so he stuck to his strategy of portraying the Transportation Agency as rife with discrimination, against women in general and against Diane Joyce in particular. Myra Beals recalled handling a complaint from Joyce in which a coworker had harassed her, and threatened to run her off with a forklift, and when Beals had met with three of the male managers, they had conceded that they knew about the situation, and had done nothing about it. As one of them had said, "If it had been two men, they would have gone outside and fought it out and settled it." Beals told a few more stories to illustrate the antifemale bias of the road workers, but all of them taken together could not establish the basic prerequisite of remedial affirmative action plans—the existence of a persistent discriminatory policy.

Dawson attempted to drive the last nails into the coffin with his final witness, Jan Davis, the woman currently responsible for affirmative action in the Transportation Agency. She confirmed that under the most recent revision of the plan, the county still called for 36.4 percent women in each category, a goal she believed unreasonable in some areas. When asked what categories she had in mind, Davis mentioned skilled crafts, because there were not enough women in the work force trained for that type of work. The agency's personnel office had been conducting extensive recruitment for road maintenance workers, but so far few women had expressed interest.

Dawson then asked her the same question he had asked Myra Beals: was she aware of any practice that she would consider discriminatory against women? No, she responded, no practice, although there had been isolated events.

When he tried to lead the witness through a review of how many incidents of promotion or appointment had been made because of affirmative action, Judge Ingram cut him off, and wanted to know what value such evidence had. Dawson started to explain that he wanted to show how unusual the Joyce appointment had been, but then stopped; he had hammered that theme throughout the trial, and there was no sense in irritating the judge over a point already made. He ended his questioning, and when Woodside indicated that he had no questions of the witness, Ingram called a short recess.

In his closing argument, Dawson claimed that the evidence showed two things. First, "but for the fact that there was a woman on the list, Mr. Johnson would have been appointed to the position." Ingram interrupted to say that was certainly clear, since Mr. Graebner had testified to that effect.

That being the case, Dawson continued, then sex had been the determining factor, and under Title VII, "there has to be a very, very good reason to make employment decisions based upon sex, as it would be on race, or any other characteristic." He repeated that Johnson did not intend to challenge affirmative action, only the Transportation Agency plan and its application in his case, and Dawson ticked off the problems that had been revealed about the plan. "There has to be some reasonable basis to use sex or race in any type of employment decision. We submit there isn't in this case."

Dawson claimed that it had been shown conclusively that Paul Johnson had been the best-qualified applicant for the job, and to deny him what he deserved under the county's own merit criteria required that the county put forward some compelling reason.

> *Dawson:* We say, No, you can't use sex, you can't use discretion, if you're the appointing authority, if you're anyone who falls under Title VII laws, unless you can tie that act into underrepresentation caused by an act of this entity, or something that is very serious and egregious, something that's well-known, like in *Weber*, the fact that blacks in the South do not get into skilled-craft positions. We simply don't think that's the case here. . . .
>
> *The Court:* In other words, it's your point that in order to have a good-enough reason to violate Title VII, they have to remedy some wrong that they were active in perpetrating, is that right, or some widespread social problem, such as black people in the South?
>
> *Dawson:* There has to be some nexus, Your Honor, between the entity itself and the underrepresentation. It can't just be general societal discrimination.
>
> *The Court:* Well, in other words, if nobody applies to work on the roads that's a woman because—for any reason, other than one induced by the county, then that would not be a good-enough reason, if that's what resulted in the underrepresentation.
>
> *Dawson:* That's correct, Your Honor.

Whether Stephen Woodside recognized it or not at this point, the momentum in the trial had swung over to Paul Johnson. James Dawson had done his work well; he had managed to keep the focus of the trial on his client. He had portrayed Paul Johnson as the

75

most qualified person for the job, ranked that way through the county's own personnel procedures, and a less-qualified person had been appointed for one reason and one reason only—gender. This blatant discrimination violated federal law, and his client deserved to be made whole for the wrong done to him.

Woodside had been dancing along a very thin line throughout the trial, and he recognized that he would have to be more explicit if he had any hope of winning his case in summation. The affirmative action plan could be justified for only one reason, if the county had in fact purposely discriminated against women. He started going over the incidents of discrimination that had been mentioned as well as the statistics showing underrepresentation when Judge Ingram interrupted him and asked point-blank, "Was the county responsible in some fashion, through discriminatory policy, for an underrepresentation of women?"

Woodside could not do the one thing that might have given him a chance, make an admission of overt discrimination, so he intimated that the county had allowed discrimination to take place, and pointed to some exhibits showing the extent of underrepresentation.

> *Woodside:* I think, as Your Honor is aware, statistics play a very prominent role in Title VII litigation. Certainly in class-action litigation, it's oftentimes the most decisive factor.
>
> *The Court:* A less decisive role in individual litigation.
>
> *Woodside:* Yes, but nonetheless a relevant role. I believe you can say that if there's a statistical aberration, that may tend to prove discrimination in an individual case.
>
> *The Court:* I think you can use it to corroborate other evidentiary acts of discrimination, but I don't—it can't carry the day, as it can in the class action, by itself.
>
> *Woodside:* That's correct, Your Honor. That's correct.

Trying to recover the momentum, Woodside went back to the argument he had been trying to make all through the trial, that Paul Johnson was not that much better qualified than Diane Joyce, and that since both had qualified for finalists, the hiring authority could take into account other criteria, including gender as it related to the affirmative action plan. Plaintiff's evidence, Woodside contended, just did not prove that Johnson had a right to that job. Before he could go on, Judge Ingram interrupted again to press him on the county's plan.

The Court: The evidence does not reveal any termination of this affirmative action plan. And there's no question but what the affirmative action plan sanctions racial and sexual discrimination, and thus violates Title VII. Right?

Woodside: It sanctions, Your Honor, that consideration be given to gender where there's underrepresentation.

The Court: Which is contrary to federal law.

Woodside: You're right, it's discrimination based on sex.

The Court: This is going to be going on in perpetuity.

Woodside: First of all, Your Honor, it is not. Our plan, unlike some others, sets up no quota system. There's no requirement that one out of three—

The Court: It sets percentage goals, apparently.

Woodside: Okay, they are goals. . . . And the plan, if you look at it from a perspective of 1978, is that that's our goal, and we're going to set out to try to do that with no particular termination date.

The Court: Is there anything in evidence before me from which I can tell how long the thing is going to last?

Woodside: Nothing at this point, Your Honor, that's in evidence.

Judge Ingram kept pushing Woodside about the imprecision of the plan in so many areas, about how it would affect individual males in the future, about when and how the county would know if it had been successful. The county's counsel struggled valiantly, but even if he had wanted to answer more precisely, the fact became evident that there were no answers to some of these questions. Ingram, in just a few short moments, had put his finger on every weakness of the Santa Clara County affirmative action plan.

James Dawson and Steven Woodside had one more task to perform for Judge Ingram: each had to prepare a proposed "findings and conclusion" memorandum, setting out what their client wanted should the judge decide in their favor. The county merely wanted

Paul Johnson's suit dismissed, and its personnel decision affirmed, leaving both Diane Joyce in her job and the affirmative action plan in place. Paul Johnson asked for the county to promote him to dispatcher, and to pay him the difference in wages between what he had earned in his current job and what he would have earned as dispatcher in the two years since the event, as well as reasonable attorney's fees for James Dawson. The memoranda also had to support these findings in terms of the relevant law and the facts presented at the trial.

Both men turned in their proposals to the court within a week after the trial ended in May, and then waited almost three months while Judge Ingram wrestled with the problem. The facts made it clear enough that Paul Johnson had been discriminated against on the basis of his sex, a violation of Title VII of the Civil Rights Act. The testimony also seemed to support his contention that he had been the better qualified of the two. However, the county did have the right to choose any of the qualified finalists. Moreover, the Supreme Court in *Weber* had approved race- or gender-conscious plans that responded to a record of past discrimination, and in an earlier line of cases had endorsed the use of statistical imbalances as proof of discrimination.

Ingram was not about to start second-guessing the county's personnel department on whether the dispatcher should be rated as skilled or clerical; that classification had been made well before Diane Joyce had applied for the job. In any event, courts should not be involved in such questions, so long as the agency's personnel policies followed accepted practice and had been applied fairly and in a consistent manner. So if he accepted the county's rating of the job as skilled, then he would also have to accept the county's statistics showing no women in a skilled-job category that had 238 men. From this, as the county had argued, one could infer discrimination and justify the affirmative action plan.

But Ingram had trouble: not with the concept of affirmative action, but with the county plan. The goal of 36.4 percent women in every job category had been admitted by one of the county's own personnel officers as unrealistic. Moreover, it appeared so rigid as to be less a "goal" and more of a "quota" which, except in rare cases of blatant discrimination, the Supreme Court had refused to endorse. The open-ended nature of the plan also bothered him, along with the wide discretion given to individual hiring officers to fine-tune the program as it went along.

In early August the clerk of the court called Woodside and Dawson to tell them that Judge Ingram had reached his decision, and wanted to meet with them. When they arrived in his chambers, he laid it out very simply. The county's affirmative action plan did not measure up to the *Weber* criteria;[17] Paul Johnson, therefore, should be promoted and should receive the differential in pay ($5,654.48), and the amount of attorney's fees would be computed later. Ingram's ruling relied almost entirely on Dawson's proposed findings, but the judge did not accept his rationales. He finessed the questions of job classification and statistical imbalance by relying on the plan's defects, a strategy that allowed him to reach this decision but would become an issue down the road.[18]

"I'll never forget Steve's face," Dawson later recalled. "I mean, it was the biggest shock in the world that he had lost the case, since it's sort of difficult to lose in a Title VII defense case if you represent a public institution."[19]

The decision awarded Paul Johnson what he had asked for, and vindicated his claim that he had earned the job and then had been deprived of it because of discrimination. Although the county would drag its feet in implementing the decree, it could also breathe a sigh of relief that Ingram had handed down a fairly narrow ruling. The county affirmative action plan remained intact, and future suits of this kind could easily be avoided by some simple and straightforward changes in the plan and its rationale. The county could live with that.

A jubilant Jim Dawson left Ingram's chambers to give his client the good news. Steve Woodside reported back to 70 Henning Street, the county government's headquarters, to tell his boss and the county executive that they had lost, and what they now had to do. When Diane Joyce learned about the decision, she called the union.

5

The Road
to the Marble Palace

When Kristy Sermersheim picked up her phone, she heard an agitated Diane Joyce exclaim, "We lost!" "What do you mean, 'We lost'?" Kristy asked. "Ann Ravel said it wasn't even going to go to trial. Do you mean it went to trial?" Joyce told the SEIU representative what she knew, and then waited to learn not only whether the union would help her, but what the county planned to do in response to Judge Ingram's order.

After hanging up, Sermersheim ran down the hall, burst into Michael Baratz's office, and demanded that the union do something. "They're going to kick Diane out," she said, "and we can't let this happen. She's entitled to the appointment under the rule of seven, and the boss was nuts not to pick her in the first place. It's because she's smart, and she's a woman, and she's a steward. The union has to help her." Aside from questions of principle, Sermersheim said, the whole case smacked of union-bashing, "of a union steward getting ousted by a heavy-duty, really antiunion, nonmember man."[1]

Baratz agreed something had to be done, but so far the union had not been involved in the case. While Local 715 of the State Employees' International Union backed affirmative action, it would be better if the county showed a real commitment to the concept by defending its own plan. Baratz began to make some phone calls and, as he later recalled, discovered that the Board of Supervisors had little interest in appealing. Both Suzanne Wilson and Rod Diardon, whom the union considered liberal and friendly to labor interests, reported that the county counsel had advised the board that an appeal could open a can of worms that could scuttle the entire affirmative action plan.

Steven Woodside remembers the story somewhat differently, and claims that from the beginning the board stood willing to appeal Ingram's decision. Even before the briefing by the counsel, one member, Rebecca Morgan, had come to the conclusion that the judge had been wrong and that the county should fight the ruling. The judge had not even looked at the statistics, which in her opinion showed a definite bias against women, and she strongly disagreed with Ingram that the lack of a specific end date made the plan defective. And that, according to Woodside, "was the reaction of the whole board."[2]

Eventually the Board of Supervisors did decide to fight, but the evidence seems to support the union view that it took some pressure to achieve that result. Several weeks passed and nothing happened; the union suspected that Woodside was dragging his feet and decided to force his hand by making a public appeal to the supervisors. At its regular Tuesday morning meeting, the board had a so-called one-minute calendar, an opportunity for people not on the regular agenda to request consideration of a particular issue. Michael Baratz told Kristy Sermersheim to get on the one-minute calendar.

She went down the next Tuesday and when her turn came asked the board if they knew that the county only had two more weeks to appeal Judge Ingram's decision. Diane Joyce, she reminded them, had been picked in pursuance of the affirmative action plan, and now she would be out. Were they going to do anything about this? This news, she recalled, seemed a big surprise to the board, and several members looked quite startled by it. They promised to "get back" to her, the standard reply to one-minute requests, but a day or so later, Suzanne Wilson came over to union headquarters, a few blocks from the county seat. After discussing the case for a while, she said, "This is really a problem, isn't it?" Yes, it is, they agreed.[3]

Wilson went back to the board, which now agreed that the county counsel should file an appeal. Local 715, in the meantime, decided that it needed to get more involved. Since it had not been a party to the original suit, it had no standing to present arguments or file appeals. If the county had decided not to pursue the case, the union would have been unable to do anything about it. Michael Baratz first went to speak with David Rosenfeld, a San Francisco labor attorney whose firm had long represented the SEIU, to find out what options the union had. He learned that in order to have a voice before the courts, the union had to intervene in the suit, and in essence become a party to the case. "If we intervene," Rosenfeld told him, "then the county can't screw it up anymore, since we can be there watching what is happening."

Baratz then went to the governing board of Local 715 to explain what had happened, and to emphasize the importance of backing Diane Joyce for the sake of affirmative action. He also told them that he doubted the will, and by implication the competence, of the county counsel, and asked the board to authorize Dave Rosenfeld to intervene on its behalf. Just as Jim Dawson represented Paul Johnson, so Dave Rosenfeld would now be working to protect Diane Joyce. After a brief discussion, the board agreed that Rosenfeld should proceed and that it would pay the necessary legal expenses.[4] Even while county officials had been debating whether or not to act, Rosenfeld had filed a motion with Judge Ingram to allow Local 715 to intervene; after a brief hearing on October 25, 1982, Ingram ordered that the union could intervene solely for the purposes of arguing a motion for a new trial and participating in any appeals taken by the county to a higher court, but for no other purpose.

Judge Ingram had handed down his decree on August 10, 1982, and denied a rehearing on October 27; at that time he gave the county until December 27 to file an appeal in the Ninth Circuit. As Christmas approached, Steven Woodside hurried to write his brief.[5] Dave Rosenfeld prepared the SEIU brief, setting forth the union's interest in the case, and why it believed the district court decision to have been wrong. Michael Baratz kept up the political pressure on the Board of Supervisors to maintain its interest in affirmative action and dispatched his assistant, Kristy Sermersheim, to keep Diane Joyce calm and focused. In the meantime, an increasingly angry Jim Dawson wanted to know why the county was dragging its feet in implementing Ingram's decree giving Paul Johnson the dispatcher's mike.

In preparing his brief for the appeal, Woodside faced the same problem that had bedeviled him at the trial: how to defend a program based on an assumption of prior bias without admitting that the county had, in fact, discriminated against women.[6] He could not and did not—with one exception—challenge the findings of fact, since there had been no disagreement at the trial over what had happened, only about how the facts should be interpreted. The county did challenge Judge Ingram's finding the affirmative action plan defective because of its allegedly open-ended nature, but by itself this did not appear to be sufficient grounds on which to reverse the ruling. James Dawson described the county's appellate brief as "a perfunctory effort at best . . . not a very good brief."[7] In his reply, he pointed out that appeals had to be based either on law or on fact, and that a disagreement with a judge's interpretation of one aspect of the record did not constitute sufficient grounds for reversal. The case had been docketed by the clerk of the Court of Appeals on January 19, 1983, and all the briefs and replies had been filed by the end of July. Now the attorneys waited until the court could schedule a hearing.

Looking back a year after the case had been decided in the Supreme Court, Dawson admits that he went up to the Ninth Circuit "overly confident," sure that he couldn't lose. Events prior to the actual hearing bolstered this sense of victory. In the Ninth Circuit, staff attorneys who work for the court meet with both sides to see if a settlement can be reached so that the time and expense of a full panel can be avoided. When the staff attorney met with Dawson, Woodside, and Rosenfeld in the fall of 1983, he asked Woodside why he was even bothering to appeal. Rosenfeld, however, jumped in and said there could be no settlement because the union wanted to uphold the affirmative action plan.

A short time later, both sides received notice that their case, docket number 83–1532, would be heard on February 14, 1984, at 9:00 A.M. The case also had an asterisk next to it, indicating that the court had placed it on the so-called short calendar, in which both sides together had only fifteen minutes to present their arguments. Attorneys practicing in the Ninth Circuit knew that a case on the short calendar meant the judges did not see any major mistakes in the lower-court decision, and there would be little chance of reversing the original ruling. Dawson figured that he would be finished at nine-fifteen, or nine-thirty at the latest, and planned to take the rest of the day off, visiting some friends in San Francisco and perhaps doing a little shopping. Steve Woodside and David Rosenfeld also knew what the asterisk meant—Woodside termed it the "kiss of death"—and realized that unless something dramatic happened in oral argument, they had little chance of winning on their appeal.

When a case is appealed from a federal district court to a circuit court, it is heard by a panel of three judges drawn from the larger number of judges appointed to that court. Case 83–1532 had been assigned to a panel consisting of J. Clifford Wallace, Warren J. Ferguson, and Betty M. Fletcher.

Wallace, the senior of the three, had been appointed to the Court of Appeals in 1972. A native of San Diego, he had practiced law there from 1955 to 1970, when President Nixon named him to the federal district court; two years later, Nixon elevated him to the Ninth Circuit. One of the most conservative members of that court, he wrote in his *Who's Who* entry: "My principles, ideals and goals, and my standard of conduct are embodied in the Gospel of Jesus Christ. They come to fruition in family life, service, industry and integrity, and in an attempt in some small way to make my community a better place within which to live." In 1988, following the Senate rejection of Robert Bork to the High Court, the Reagan Administration considered Wallace as a possible appointee, but in the end chose his colleague Anthony Kennedy. David Rosenfeld described Wallace as a judge with a conservative agenda, but very bright and courteous to all the attorneys who argued before him.[8]

At the other end of the ideological spectrum stood Judge Betty M. Fletcher of Seattle. An extremely bright woman, she had graduated with honors from Stanford, but did not enter law school for another decade. She then practiced law in her hometown until President Carter named her to the court in 1979. A friend and admirer of

William O. Douglas, she shared many of his interests and political views as well.

In the middle stood Warren J. Ferguson, another 1979 Carter appointee. A native of Nevada, he had moved to California after service in World War II and built up a successful practice in Fullerton, a growing community south of Los Angeles. In 1959 he held the first of several state court positions, and President Johnson named him to the federal district court in 1966. During his years of private practice as well as after he became a judge, Ferguson taught law as an adjunct instructor at several area law schools. A man with a wry sense of humor, he declared that he had adopted as his philosophy of life the old Nevada miner's creed: "Live today; look every man in the eye; and tell the rest of the world to go to hell."

An observer could reasonably anticipate that Wallace would not be overly sympathetic to affirmative action, Fletcher would be, and the decision, then, would rest with the centrist Ferguson. Like any good appellate judge, however, he would have to be convinced that sufficient grounds existed to overturn the lower-court decision. Dawson did not know any of the three, but Rosenfeld, who had argued often in the Ninth Circuit, believed that Ferguson could be won over, and he and Woodside, for the first time, saw a glimmer of hope. It would all depend, however, on whether Woodside could catch the court's attention, and move at least two of the judges to believe that the lower court had decided the case incorrectly.

Woodside began his argument[9] by noting that employers in cases like this one faced litigation one way or the other. If one went by the disparity in numbers, then women and minorities could sue on the grounds that they had been systematically excluded. If in an effort to open up opportunities the employer established an affirmative action program, it faced claims of reverse discrimination by white males. Before he could get very far with this argument, Judge Wallace interrupted him with a question about the facts. Rather than fazing him, the question bolstered Woodside's confidence; he had studied the record until he knew it cold, and could practically cite the pages on which the court would find this particular set of numbers.

As Wallace pushed on, Ferguson and Fletcher began listening

more closely, and soon they joined in as well. The fifteen minutes allotted to the case passed, and the questioning went on, first Woodside, then Rosenfeld, then Dawson. Wallace pressed Woodside that if the county made employment decisions on the basis of race, sex, or some other characteristic, then did it not have a very heavy burden to bear in the nature of an affirmative defense—that is, proof of prior discrimination as a justification for otherwise illegal practices? Did the facts support such a record? Woodside again had to avoid the pitfall of conceding prior discrimination, lest he open the county to a flood of Title VII suits from women, blacks, and Hispanics. All he could do was point to the disparities shown by the numbers.

Betty Fletcher went after Jim Dawson as aggressively as Wallace had questioned Woodside. At one point in his argument he attacked the county plan as "social engineering," and she launched into what Dawson considered a tirade about "the march of history," and the "invisible impediments" that women and other minorities face. Dawson, who does a great deal of trial work in his practice, said he could not recall when he had ever been on the receiving end of so much hostility and *ad hominem* attacks from a results-oriented judge.

Judge Ferguson did his best to mediate between the two extremes, and finally interrupted the proceedings to apologize to the other attorneys in the audience who had expected to march through their cases on the short calendar and get back to their offices. Evidently, Ferguson explained, they were not going to get through with this case for a while, and would probably not hear any other cases until that afternoon.

At some point that morning, Paul Johnson's efforts to reverse what he considered the county's shameful treatment of him—what the lawyers involved termed a "minor" Title VII case—became something far bigger. As Jim Dawson later recalled, his whole effort had been on behalf of a client whom they both believed the county had wronged. The case "didn't seem important to me other than because of Paul Johnson, who for the first time in his life was going against his employer. That was a tough thing for him to do. This was a case having to do with Paul Johnson; it had nothing to do with social policy."

Certainly the Ninth Circuit had not seen anything terribly significant in the case when it had assigned the appeal to the short calendar. The briefs filed by the county and the union had not questioned Ingram's decision on the basis of overarching policy questions; they believed he had erred in a relatively minor way. Jim Dawson had not raised large constitutional issues such as equal protection; he had won on Title VII grounds in the district court, and he saw no reason to change his tactics. The county also did not care to get into the equal-protection morass, realizing it could backfire. All in all, the original judgment of the court in placing an asterisk next to case 83–1532 appeared fully justified by the record.

By the time the oral argument ended, however, both sides realized that whether they had wanted to or not, they had stumbled onto a legal and social mine field. Dawson still thought the panel would affirm Judge Ingram, but he appreciated that far larger issues surrounded Paul Johnson's suit than just remedying what one person perceived as a wrong done to him. Paul Johnson probably had understood from the start that if he could be stripped of a job that he believed he had won—had earned—on merit in order to placate a politically vocal minority, then not only would white males suffer, but the whole idea of merit and ability and perseverance as virtues to be rewarded would be lost. Johnson never considered himself an oppressor, part of a majority that had for decades discriminated against women and minorities, because he personally had never seen himself involved in such bias. For him, this had begun as an individual complaint—he had been the victim of reverse discrimination—but he had intuitively understood the greater questions involved.

Diane Joyce, like Paul Johnson, recognized that the outcome of the case affected far more than her own job status. If affirmative action succeeded, women like her, who had been discriminated against throughout their lives for no reason other than gender, would now have a chance to be judged—just as Paul Johnson wanted to be—on merit alone. If affirmative action failed, then women and other minorities would continue to be shut out of better-paying jobs and promotional opportunities not because they lacked the ability, but because they happened to be women or black or

Hispanic. At least some of these issues had been raised in the oral argument; now Judges Ferguson, Fletcher, and Wallace would have to wrestle with them in deciding whether to affirm or reverse the lower court.

Normally, after a three-judge panel hears its morning cases, it will meet to take a preliminary vote and report the results to the senior judge on the circuit. The opinion will be assigned to one of the panel judges in the majority, and when ready will be circulated to the other judges on the panel; if there is a disagreement over the result, the dissenting judge will also circulate his or her opinion. When all three are satisfied that the written opinions reflect their views accurately, the decision is released. In simple cases, the opinions may be very short, and the results announced within a few weeks of the hearing; more complicated cases, or cases in which the judges have difficulty reaching or explaining their decision, may take many months. In *Johnson*, the panel heard the case on February 14, 1984, and did not hand down its decision until December 4, almost ten months later.

Judge Fletcher wrote the majority opinion, joined by Ferguson, reversing the lower court and upholding Santa Clara County's affirmative action plan as meeting the *Weber* guidelines.[10] She ruled that Judge Ingram had interpreted Title VII and *Weber* too narrowly; Congress had specifically declared its hope that Title VII would trigger similar efforts at the local level, and the Supreme Court had indicated its willingness to permit some latitude in dealing with problems of prior discrimination.

All courts, state as well as federal, are bound by the decisions of the Supreme Court. But if the High Court has not yet addressed a particular issue, the circuits may fashion their own remedies and look to their own precedents for guidance.[11] In this case, the Ninth Circuit had an applicable precedent, *LaRiviere* v. *EEOC*,[12] in which it had upheld an affirmative action plan to hire and train women as traffic officers to remedy a long-standing gender imbalance in the California Highway Patrol. The court had held that those excluded from the plan because of their sex could not sue for redress, since the plan operated consistently with the intent of Title VII.

The Santa Clara plan, according to Judge Fletcher, had many characteristics similar to the Highway Patrol scheme the court had earlier approved.

As for Judge Ingram's concern that the county plan had no fixed end date, she noted that neither did it make any claims to permanency, and believed the lower court had been misled by Graebner's description of the plan as "a permanent part of the agency's basic operating philosophy." She took that to mean only that in the future the agency would always be alert to gender or racial imbalances in the work force, and seek to avoid such problems. The plan, therefore, met the *Weber* criteria in that it had long-term goals, was remedial in nature, and did not unduly trammel the rights of white males. While, unlike *Weber*, the Santa Clara plan did not create additional job opportunities, neither did it foreclose them. To view Diane Joyce's selection as a complete bar to future opportunities for Paul Johnson, she concluded, constituted far too narrow a view of what the county had tried to do and what the law permitted:

> We conclude that the Agency plan, like the *Weber* plan, "falls on the permissible side of the line." We hold that the Agency's selection of Joyce, pursuant to the plan, was a lawful effort to remedy an entrenched pattern of manifest imbalance. We are not unsympathetic to the complaint of Johnson and others before our court that employers' attempts to remedy past discrimination sometimes visit burdens upon individual members of the non-minority group. As the Agency plan recognizes, however, "the mere existence of an opportunity for members of [discriminated] groups to apply for jobs . . . will *not* by itself result in timely attainment of parity for currently under-represented groups." Affirmative action is necessary and lawful, within the guidelines of *Weber*, to remedy long-standing imbalances in the work force.

As a result, the court reversed the lower-court decision that had given Paul Johnson the dispatcher's mike; Graebner's selection of Diane Joyce would stand.

Judge Wallace concurred in part and dissented in part. He believed that the lower court had not explored the problem of numerical disparity sufficiently to warrant the court making "broad pronouncements of judicial policy," and he would have preferred remanding the case for further hearing. Wallace, however, disagreed with the majority's interpretation of Title VII. The "ultimate question," he noted, is "discrimination *vel non*. . . . The existence of an affirmative action plan does not change this essential inquiry."[13]

When plaintiffs such as Johnson challenged promotion decisions under Title VII, they had to prove either disparate treatment—they had been treated unfairly because of specific criteria aimed against their group—or they had to show disparate impact—while the criteria did not explicitly single out their group, they had the same effect as if they had. Once the plaintiff had carried the burden of showing that he or she had been discriminated against, the employer could enter an affirmative defense that there had been past discrimination which had to be remedied by a legitimate affirmative action plan.

Wallace then went into a fairly rigorous analysis of what each side had to do, and what criteria courts should use to determine whether the plaintiff had met the minimal burden of proving discrimination, and what an employer had to show to justify an affirmative action plan as an affirmative defense. He faulted the majority for only requiring a vague showing of "some evidence" of a statistical disparity, and "some evidence" that the plan addressed the imbalance. Wallace did not say that Ingram had gotten it either right or wrong, but merely that he had not asked the right questions and produced a sufficient record to justify either the lower-court decision against the county, or the appeals court reversal.

In terms of rigorous analysis, there is no question that Wallace's opinion is far more logical than Fletcher's. Technically, he did not disagree with the conclusion that the district court had erred, but:

I cannot join this opinion . . . because I disagree with the majority's allocation of the burdens of persuasion and production, and because I believe that the district court should have the first opportunity to correct its own errors and conduct the intense factual analysis necessary to resolve these issues. In order for the majority to uphold the plan, it has taken several unnecessary doctrinal steps that weaken the Supreme Court's test in *Weber* as interpreted by *LaRiviere*. From these pronouncements, I dissent.

The purpose of his intense questioning of Steven Woodside had been to determine whether there had been past discrimination sufficient to justify an affirmative action plan, and that, of course, is what Woodside did not want to admit. Wallace did not oppose a bona fide plan, but numerical disparity, by itself, did not in his view justify a plan that did, in fact, discriminate against other groups. In many ways this position proved far more moderate than that of the Reagan Administration, which would have allowed relief only to those actually discriminated against. Wallace would not, however, as the majority seemed willing to do, accept allegations of disparity as proof of discrimination.

The Court of Appeals had affirmed the Transportation Agency plan, but the county now had another problem. After dragging its feet for nearly a year, it had finally implemented Judge Ingram's decision and in the late spring of 1983 had given Paul Johnson the dispatcher's mike at the East Yard. To show its commitment to affirmative action, however, it had created another dispatcher's job by upgrading a position at the South Yard, and had assigned Diane Joyce there. From her point of view this was a less than satisfactory arrangement, since it added on over forty miles of commuting every day; she wanted to return to her original assignment at the East Yard. The county, however, decided to leave Johnson and Joyce where they were, and hoped the issue would now die down. After all, Johnson had the dispatcher's job and the back pay he had sought and won in the district court, even though the Court of Appeals had overturned that ruling, and Joyce had the position and salary she had wanted. The county affirmative action plan seemed safe, and with the appellate decision another lawsuit appeared unlikely should a woman or minority be chosen over a white male in the future. Steven Woodside could take satisfaction that a good oral presentation had literally snatched victory out of the jaws of defeat. He assumed the Ninth Circuit decision would end the matter, and he prepared to close the file on the case and send the folder to storage.[14]

Paul Johnson, however, felt frustrated. He had been vindicated by Judge Ingram, but the victory had been spoiled by the Court of Appeals. From his point of view, the appellate decision meant that under the law one could discriminate against white males and they could do nothing about it. Even though he had the dispatcher's job, Johnson was too honest a man not to recognize that he was keeping the job only because the county hoped to keep things quiet.

Following the Court of Appeals decision, Dawson and Johnson made one last effort, and on December 21, 1984, asked the panel to rehear the case and suggested that the Ninth Circuit hear the case *en banc*. Under this procedure, the losing party in essence says that this particular three-judge panel got it wrong, that its decision does not correctly reflect either the law or the views of a majority of the members of the circuit, and had there been a different lineup, the result might have gone the other way. A case on appeal is supposed to be judged by the law, and theoretically the result should be the same no matter what the panel composition is. If a majority of the circuit judges disagrees with the panel decision, or if in a split decision it believes the law is not that clear, it may agree to rehear the case with all the members of the circuit sitting together.

But just as a three-judge panel is unwilling to overturn a trial court decision unless there is clear error, so a full circuit is unwilling to rehear a case decided by three of its members unless there are significant problems with the result. Moreover, a rehearing *en banc* is not a right; a party may not "petition" but only "suggest" that it occur. It is then up to the dissenting judge to decide whether to circulate that suggestion among his or her colleagues. If the dissenter feels very strongly about the case, and believes that a majority of his or her colleagues agree, then the dissenter will attempt to secure the votes for an *en banc* hearing. Most circuit judges do not like to sit *en banc*, and it is a rare case when it happens.

Because of the importance of the questions, Fletcher and Ferguson agreed that the suggestion for an *en banc* hearing should be circulated, but none of their colleagues requested a vote. While a majority of the circuit may or may not have agreed with the decision reached by Ferguson and Fletcher, the opinion appeared to conform to the general criteria of *Weber*, and the court refused to rehear the case. But in its denial of the petition for rehearing and the suggestion for an *en banc* on September 5, 1985, the panel in an unusual step amended its earlier opinions.

Fletcher added several short sections in an effort to show that her opinion did not take a casual attitude toward the requirements of a legitimate affirmative action plan, and claimed that her analysis met the *Weber* criteria. Moreover, she claimed that Wallace had mistaken the law and incorrectly cited Justice Blackmun's concurrence in that case.[15] This brought an angry retort from Wallace, and an addition to his opinion as well, that he had "correctly cited the law" and that the majority decision ran contrary to *Weber*.[16]

A thoroughly disgusted Paul Johnson decided to call it quits, both on the case and on the job. At age sixty he had enough years of service and enough money saved to take early retirement, and while normally he would have worked until sixty-five, "I just wanted to get the hell out of there." He went to Dawson's office and told him to figure up his bill; it had been over five years since he had initiated the suit, and he could not afford to fight the case any more.[17] Dawson understood the situation, but told Paul that if he wanted to try to take the case to the Supreme Court, there were some public interest firms that might take it on. They would pay the costs, and only needed his permission. "Fine," Johnson said, "but I can't afford any more."[18]

Public interest law firms are a fairly new development in American law. Many lawyers devote some of their time to *pro bono* work, that is, work for a good cause for which they accept no remuneration. This may take the form of advising poor clients on civil law (family matters, bankruptcy, etc.) at a legal clinic, or working with indigent prisoners on their appeals. Some pioneering attorneys, such as Louis D. Brandeis, devoted their time to representing reform groups or even cities and states in defense of particular programs.[19] The efforts of the NAACP to break down the walls of segregation led to the creation of the NAACP Legal Defense Fund, Inc., a separate and independent entity that did nothing but civil rights litigation, and which depended for its financing almost entirely on donations.[20] The "Inc. Fund" became the model for other public interest firms that specialize in such areas as women's rights, consumer protection, and the environment, as well as some that have particular liberal or conservative ideological agendas.

Several conservative firms expressed an interest in Paul Johnson's case, and after looking over their credentials, Jim Dawson arranged a "beauty contest" between the Pacific Legal Foundation of Sacramento and the Denver-based Mountain States Legal Foundation, where both firms would meet with him and his client, and they could decide who would get the case.

Looking back later, Dawson somewhat wistfully said he wished they had gone with Pacific, since it had appeared willing to allow him a larger role should the Supreme Court accept the case. But Mountain States seemed better qualified, and it boasted the talents of K. Preston Oade, who had recently argued a reverse discrimination case in the Supreme Court,[21] and who had a great deal of experience in affirmative action and employment discrimination law. Johnson and Dawson looked over his impressive résumé, as well as copies of decisions in cases he had won. If Mountain States took on the case, it would pick up all the costs, but it would also have sole control of the appeal. Their attorneys would consult with Jim Dawson, but they would have the final word on the structure of the appeal, and would handle oral argument. Dawson did not particularly care for this arrangement, but both he and Johnson thought Oade the best-qualified person to argue the case. Dawson agreed to take the backseat, and Johnson signed a consent form to allow Mountain States to appeal the circuit court decision to the United States Supreme Court. Shortly afterward, Preston Oade left Mountain States.[22]

From here on in, Paul Johnson's case would be handled by Constance Brooks, who had joined Mountain States as a senior attorney in 1982. After graduating from Tulane Law School in 1977, she had worked for a private law firm in Washington, D.C., and had been fascinated by the public interest litigation that it did as part of its larger work. But as she grew more experienced, it became less cost-effective, as she put it, for the firm to assign her to that type of case. Mountain States offered her not only a chance to return to her native Colorado, but the full-time opportunity to do public interest work.

Brooks found the atmosphere at Mountain States congenial in a number of ways. While it supported conservative economic ideas, it also endorsed libertarian positions on many social issues, and thus could, and at times did, find itself allied in certain causes with the American Civil Liberties Union.

Attorneys at the firm read about Paul Johnson's case, and then the four senior attorneys discussed whether it constituted the type of litigation the firm should join. At one time Mountain States did "cradle-to-grave" work, initiating a suit for a plaintiff and carrying it through to the last appeal. But with limited resources and rapidly changing case law, the firm had adopted a strategy of involvement at particular stages, where it believed its assistance could be most effective. By 1982, Mountain States had been involved in several types of reverse discrimination suits, and its attorneys wanted to help Paul Johnson if he agreed.

In addition to her role as head of the section on natural resource litigation, Brooks at the time served as supervising attorney at Mountain States, directing the relatively young staff in various procedures, so she had the initial responsibility for overseeing prep-aration of petitions for certiorari. When Oade left, only two attor-neys, she and Diane Vaksdal, knew anything about Johnson's case, so they stepped in full-time to finish the cert petition. Since most of the staff had been out of law school only a few years, Brooks was also one of the few lawyers at Mountain States with the five years of practice required for admission to the Supreme Court bar. She had not yet met Paul Johnson or James Dawson; over the next eighteen months she would get to know them well.

Under the rules of the Supreme Court, the losing party in a lower court has ninety days from the time of final judgment[23] in which to file a petition for a writ of certiorari, thus initiating the process by which the Supreme Court will decide whether it will accept a case on appeal. Despite the litigant's famous cry, "I'll fight this all the way to the Supreme Court," very few cases are actually heard in the Court's marble palace across from the Capitol.[24]

Cases come to the Supreme Court in one of three ways. The Constitution confers so-called original jurisdiction in a handful of instances, and in these cases, such as suits between two or more states or those "affecting Ambassadors, other public Ministers and Consuls," the suit is filed directly with the Court, which will act as a trial court. In all other cases, the Supreme Court has "appellate jurisdiction," and parties appeal from either the highest tribunal in a state or a federal court.[25] There are two types of appellate juris- diction. In a rare number of instances, a losing party has an au- tomatic right to have the High Court review the decision. This does not mean that the Court will actually hear oral arguments in these cases; nearly all the time it will rely on the briefs and dispose of the case summarily, issuing a terse statement usually upholding the decision below.

The vast majority of appeals to the Court come as petitions for certiorari, which the Court has discretion to accept or reject. The justices receive over 5,000 petitions for cert each term; of these they accept only a few hundred, many of which are disposed of sum- marily, either through upholding the lower court and thus affirming a particular point of law; overturning the lower-court decision, a common procedure in the 1960s and 1970s in civil rights cases but otherwise fairly rare; or remanding (sending the case back to a lower court) for further review in light of a particular and usually recent Supreme Court decision. Perhaps 170 cases a year will re- ceive a full-dress consideration, including oral argument before the bench.[26]

By the time Dawson and Johnson had chosen Mountain States, and Connie Brooks had been assigned the case, very little time remained of the ninety-day limit on filing an appeal, and Brooks realized that even working around the clock with assistance, she would not be able to file an effective appeal before December 4, 1985. So she requested a thirty-day extension from Associate Justice William H. Rehnquist, in his capacity as circuit justice for the Ninth Circuit.[27] Rehnquist granted the extension, and Brooks filed the petition for writ of certiorari in the case of Paul E. Johnson, Petitioner, versus Transportation Agency, Santa Clara County, California, and Service Employees International Union, Local 715, Respondents, on December 31, 1985, three days before the extended deadline. At the top of the title page, the clerk of the Court penciled in the docket number, 85–1129, the petition being number 1129 of those filed in the 1985 term of the Court. The petition listed Constance H. Brooks and Diane L. Vaksdal of Mountain States and James L. Dawson as the attorneys for Johnson, with Brooks as counsel of record.

Johnson, through his attorneys, asked the Court to grant the petition on two grounds. First, a conflict existed between two circuits. The Ninth Circuit decision in *Johnson* apparently held that a public employer could make gender-based employment decisions under cover of an affirmative action plan adopted solely on the basis of a statistical imbalance between men and women in the work force, and without any evidence of overt discrimination. The Seventh Circuit, in a decision dealing with minority hiring in the South Bend, Indiana, police and fire departments, had ruled that statistical disparity by itself did not justify an affirmative action plan; there had to be proof of actual past discrimination.[28] Brooks had firm ground on this point because it is one of the functions of the Supreme Court to resolve differences of interpretation among the circuits, so that all citizens, no matter where they live, will be subject to the same federal law.

In her second justification, she challenged the Ninth Circuit panel's conclusion that the Santa Clara plan did not violate the criteria for voluntary affirmative action plans set out in *Weber*, which since its announcement in 1979 had been the standard by which lower courts evaluated affirmative action plans. Brooks read *Weber* to hold that there had to be past discrimination "so egregious that the Court could take judicial notice," and the plan had to be designed to break down the "old patterns" of segregation and hierarchy. Beyond that, the plan could not "unnecessarily trammel the interests of white employees," and would end when the current exclusion of minorities had been remedied. None of these conditions, she claimed, existed in this case:

First, the district court found as a matter of fact and law that no discrimination against women had occurred, based on evidence and testimony presented by the Agency. Instead, the plan is based solely on statistical disparity. The plan is not intended to break down traditional patterns of exclusion, because exclusionary acts have never occurred. The plan has neither an end date nor criteria to determine the end date. In more than seven years, the percentage goals in the plan have never been reviewed, nor has any yearly review been completed as the plan requires. Thus, the plan unnecessarily trammels the interests of the male employees because it has no remedial purpose.[29]

Brooks had made no reference to equal protection, because the trial had been conducted strictly on Title VII grounds. If her only argument had been that the county plan did not square with the *Weber* holding, the chances of the Court accepting the case would have been slim. The Ninth Circuit had interpreted the facts and what *Weber* required in a way that did not seem blatantly mistaken; a majority of the judges had apparently thought the panel sufficiently right to preclude an *en banc* hearing. The need to resolve a difference between two circuits, however, would always receive close scrutiny by the bench. Whether in order to resolve that difference required a full-scale argument or merely a summary decision constituted another question.

Steven Woodside had not expected an appeal, and awareness that Mountain States had taken over Paul Johnson's case came when he learned that Connie Brooks had requested an extension of time. He did not get too concerned over this, since he knew that the Court accepted only a small number of cases for review. But he did have to get himself admitted to the Supreme Court bar, a simple procedure he arranged by mail, so he could file a response to the petition.

Santa Clara County had had only one other case go up to the Supreme Court, but that had been a question of criminal procedure under California state law, and the appeal had been handled by the state attorney general. The county counsel's office had had absolutely no experience at all with the United States Supreme Court, but after a brief discussion, the county counsel, Donald Clark, decided Steven Woodside should keep control of the case. He had argued it at trial and successfully turned around the appellate court; most important, no one knew the record better than he did.

While Woodside displayed a fair degree of self-confidence throughout the case, he also had a good sense of his own strengths and limitations. He had trial experience, and had argued a few cases before the Ninth Circuit, so he knew what had to be done at those levels. He recognized that at the Supreme Court inexperience would be a serious liability, and from the initial response to the petition for cert right on up through preparation for oral argument, he sought and accepted advice from others.[30] He prepared a response to Johnson's petition, and circulated it among his colleagues in the county counsel's office as well as to several outside lawyers for their reaction. They thought he had done a good job in hitting all the right points.

Just as Connie Brooks had framed the key question to favor her argument, so Woodside now did the same. "May an employer," he asked, "consider gender as a factor in promoting a qualified woman where none of 238 persons employed in the job category were female and where the employer's voluntary affirmative action plan set no quotas, but permitted gender to be a factor in employment decisions until such time as the employer's work force is representative of the local area labor force?"[31]

Woodside's two key points responded directly to those raised by Brooks. The Court of Appeals decision, he maintained, had been consistent with the standards enunciated in *Weber*, and presented no facts which would give rise to a new issue requiring review by the Court. He narrated the events emphasizing how the county plan had responded to a particular set of facts, and how it comported with the *Weber* criteria, the only difference being that *Weber* had dealt with race, and *Johnson* with gender. Both Joyce and Johnson had qualified for the job, and no significant difference in abilities made one clearly better than the other; in such a situation, the employer could legitimately take gender into account.

Woodside also denied that an irreconcilable difference existed between the Seventh and Ninth Circuit decisions. The *Janowiak* case had a completely different set of facts than *Johnson*. In *Janowiak* the district court had issued a summary judgment based on statistics indicating discrimination, and had never heard any evidence as to whether there had in fact been any discrimination on the employer's part. The appeals court had reversed because two public task forces had found that despite the statistical imbalance, the employer had never followed any discriminatory policies. Moreover, the Seventh Circuit itself had carefully limited *Janowiak* to its peculiar circumstances, and another more recent decision in the same circuit had been consistent with the Ninth Circuit cases.[32]

The petitioner has a right to file a reply, and Brooks exercised this right. She wanted to emphasize one point, both in terms of securing cert and also as a basis for her later argument. She devoted her reply to one issue, attempting to rebut Woodside's assertion that Joyce and Johnson had been equally well qualified. She quoted extensively from the depositions and the trial to support her claim that Johnson had been far better qualified, and thus the county's plan, in unnecessarily trammeling his rights, had violated the *Weber* standards.[33]

When the county's reply had been received, the clerk of the Court distributed it and Johnson's petition to all nine members of the Court. In each chamber, one of the clerks read the two documents and prepared a short summary of the arguments, as well as a recommendation of whether or not to grant cert. In late February, Chief Justice Warren E. Burger put No. 85–1129 on the agenda for discussion at the next conference.

For the Supreme Court to grant certiorari, four of the nine justices must agree that there is a case or controversy of sufficient magnitude to warrant the expenditure of the Court's scarce time and resources. The rule of four, as one scholar has noted, "is an intriguing institutional tradition. Four is the perfect number, striking a sensitive balance between principle and pragmatism."[34] If one allowed the Chief Justice to determine the Court's calendar, that would put too much power in the hands of a person envisioned by the Framers as no more than "first among equals." If five justices had to vote for cert, that would in effect prejudge a case, since the majority could accept only those cases it wished to reverse or affirm for ideological as well as jurisprudential reasons.

While some of the five-thousand-plus cases reaching the Court each year are frivolous, and most raise no new point of law, many do involve difficult legal and constitutional questions that may require extensive briefing and argument. The rule of four makes sure that some of these questions will be heard, and it negates the need to play tough at an early stage of the proceedings. The majority can agree graciously to the wishes of a minority to hear a particular question, recognizing that the minority is only one vote short of a majority. On the other hand, if only two or three people are interested in a case, it will not be heard. For the most part, the rule of four makes sure that insignificant issues will not waste the Court's time, and that important questions will usually get onto the calendar.

Prior to the Friday conference, the Chief Justice will circulate two lists of cases. Special List I, or the Discuss List, includes those petitions for cert which he considers ready and worth discussing. Special List II, the so-called Dead List, contains those petitions he believes not worth discussing, for a variety of reasons, and on which the conference should not waste time. The other justices will have one of their clerks check the list, and if there are no cases that they have a particular interest in, they will agree to deny cert. Discussion will then be confined to just those cases where one or more justices believe significant issues are involved. Ideally, the justices agree to grant or deny cert because of the questions of law involved; in fact, personal views about particular issues will also affect how each justice votes.

At its conference on February 24, 1986, the four most liberal members of the Court—William Brennan, Thurgood Marshall, Harry Blackmun, and John Stevens—voted to deny cert. All of them had voted to sustain affirmative action plans in prior decisions, and saw no reason to disturb the Ninth Circuit's ruling. Justice Louis Powell, the Court's leading centrist, believed that cert should be granted, but that the Ninth Circuit decision should then be vacated and the case remanded for review in light of the Court's as yet unannounced decision in No. 84–1340, *Wygant* v. *Jackson Board of Education,*[35] another affirmative action case. Chief Justice Warren Burger, joined by his three most conservative colleagues, Byron White, William Rehnquist, and Sandra Day O'Connor, voted to grant cert; the rule of four had been met. The justices agreed that notice that cert had been granted in the *Johnson* case should be held until after the opinion in *Wygant* had been delivered. On July 7, 1986, the United States Supreme Court announced that it would hear argument in Paul Johnson's case the following term.

6

The Changing Law
of the Eighties

Steve Woodside walked into 70 West Hedding Street on Monday morning July 14th feeling pretty good after enjoying a few days' vacation with his family in northern California. He got off the elevator at the ninth floor, and as he walked to his office someone said to him, "Gee, isn't it wonderful about the case?"

Steve said, "What case?," thinking he had won a suit then pending in a local court.

"The affirmative action case, you know, the one about Diane Joyce. The Supreme Court is going to hear your case."

"Oh, Christ no, tell me it isn't so!" Woodside said, and ran down the hall to his office. There he found his desk piled with letters and telegrams from all over the country, ranging from "You have to settle this case or the Supreme Court will dump affirmative action" to "Boy, we can help you and we can argue the case for you."

To put it mildly, Steve Woodside was not thrilled. Looking back on it later, he said, "Now it's easy to say this is a highlight of my career and all that, but at the time all I could see was a lot of work and a lot of problems. I kept telling myself, 'Keep your mind on your job; your job is to do the best for your clients.' "

Woodside knew that the Court had been split on affirmative action cases, and that it could very easily reverse the victory he had won in the Ninth Circuit. He looked through a stack of telephone messages, and began calling people—Barry Goldstein of the NAACP Inc. Fund and Benna Solomon at the Council of State and Local Governments—asking them what they thought the Court might do. He soon discovered that no consensus existed on either the Court's proclivities or the best way to deal with the issue. Several people suggested that he come to Washington, where they would arrange a meeting of interested groups to discuss strategy. Within a week, Woodside flew east.[1] In the meantime, he reviewed some of the recent High Court cases to see whether the law had changed significantly since the Johnson suit had first begun.

Following the *Weber* and *Fullilove* decisions, it appeared that the Supreme Court would endorse affirmative action as consistent with both Title VII and the equal-protection clause. But in the three years since Judge Ingram had first heard Johnson's suit, the High Court had decided several other cases which now made approval of the Santa Clara plan problematical. Moreover, the Reagan Administration in general, and the Justice Department in particular, had declared war on affirmative action, launching one suit after another in efforts to reverse previous settlements, and pressuring state and local governments to withdraw from consent decrees that had established preferential hiring programs.

The first case before the Court involved a clash of competing rights, a problem frequently associated with affirmative action programs. In 1980 Memphis, Tennessee, had entered a consent decree following a class-action suit initiated by Carl Stotts, a black fireman who charged the city with discrimination in hiring and promotion practices in the fire department. The city agreed to promote certain individuals, and established interim goals of filling one-half of job vacancies and 20 percent of promotions in each job category with qualified black applicants. The decree did not contain any provisions for layoffs or for awarding competitive seniority.[2]

The following year, in the face of budget deficits, the city announced that it would have to reduce personnel in nearly all departments, and in doing so would follow a "last hired, first fired" rule based on an employee's length of continuous service with the city. Since most black employees had only recently been hired or promoted under the consent decree, nearly all of them—including Carl Stotts—would be let go in the layoff. He went to court and got a temporary restraining order forbidding the layoff of any black employees. The firefighters' union, which had not been a party to the consent decree but which had negotiated the seniority system with the city, intervened, and from here on the fight over the seniority system pitted the black firemen against the predominantly white union.

In May 1981, the district court issued a permanent injunction against the city. While it noted that the consent decree had been silent on the question of layoffs, the judge found that the city did not have a bona fide seniority system, and therefore could not use seniority as a basis for reducing staff. The Sixth Circuit affirmed the district court's findings, and the union appealed to the Supreme Court. In the meantime, the city's fiscal problems eased, and all the white employees laid off had been hired back. The Court could easily have avoided this case by declaring it moot, but at least four justices wanted to deal with the issue, and under the rule of four, the Court granted certiorari.

Justice White handed down the Court's opinion in June 1984, and by a vote of 6–3 upheld the vested rights in valid seniority systems against affirmative action plans.[3] Title VII specifically permitted bona fide seniority plans as justification for differences in compensation and conditions of employment and discharge, and the district court could not ignore the plan in attempting to fashion a remedy against discrimination. Neither the union nor non-minority workers had been parties to the consent decree, and therefore had not agreed to give up their rights under the system negotiated with the city.

Chief Justice Burger and Justices Powell and Rehnquist joined White's opinion. Justice Stevens concurred only in the result, and thought White's discourse on the meaning of §703(h) of Title VII, the section on seniority, wholly unnecessary; he would have decided the case on the simple fact that the district court misinterpreted the facts and "abused its discretion."

Justice O'Connor, rapidly becoming a critical centrist vote on affirmative action cases, also concurred with the results, but not with the plurality's reasoning. She agreed that a district court could not unilaterally modify a consent decree in a way that impinged on legitimately vested rights, and she pointed out that in their original suit, the black firemen had chosen to ignore the union. They had, she implied, taken the easy way and avoided both the expense of litigation and the burden of identifying the specific victims of the city's discriminatory practices. The bargain they struck included the existing seniority system as part of the city's permitted employment practices, and now they had to live with that bargain. O'Connor differed from the majority in that where White implied that no affirmative action plan could take precedence over a bona fide seniority system, O'Connor said that it could, if the appropriate steps are taken in the beginning. The process is more difficult, but that is as it should be when competing sets of rights are concerned.

Reagan Administration officials crowed with delight over the *Stotts* ruling. Clarence Pendleton, chairman of the Civil Rights Commission, called the decision a "milestone in . . . limiting the use of so-called remedies such as quotas and similar devices."[4] William Bradford Reynolds, the head of the Justice Department's Civil Rights Division and the Administration's point man in the war on affirmative action, declared that *Stotts* fully justified the Administration's policies. Invoking the case as authority, he called for fifty-one jurisdictions to "cleanse" past consent decrees of anything that even faintly resembled hiring quotas.[5] Union officials such as Albert Shanker, president of the American Federation of Teachers, praised what he termed "a very important decision," and said that seniority systems, with their built-in objectivity, would in the long run prove beneficial to minorities.[6]

At the other end of the emotional spectrum, civil rights leaders believed the case a disaster. Richard Fields, the attorney for the black firemen, said the decision would allow cities to thwart all the gains made through affirmative action. Benjamin Hooks of the NAACP bitterly complained that to uphold the "last hired, first fired" rule "is to turn our backs on the reality that such discriminatory practices have had and continue to have on excluded groups." Judy Goldsmith of the National Organization for Women worried that the decision would erode affirmative action as a remedy against race and sex discrimination.[7]

Those who stopped to read the opinions carefully noted—correctly—that *Stotts* did not sound the death knell for affirmative action. Linda Greenhouse, the Supreme Court reporter for *The New York Times*, pointed out that the Court traditionally walks a fine line on sensitive issues, avoiding broad, sweeping opinions in favor of narrow rulings on one question at a time. The decision did not break much new ground, and did little more than affirm Title VII's explicit protection of seniority systems.[8] Douglas Seaver, a partner in a Boston firm specializing in civil rights and employment law, called the ruling "fairly narrow, and not unexpected." It would require plaintiffs alleging discrimination not only to prove that bias exists, but in securing a remedy, they would have to involve unions representing the nonminority workers, and negotiate an arrangement regarding seniority. The real problems, he predicted, would be for union leaders caught between their female and minority members seeking modification of seniority rules, and white males demanding full protection of their vested interests.[9]

Some people seemed less worried by the actual decision and more concerned by how the Court had seemingly gone out of its way to reach that decision. At the American Bar Association meeting in Chicago that summer, Justice Stevens, even though he had concurred in the result, strongly criticized his colleagues for their "far-reaching pronouncement" and for "casting aside judicial restraint to move the law to the right."[10] *The New York Times* editorialized that the Court should not have taken *Stotts*, when the issue had already been mooted. Instead, the Court "labored very hard to hand the Administration a victory." For a Court that had led the way in the fight against bias, "the decision signals a troublesome retreat."[11] In a similar vein, Vanderbilt law professor Thomas McCoy wondered if *Stotts* would be the first piece in the puzzle, the beginning of the judicial dismantling of affirmative action.[12]

The following term, however, the Court sent contradictory signals on just how it did view affirmative action. First, it apparently struck a strong blow against preferential hiring plans. Then, in two cases decided at the end of the term, it seemed to reject the broad dicta in White's opinion in *Stotts* and held that under some circumstances race-conscious remedial plans could be instituted that benefited those who were not the actual victims of discrimination.

In *Wygant* v. *Jackson Board of Education*,[13] the Court dealt with a situation somewhat different from that of *Stotts*, in that the union had been a party to a collective bargaining agreement incorporating minority protection during layoffs. In 1972, the Jackson, Michigan, school board, in the face of considerable racial tension in the community, negotiated an agreement with the union that in case of layoffs, seniority would be the guiding rule, but that the percentage of minority personnel (the last hired) laid off would not exceed the percentage of minorities in the system. The school system, as everyone agreed then and later, had not itself discriminated against minorities, a fact that would become very important to the High Court. As a result of the agreement, during two layoffs in 1976–77 and 1981–82, the school administration retained minority teachers while letting go nonminority faculty with greater seniority. The white teachers sued, not only under Title VII but also under other civil rights statutes as well as the equal-protection clause, which established a high level of scrutiny for racial classification.

The district court dismissed all of the white teachers' claims. With respect to the equal-protection claim, the court held that the racial preferences in the collective bargaining agreement did not have to rely on a finding of past particular discrimination. Rather, the school board could utilize such classifications to provide role models for minority students in an attempt to remedy societal discrimination. The Sixth Circuit agreed with this logic, but the Supreme Court did not.[14]

In what had become a familiar pattern, Justice Powell's opinion for the Court had the full endorsement of only the Chief Justice and Justice Rehnquist, although Justice O'Connor concurred in most of the major points. Justice White gave Powell his fifth vote, but concurred only in the result. Justice Marshall dissented, joined by Brennan and Blackmun, while Justice Stevens dissented separately.

Because the challenge invoked equal protection claims, the school plan had to support a "compelling state purpose," and the means chosen had to be narrowly tailored to that purpose. Just as he had in *Bakke*, Powell rejected the notion that "societal discrimination alone is sufficient to justify a legal classification." There had to be proof that the governmental agency involved had engaged in discriminatory practices which it had attempted to remedy. The Jackson school system had no record of prior discrimination, and its plan, to provide role models to counter societal bias, struck Powell as vague and far too broad. "Carried to its logical extreme," he wrote, "the idea that black students are better off with black teachers could lead to the very system the Court rejected in [*Brown*]."

Powell went out of his way, however, to acknowledge that "in order to remedy the effects of past discrimination, it may be necessary to take race into account." But such a plan had to be narrowly tailored in order, among other things, to minimize the burden placed upon innocent nonminority workers. Hiring goals diffuse this burden and impose a lesser hardship than layoffs. "Denial of a future employment opportunity is not as intrusive as loss of an existing job." The Jackson plan, without proof of prior discrimination and an insufficiently narrowly tailored plan, did not meet the strict standards of scrutiny the Court had established for equal-protection clause claims.

During the time the Court had prepared its opinions in *Wygant*, the Reagan Administration had made quite clear what it thought the law should be. Attorney General Meese had declared that the very idea of using racial quotas "to remedy the lingering effects of past discrimination is nothing short of a legal and constitutional tragedy." Following announcement of the decision, William Bradford Reynolds claimed a victory for the Administration, and charged that *Wygant* exposed "a serious constitutional flaw" in the federal government's set-aside requirements.[15] Conservative legal analyst Bruce Fein of the American Enterprise Institute predicted that the ruling would "unravel hundreds of affirmative action plans" across the nation.[16]

Outside the Justice Department, most people did not see *Wygant* as so clear a signal. Paul Gerwitz, professor of civil rights at the Yale Law School, accused Reynolds of "twisting the Court's decision to reach a result that he wants." Barry Goldstein of the Inc. Fund saw the ruling as a victory for civil rights, in that the Court had rejected the Justice Department's argument that only identifiable victims of past discrimination could benefit from remedial plans. A survey of editorial opinion led a major news magazine to headline the article "Did Court Flash Red, Green or Amber?" It took the title from the *Denver Post*, which charged that the Court had been unable to give either a red or a green light to affirmative action, and so had "once again flashed its favorite color: amber."[17]

A few weeks later, just before the Court recessed for the summer, it announced two more affirmative action decisions that muddied the water still further. In *Firefighters* v. *Cleveland*,[18] Justice Brennan put together a 6–3 coalition that gave lower courts broad discretion in fashioning consent decrees that included hiring programs with explicit racial preferences. Brennan distinguished the facts in this case from that of *Stotts* by claiming that the plan in Cleveland, designed to eliminate past patterns of racial discrimination, was a true consent decree, whereas the case in Memphis had arisen out of a dispute over modification of a consent decree.

In a far more complicated decision, the Court by a narrow vote upheld a court-ordered goal of 29.23 percent minority membership in a New York union.[19] The sheet metal workers had originally had a whites-only clause, and even after the state civil rights commission ordered the clause eliminated, it still took no black applicants for membership. The EEOC tried to reason with the union, and when all efforts at mediation failed, the commission, joined by the city and the state, initiated a suit in 1971. In 1977 a federal judge found that not only had the union discriminated, but it had violated repeated state and federal orders to cease discrimination. He established a nonwhite membership goal of 29 percent, based on the percentage of nonwhites in the relevant local labor pool, and gave the union four years to reach that goal. The union refused to comply, and in 1981 a federal court found Local 28 in contempt of court for its "willful disobedience," and fined it $150,000.

The Supreme Court had no problem with the finding of past discrimination, but did the remedy benefit those who had suffered from that discrimination, or a larger group that included those who were not "identifiable victims"? Justice Brennan, joined by Marshall, Blackmun, and Stevens, upheld the use of explicit racial classification as a remedy for past discrimination, although he conceded that the Court had not agreed "on the proper test to be applied in analyzing the constitutionality of race-conscious measures." Brennan got his majority when Justice Powell concurred in the judgment, agreeing that in some instances goals were necessary. Justice O'Connor concurred in part, but dissented from the judgment, believing the court-ordered plan a mandatory quota rather than a goal. White, Rehnquist, and Burger also dissented, on the grounds that the plan not only constituted a quota, but benefited those who had not been the victims of discrimination.

Just as civil rights advocates had wept over *Stotts*, they now exulted over these cases. Ralph Neas, the director of the Leadership Conference for Civil Rights, termed the two decisions "a tremendous and historic victory."[20] Barry Goldstein of the NAACP Inc. Fund noted that the Justice Department had wanted to scrap affirmative action altogether; now the Court had ratified affirmative action as an important and legitimate tool in the fight for equality.[21] O. J. Silas, director of affirmative action for Minneapolis, one of the cities under pressure from the Justice Department to annul a consent decree, declared, "It will give us a feeling of not being out there fighting the battle all alone."[22]

Conservatives, on the other hand, took a more pessimistic view. Attorney General Edwin Meese tried to put the best light on the decisions, claiming that even though affirmative action plans had been upheld, the Court had "accepted the general position of this Administration that racial preferences are not a good thing to have. What they have done is carve out various exceptions to that general rule, even while affirming the rule itself." Paul Kamenar of the conservative Western Legal Foundation took a far less sanguine view. "It's obviously a defeat for us. If '29.23 percent' isn't a quota, I'd like to know what is."

In fact, the decisions in all these cases did not mark any significant shift in the Court one way or the other, but mirrored the lack of consensus within the Court. To begin with, the justices split deeply in all the opinions, with no five members endorsing any particular point of view. A majority did, however, firmly reject the Reagan Administration's view that court-ordered racial preferences in hiring and promotion were illegal, except to benefit those victims who had personally suffered discrimination. On the other hand, a somewhat different majority agreed that judges should impose affirmative action with racial quotas only as a last-ditch remedy for "egregious" discrimination, the kind encountered in the sheet metal workers' union.[23] In an analysis of *Wygant* which applied equally well to the Court's entire collection of affirmative action decisions, Daniel Seligman wrote: "We still cannot figure out when it is naughty to reverse-discriminate and when it is nice. There now seems to be absolutely nobody under those robes willing to just haul off and say you can't discriminate. So the forecast here is for additional decades of ontological hairsplitting over the difference between a 'compelling' governmental interest and one that is merely 'important.' "[24]

The Court during these years had also handed down some additional opinions regarding gender discrimination in employment, and while none of these involved affirmative action plans, they signaled the importance the Court attached to this issue.[25] In 1981 the Court, by a 5–4 vote, held that women could file certain claims alleging sex-based wage discrimination under Title VII, even if no man held an equal but higher paying job.[26] The issue revolved around the interaction of the Equal Pay Act of 1963, which did not apply to municipal and state employees until 1974, and the Bennett Amendment, §703(h), to Title VII, adopted at the time of its passage in 1964. The section incorporated the so-called affirmative defenses of the earlier act, in which employers could support sex-based wage differentials because of seniority, merit, quantity or quality of production, or "any other factor other than sex."

Female prison guards in Washington County, Oregon, made substantially less than their male counterparts; in 1973, the monthly pay scale for female guards ranged from $476 to $606, while male guards earned from $668 to $853. The county argued that the male guards supervised ten times as many prisoners per guard as did the women, who spent much of their time doing less valuable clerical work. On this basis, the district court dismissed the suit by the female guards. While the Court of Appeals agreed that on the basis of work alone the county did not have to pay the women the same as the men, it nonetheless held that Title VII permitted wage-discrimination suits, even if the women's jobs were not equal to those of the higher paid males, if it could be shown that the lower wages resulted at least in part from intentional discrimination.[27]

The High Court agreed, and Justice Brennan emphasized the narrow question before the Court. The Equal Pay Act had resolved the issue of equal pay for equal work, so that if the women guards performed the same tasks as the men, and supervised roughly the same number of prisoners, any wage differential would be illegal. Here the county had proved that the men and women had different levels of responsibility, which would justify some of the discrepancy in wage rates. If women could prove that sex discrimination accounted for at least part of the differential, then they could sue under Title VII. This meant that women could go beyond the straightforward equal-pay-for-equal-work standard and seek redress even if one of the affirmative defenses existed, provided they could offer proof of gender discrimination.[28]

In 1983, the Court decided two cases affecting gender discrimination in employment. In the *Manhart* decision in 1978, the Court had held that, despite actuarial tables showing that women as a class lived longer than men, employers could not require women to make larger contributions to a retirement plan and then receive the same monthly payments as men. In *Arizona Governing Committee v. Norris*, a closely divided Court held that if men and women had paid the same retirement premiums, they could not be paid lesser monthly benefits.[29]

In another case that term, the Court held that employers had to provide the same medical coverage for pregnancy in the benefits plan offered to male as to female employees. In 1976, the Court had ruled that Title VII did not prohibit gender discrimination based on pregnancy,[30] and two years later Congress amended the law to explicitly prohibit such discrimination. An employer immediately changed its health insurance package to provide better pregnancy coverage to its female workers, but did not provide the same level of coverage in its family plan to the wives of male workers. Some male employees filed a gender-discrimination suit, and Justice Stevens, speaking for a 7–2 majority, upheld the EEOC determination that the amendment required equal health care packages.[31]

In its next term, the Court handed down a unanimous decision in a well-publicized case involving discrimination against women in law firms. Following her graduation from law school, Elizabeth Hishon had accepted a position with the large Atlanta firm of King & Spalding, assuming that if she performed well, she would, like her male associates, be made a partner. In 1978 and again in 1979 the firm passed her over for partnership, and she had to leave the firm. At the time, King & Spalding had fifty partners and fifty associates, but not a single female partner. Hishon went to the EEOC, claiming that she had been discriminated against on the basis of her sex in violation of Title VII, and the commission issued a right-to-sue letter. The lower courts dismissed her suit, however, on the grounds that Title VII did not apply to the selection of partners by a partnership.

Chief Justice Burger spoke for the entire bench in rejecting the law firm's contention that as a partnership it did not come within the reach of Title VII. Modern large law firms differed significantly from nineteenth- and early-twentieth-century arrangements involving only a handful of lawyers. Modern firms had dozens, perhaps hundreds of attorneys, with associates on a salaried basis, as well as many more people in support positions, and as such qualified as employers within the definition of Title VII. When hiring new associates, the assumption that good work would ultimately be rewarded by partnership constituted part and parcel of the contractual relationship. Gender could not be the grounds for withholding partnership, and discrimination on that basis would violate Title VII.[32]

The final days of the Burger Court brought another decision that cheered feminists both by its holding and by the near-unanimity of the Justices. William Rehnquist, whom many women believed the justice least sympathetic to feminist claims, spoke for the Court in holding that sexual harassment constituted sex discrimination under Title VII. The law not only forbade the demand of sexual favors as a *quid pro quo* for hiring or promotion, but also reached situations in which harassment had created an abusive work environment.

Sidney Taylor, a vice-president of the Meritor Savings Bank and manager of one of its branches in northeast Washington, D.C., had hired Michelle Vinson as a teller. Four years later, by which time Ms. Vinson had advanced to assistant branch manager, the bank discharged her for excessive use of sick leave. She then brought suit, charging that she had been sexually harassed by Taylor, and that she had agreed to sleep with him out of fear of losing her job. The bank had responded that no grounds for a suit existed, and that because Vinson had voluntarily agreed to Taylor's advances, there had been no harassment. It also introduced evidence about Vinson's dress and personal fantasies to buttress its claim that the woman had voluntarily become Taylor's sex partner.

Rehnquist's opinion for a unanimous Court displayed a great sensitivity to the first issue, and the psychological pressures on employees told that their advancement rested on submitting to unwanted sexual advances. The district court had ruled that because of the "voluntary" nature of the sexual conduct, Ms. Vinson had had no grounds for a suit. Rehnquist rejected this view, and announced that "the correct inquiry is whether respondent by her conduct indicated that the alleged sexual advances were unwelcome, not whether her actual participation in sexual intercourse was voluntary."[33]

The Court did, however, agree that the evidence regarding Ms. Vinson's dress and alleged fantasies might be admitted, and would depend upon the judge's evaluation of whether it would be relevant or prejudicial to the case. This ruling angered a number of feminists, who wondered what relevance a woman's private dreams would have in a harassment case. Leaving the issue of admissibility up to individual judges, Wendy Williams charged, recalled the days when a woman's sexual history had been deemed "obviously relevant" as to whether or not she "voluntarily" consented to intercourse with an accused rapist.[34]

Looking at the law that would govern the *Johnson* case in the summer of 1986, one could not predict which way the Supreme Court would go. Attorneys on both sides believed that they could win, but only by a close vote. In terms of affirmative action, the Court since *Weber* had upheld the idea of affirmative action, especially in circumstances where the record showed a clear pattern of past discrimination. But when preferential hiring plans came up against other rights, such as seniority, the Court had been less sympathetic. On the other hand, the Burger Court had taken the lead in moving women out of the legal dark ages, and a clear majority on the Court viewed Title VII as a clear barrier to gender discrimination.

The Burger Court, however, would not be hearing the case. A few days before the end of the 1985 term, Warren Burger announced his retirement from the center chair. President Reagan promptly named William H. Rehnquist, the Court's most conservative member, to be the sixteenth Chief Justice of the United States. To take Rehnquist's seat as associate justice, the President nominated Antonin Scalia, a member of the Court of Appeals for the District of Columbia and widely recognized as a brilliant and very conservative jurist. The addition of Scalia and Burger's departure would not affect the general lineup of the Court, but the trio of Rehnquist, O'Connor, and Scalia now provided a conservative bloc that, for the first time in years, could provide a cohesive jurisprudential rationale for moving the Court to the right.

7

Preparing for Battle

Arguing a case before the United States Supreme Court is a daunting proposition, even for the experienced trial lawyers. A Daniel Webster, a Felix Frankfurter, or an Abe Fortas may feel comfortable at the lectern, but for most attorneys, the thirty minutes or so they have to present their argument may well prove the most frightening, as well as the most exhilarating, thirty minutes of their professional career.

Between the time that the Court grants certiorari and when it actually hears a case, the attorneys must meet certain requirements established by the Court both in terms of their own qualifications and in the written materials they submit. Both sides have to plot a strategy, as well as contingency plans should the justices decide to pursue particular issues. Negotiations have to be conducted with each other and with interested parties who file *amicus* briefs. And while the tension mounts until the clerk sets the argument date and the Court actually hears the case, one has to look after the client's best interests, which means following other cases and business for one's employers.

Both Steve Woodside and Connie Brooks had filed for admission to the Supreme Court bar, a qualification necessary to practice before the nation's highest court. The Supreme Court bar has thousands of members, the vast majority of whom join for the cachet of hanging the certificate on their office walls. Others join in the hope that someday they may, in fact, have a case to argue at the

117

Marble Palace, or, if they are members of the solicitor general's office, because they can reasonably expect to represent the government before the Court. When lightning does strike and an attorney suddenly learns that cert has been granted, he or she can then send the application form and a check for $100 to the Clerk of the Court. There is no examination; one need only be a member in good standing of a state bar, and have had five years' experience as a practicing attorney.

At Mountain States, with its limited budget and small staff of young lawyers, most of them only a few years out of law school, there was no question that Connie Brooks would argue the case. Santa Clara County, on the other hand, had the resources to hire an outside attorney, but the Board of Supervisors had faith in Steve Woodside. He had, after all, argued successfully in the Fourth Circuit, and he knew the record in a way that no one coming in at this date could hope to match. So the board, which had now become *very* interested in the case, expressed its confidence in their staff attorney, and authorized him to secure outside help to assist him in his preparation.[1]

Other people, however, did not know Woodside or share the board's confidence, and this became apparent at the meeting in Washington in early August 1986. Representatives from a number of civil rights groups gathered to discuss the implications of *Johnson* and another affirmative action case scheduled to be argued around the same time, *United States* v. *Paradise*.[2] On the way to Washington Woodside had decided that these people needed above all else a clear statement of the facts in the case, an account similar to what he would prepare as part of his brief.

At the meeting Woodside sensed that many of the participants looked somewhat askance at him. With a parochialism typical of many East Coasters, they saw a boyish assistant counsel from what they considered a little California town. He had never been before the Supreme Court before. He worked for a local agency, and therefore did not see himself as a plaintiff's attorney pursuing civil rights goals. He had limited Title VII experience. Without coming right out and saying it, many of them indicated that they thought this guy would lose.

They were smart enough, however, to recognize that as the

named respondent in the suit, Santa Clara County could choose whichever lawyer it wanted. So they refrained from expressing their reservations, and began to ask serious and difficult questions about the case, especially about the Ninth Circuit opinion, which they thought absolutely terrible.

Woodside, in turn, went out of his way to show them that he knew the case. "In addition to what you're hearing about the Ninth Circuit," he said, "there are other factors relevant to this case, including Diane Joyce being denied opportunities earlier in her career." Moreover, his client still preferred to reach an agreement with Paul Johnson and moot the case, thus shielding its affirmative action plan from a possible invalidation by the High Court.[3] Finally, Woodside wanted them to know that he felt competent and confident about handling the case. "I'm not an expert in this field of law," he conceded, "but I know enough about it to think that the Court is divided, that there are some key swing votes, namely O'Connor and Powell, and I think I can convince."[4]

Woodside's candor won over some of the skeptics; the rest, whatever their private feelings, realized that he had no intention of giving up control of the case. So they offered him their help, some of which proved quite valuable later on, and he in turn agreed that some of the organizations there ought to enter *amicus* briefs in support of the county plan. Feeling that he had hurdled a considerable barrier, Woodside returned to San Jose to begin serious preparation of his brief.

One reason that there are so few unanimous decisions in the Supreme Court is that it takes only difficult cases that raise new and/or complex issues of law. If the question is simple, the lower courts should have had no difficulty in answering it correctly.

At the beginning of a suit, in the original trial phase, the burden of evidence is on the party bringing the complaint. In this case, Paul Johnson, through his attorney, had had the burden of proving to Judge Ingram that the county had discriminated against him. The defendant, in turn, has no burden unless and until the plaintiff can make a reasonable case that discrimination did occur, and then it has the burden of rebuttal.

At the Court of Appeals, the burden is on the petitioner, the party that has lost and is appealing the lower court's decision. Counsel has to make the oftentimes difficult argument that the trial judge got the law wrong; the winning party has the easier time in that he or she is telling the court, "Look, one of your fellow judges decided it this way, and that judge knows the law, so the decision should be left alone."

In the Supreme Court, one might expect that there would be a similar burden on the petitioner, a greater barrier to hurdle than that facing the party that won below. This is, in fact, the situation when one party is seeking to overturn a long line of precedents and have the Court announce a radical departure in the law. That burden, however, comes not from saying that the lower courts made a wrong decision, but that the honorable justices of the Supreme Court of the United States made an error. Precedent is a powerful conservative force, but the Court has on a number of occasions admitted that it had been wrong in the past, on issues such as racial segregation,[5] the right to counsel,[6] and legislative apportionment.[7] Otherwise the very difficulty of the cases confronting the Court tends to place both parties on a more or less equal basis. In new questions, the Court is not bound by its own prior rulings on the issue, and very often there is a difference among the circuits, so both sides have to argue that at least one of the courts of appeals decided incorrectly. In some ways, there is a slight advantage to the petitioner. Having lost below, this is the last chance, so counsel can risk pursuing a more aggressive line of argument, while the respondent is confined to the more conservative stance of defending the opinion of the lower court, no matter how weak or poorly reasoned it may be.

In deciding cases before it, the Supreme Court relies on the written briefs and responses to determine the relevant facts and law about a case. There is a great deal of debate over whether or not oral argument affects how the justices vote, but there is no question that a poor brief will work against a litigant's position. Under the rules of the Court, each side must present a brief that follows a set format, and does not exceed fifty pages. First comes the central question or questions in the case, followed by a table of authorities, a narrative of the case, a summary of the argument, and then the argument itself, with the main points set off in a different type face. The petitioner's briefs and replies must be bound in blue, those of the respondent in red. Both sides agree to a so-called joint appendix, which includes relevant evidence from earlier stages in the suit, such as copies of exhibits, excerpts from the trial transcript, and affidavits.[8] The joint appendix provides the record the justices will use in reviewing the case.

Both sides also have a great deal of law on which to rely, and in the briefs they present—in as strong a manner as possible—what they believe to be the correct interpretation. In the brief for Paul Johnson, Connie Brooks elected a strategy of focusing on a single question, and phrased that question in a way which, if the Court adopted it, would make it impossible to rule for the county: "May a public employer lawfully promote a less-qualified female candidate over a more-qualified male employee allegedly pursuant to an affirmative action plan adopted solely to eliminate a statistical disparity in the work force, unrelated to sex discrimination?"

By wording it this way, Brooks reminded the Court that in prior decisions it had held that employers, for the sake of affirmative action, did not have to hire or promote less-qualified minority applicants. By claiming that the statistical disparity had no relationship to gender discrimination, she referred to the several cases in which there had been a finding of prior discrimination as a necessary predicate for an affirmative action plan. Look, she was saying, the law cannot possibly mean that an employer can discriminate against a well-qualified white male when there had never been any bias against women and minorities. Her legal arguments all buttressed this line of reasoning:[9]

- The agency plan lacked any remedial justification, because the agency had never been guilty of sexual discrimination. Moreover, according to the Court's recent decision in *Wygant*, one could not adopt affirmative action in response to alleged general societal discrimination.
- Even if there had been a legitimate remedial purpose, the plan failed because it had not been narrowly tailored so as to avoid unnecessarily trammeling the rights of white males like Paul Johnson.

- *Weber*, which involved a private employer, did not apply to a public employer, but even if it did, the agency plan did not meet the *Weber* guidelines.
- Because the county had admitted that Johnson had been denied promotion solely on the basis of his sex, the county had to bear the burden of proof to show that it had not violated his Title VII rights. In other words, the county had to prove the necessity and appropriateness of the affirmative action plan; Paul Johnson did not have the burden of proving its inappropriateness.

In all these points, Brooks pointed to the very points of law that had become the norm in suits challenging affirmative action plans, questions concerning the remedial nature of the plan, its scope of operation, the fact situation that made it necessary, and the evidentiary criteria applicable in such cases. But with *Wygant* so recently decided, she also tried to hook in a new argument that had until this point been absent from the case: the equal-protection claim that would have shifted the focus of the case from a question of statutory interpretation—did Title VII permit such a plan?—to that of whether the plan violated the Constitution, thus invoking a much higher level of scrutiny and a much greater burden on the county to justify its plan.

> A voluntary affirmative action plan by a public employer must be reviewed under the Fourteenth Amendment's strict scrutiny standard even though the Petitioner only claims violation under Title VII. . . . Even though this case concerns a sex-based classification, it should be subject to strict scrutiny because neither Title VII nor the Fourteenth Amendment countenance discrimination and any exception to that principle established by this Court should be very narrow.

Here Brooks invited the Court to take a major step in employment discrimination jurisprudence, elevate sex to the same level as race, and impose the same strict scrutiny standard on any plan designed to alleviate alleged gender bias as it applied to racial classification. This question had been raised before the Court in previous cases, and a majority had never been willing to go that far.

In order to take that step, however, the Court also had to accept constitutional claims raised under the equal-protection clause, and those claims had not been raised in this particular case. Johnson had won on Title VII in the district court, and the court of appeals, in overturning that judgment, had also limited itself to Title VII questions. It had been Jim Dawson's strategy from the start to go with Title VII rather than constitutional claims because Title VII law in 1981 seemed much clearer on the subject. At the time, *Bakke* and *Weber* had been the controlling cases, not *Wygant*, and now Brooks wanted the justices to inject a new issue, one that had not been litigated below. If they accepted her invitation, Paul Johnson had a good chance of winning.

Brooks had contacted Rex Lee, the former solicitor general of the United States and a leading conservative, right after cert had been granted, and asked for his assistance.[10] In the fairly short turn-around time they had had to prepare the brief, he had been one of the people to critique it; he also put Brooks in touch with people in the Justice Department who could provide information and assistance. She had known Lee for a number of years, and his knowledge and experience of the Court would prove very useful.

After filing her brief, Brooks began to prepare for oral argument. She had never considered herself a civil rights expert, so she had to be sure that at the least she knew the major recent cases in that area. An associate at Mountain States, Diane Vaksdal, had worked on preparing the *Wygant* case and had also helped Brooks do the *Johnson* brief. Vaksdal put together a briefing book consisting of all the major statutes and decisions of the last ten years. "Here it is," she said, and handed the thick binder to Brooks. "Learn it." Brooks did. As part of her preparation, she outlined in detail every one of the Supreme Court's civil rights decisions in the past decade. She not only wanted to see what key issues had been common to several cases, but how the individual justices responded to these questions. She also had to master the record in Paul Johnson's case. While she might never have as intimate a knowledge as Steve Woodside, she had to know the material so that she would not make a factual error in responding to a question from the bench.

In preparing her argument, Brooks followed a pattern she had used in other cases: make the points so clear that her mother (the archetypical layperson) would understand them. While the law can often be complex and obtuse, one mark of a good lawyer is the ability to state the legal issues clearly and succinctly, a talent prized by judges as much as juries. Loading up her argument with extensive quotes and citations would not be effective.

Brooks knew that out of the thirty minutes assigned to her argument, she would be lucky if she had five minutes to make the statement of her case, with the rest of her time spent answering questions. So she wrote out fairly lengthy narratives, and then boiled them down as far as possible. This way, she hoped, she would be able to get back on track quickly after a question. Her husband, Vaksdal, and other people helping her all wrote down questions they thought the justices would ask, so she could have answers ready; as it turned out, every question from the bench had been anticipated in these sessions.

Like Steve Woodside, Connie Brooks had had a great deal of experience in the lower courts, but the Supreme Court would be different. To help her prepare for the hearing, the Justice Department (which endorsed Johnson's argument) set up a moot court where she could practice her argument and respond to questions. A moot court is a mock trial, in which real issues are argued before stand-in judges. In law school, students are assigned sides in a case, and get their first experience arguing before a jury of other students or a panel of judges drawn from the faculty. For this panel, scheduled a few days before the Court hearing, the leading lawyers in the Civil Rights Department, including Brad Reynolds, peppered her with questions and critiqued her responses. She felt ready—scared, but ready.

Down in San Jose, Steve Woodside went through his own preparations for battle, and, like Brooks, had no hesitation in bringing in some outside experts on the Supreme Court. One of the most knowledgeable Title VII attorneys on the West Coast, Morris Baller, helped with the brief, offering suggestions and editing drafts. Russell Galloway of the University of Santa Clara Law

School had recently spent a year observing oral arguments in the Court, and had a clear view of the different styles and interests of each justice. Edward Steinman, another member of the Santa Clara faculty, had argued a half-dozen cases in the Supreme Court, and Woodside spent a lot of time with him trying to get a feel for what, at best, would be an unpredictable experience.

The respondent's brief is, at least in part, a response to that of the petitioner, and once the county had received a copy of the Mountain States brief, it had thirty days to do two things—rebut the petitioner's claims of law and fact, and put forward its own interpretations. Woodside used the same question he had employed in his earlier brief responding to Johnson's petition for cert, emphasizing that the county plan, with no quotas or rigid preferences, took gender as one consideration in promoting a fully qualified person into a job category which had hitherto not had any women. In his narrative of the facts, he also placed great emphasis on the fact that Diane Joyce had qualified for the job, and that under the county's accepted personnel procedures, she had been considered as well qualified for the position as Paul Johnson.

The county's argument had two points. Just as Brooks had rung changes on most of the arguments made against affirmative action, Woodside now lined up all of the traditional arguments in favor. He spent nearly thirty pages demonstrating that the county plan met all of the *Weber* criteria. The county had a firm basis to believe a plan necessary; the facts supported the county's conclusion to initiate a remedial program; that plan had been narrowly tailored to meet its objectives; and the decision to promote a fully qualified woman did not violate the petitioner's Title VII rights.

In his second point, Woodside argued that the Court should reject Brooks's "belated" effort to ground her case on the equal-protection clause. That claim had not been raised in the lower courts, but even if it had, the county's plan would have met the test.[11]

Local 715, which had intervened in the case following Judge Ingram's decision, was also a respondent in the case, and David Rosenfeld filed a separate brief. While he concurred in the major points put forward by the county, the union attorney wanted to emphasize that the facts, even without a formal finding of discrimination, justified both the affirmative action plan and Diane Joyce's promotion. The union had been a prime mover in getting the plan adopted, and it wanted to drive home the fact that sufficient evidence existed to warrant what the county, and the union, had done.[12]

Once the briefs had been submitted, Woodside began his preparation for the oral argument by participating in several moot courts, both in California and later in Washington. Woodside had experience both in bench[13] and jury trials, and before three-judge panels in the Ninth Circuit. But how did one handle a panel of nine judges? Would it be possible to look at all of them at the same time? (It would not!) How did one retreat, with a minimum of damage, from hostile questioning?

David Rosenfeld helped set up some moot courts in the Bay area, with participants who knew Title VII law and could pepper Woodside with the type of questioning he would face in the Supreme Court. In October, Woodside flew to Washington to watch an old friend and colleague, Mary Johnson, argue her first case in the Supreme Court.[14] He had never been in the Marble Palace, so he took a tour of the courtroom and the library, all part of a plan to "feel at home" on November 12, the day the Court had set for the oral argument.[15]

In addition to briefs from the litigants, the Supreme Court will also accept written arguments from other parties who have a strong interest in the results of the case. In some instances, such as the desegregation cases, the Court may ask the attorneys general of some states to file *amicus curiae*, or "friend of the court," briefs. The more likely situation is that different interest groups, recognizing the importance of the case, will file briefs presenting their particular views;[16] the more important or controversial the issue, the greater number of *amicus* briefs the Court is likely to receive. When it heard the *Bakke* case in 1978, 120 organizations signed fifty-eight *amicus* briefs; eighty-three supported the position of the University of California, thirty-two backed Bakke, and five had earlier urged the Court not to accept the case.[17]

In *Johnson* v. *Transportation Agency*, forty groups entered eight

126

amicus briefs supporting the county and the idea of affirmative action:

- National League of Cities, together with the National Association of Counties, the U.S. Conference of Mayors, and the International City Management Association;
- City of Detroit, with the District of Columbia and the City of Los Angeles;
- Equal Employment Advisory Council;
- Lawyers' Committee for Civil Rights under Law, together with the Mexican-American Legal Defense and Education Fund, the NAACP, and the Puerto Rican Legal Defense and Education Fund;
- National Organization for Women Legal Defense and Education Fund, joined by the National Organization for Women, the American Civil Liberties Union, California Women Lawyers, the Employment Law Center, Equal Rights Advocates, Federally Employed Women Legal and Educational Fund, the League of Women Voters of the United States, the NAACP Legal Defense and Educational Fund, the National Women's Law Center, Women Employed, Women's Equity Action League, the Women's Law Project, and the Women's Legal Defense Fund;
- The State of California and the California Fair Employment and Housing Commission, joined by the states of Idaho, Louisiana, Maryland, Michigan, Minnesota, Nebraska, New York, Oregon, Wisconsin, and the Pennsylvania Human Relations Commission;
- American Federation of Labor–Congress of Industrial Organizations;
- American Society for Personnel Administration.

Only two public interest groups, the Mid-Atlantic Legal Foundation and the Pacific Legal Foundation, entered *amicus* briefs in support of Johnson.

For the most part, the *amicus* briefs presented essentially the same legal arguments as could be found in the principal briefs, although slanted to make the point in a way that related to the group's interests. The National Organization for Women, for example, emphasized the discrimination faced by females in entering tradi-

127

tionally male job markets, and pointed out that once the barrier had been breached, women did in fact want to work at those jobs. The AFL-CIO differed somewhat with Local 715 and the county in its interpretation of what *Weber* required as proof of prior discrimination to establish an affirmative action plan. The AFL-CIO wanted *Weber* read very liberally, so that employers and unions could have wide latitude in their efforts to remedy past subtle as well as overt discrimination.

All the employer groups supporting the respondent, including the states, operated some affirmative action plans under their aegis, and whether private employer or public, wanted the idea of affirmative action upheld. To have struck down the Santa Clara plan would have called into question nearly every public preferential hiring plan in the nation. That, of course, is exactly what the Reagan Administration wanted, and it had its say in this case in the *amicus* brief submitted by the solicitor general, Charles Fried.

The solicitor general's office in the Justice Department, ever since the creation of the position in 1870, has been responsible for representing the federal government in court, and especially in the Supreme Court.[18] From the Court's viewpoint, the office performs some very valuable work. It screens all potential appeals and petitions in which the government is involved, and decides which should be taken to the Court. While the justices will not automatically grant cert to every petition filed by the solicitor general, the fact that he has screened out a large number does make them more sympathetic to the ones that are filed. Between 1977 and 1981, the Court granted review in 70 percent of the cases filed by the government, but in only 6 percent of all other cases.[19]

Whenever the Supreme Court grants cert, it automatically sends a copy of the petitions to the Justice Department to see if the government has an interest in the issue of a sufficient degree to warrant its participation, either as an *amicus* or in cooperation with one of the litigants. The briefs are routed to that division which has responsibility, and it in turn sends a report to the solicitor general, who makes the final determination of whether or not to get involved. In Paul Johnson's case, the briefs had gone to the

Civil Rights Division, which under William Bradford Reynolds opposed any affirmative action plan that involved quotas and which did not result from a clear pattern of prior discrimination. The division recommended that the federal government join Johnson's case; the final decision would be up to the solicitor general.[20]

While the Justice Department always has the right to submit an *amicus* brief, the solicitor general does not have an automatic right to participate in oral argument. Each side is normally given thirty minutes for oral argument, and if a litigant wants to have the solicitor general speak on his or her side, that time is deducted from their thirty minutes. Fried very much wanted to appear before the Court in *Johnson*; ever since he had joined the Justice Department a year earlier, he had been firmly aligned with the conservative bloc in opposition to preferential hiring. At a banquet in November 1985 in honor of William Bradford Reynolds, Fried had sounded the clarion call of the Reagan Administration:

> By 1980, this country was in danger of becoming a quota society. By 1980, we were in danger of a situation with jobs—private and public sector—educational opportunities, housing, judgeships—all the good things were being handed out, not on merit, but by a racial and ethnic and religious and gender spoils system. The American people elected Ronald Reagan to restore the idea of equality of opportunity and the great ideal of the unity of all mankind. Today that danger is further from us than it was in 1980. And if Ronald Reagan has been able to keep his promise, it is largely because of the work of Brad Reynolds.[21]

Fried had pressed the Administration view in a number of cases, with only minimal success, and by the time the *Johnson* brief came across his desk, he had recognized that only a more moderate position could hope to win judicial approval. The hard-line conservatives would permit only victim-specific remedies; if a particular black or woman or Hispanic could prove that he or she had been discriminated against, then the courts could order a hiring or promotion to make that particular person whole. Paul Johnson had essentially done this at the district court level; he had proven to the judge that he had been the victim of discrimination, and the court had ordered the county to promote him and pay him the differential in wages. If a black or a woman could make the case, then he or she should be helped. But plans addressed to groups or to remedy societal discrimination did no more than substitute one bias for another.

Fried also opposed quotas but would have allowed a preferential hiring plan for groups if there had been actual discrimination against that group. If an employer could be shown to have deliberately refused to hire or promote blacks, that would be the factual basis for justifying a limited affirmative action plan, one narrowly tailored to address this particular situation.

He saw no factual predicate in Santa Clara County. The fact that there had been no women on road crews did not, by itself, prove discrimination; one would have to show that the employer had erected barriers against women. "If there are no barriers, then there's no discrimination," he said. "Just because you think it would be nice to have a certain representation of women, what I call the United Nations model, that is not enough reason to prefer a woman over a man, a black over a white."

The problem, as Fried saw it, centered on how one established that discrimination really existed. Did statistics showing a disproportionate lack of a particular group in certain jobs prove discrimination? Or did the numbers themselves constitute the sin—i.e., was it terrible that there were none or only a few blacks, women, Hispanics in these jobs, regardless of whether the employer had deliberately kept them out or if other, possibly benign, factors were at work? *Johnson* seemed an ideal case in which Fried could make this argument.

Connie Brooks, on the other hand, believed the liabilities of having Fried appear far outweighed any possible benefits. The government had just recently lost the two major civil rights cases of the 1985 term, the Cleveland firefighters' suit and the New York sheet metal workers' union decision.[22] These had been two high-profile cases that, according to Brooks, Charles Fried had not only lost, but the Court had in each instance handed down opinions highly critical of the government's position. Along with Reynolds,

Fried had emerged as the Darth Vader of the civil rights movement, the point man for the Reagan Administration's efforts to undo thirty years of civil rights progress which the Justice Department had previously championed, a situation that the plurality opinions in several cases had commented upon critically. Brooks wanted to find a middle ground on which at least five justices could agree; Fried, in her opinion, would only polarize the Court. She also knew that the year before, Mountain States had turned down Fried's request to share time in *Wygant*, and that apparently had been the proper strategy.

Upon learning of Brooks's opposition, a very piqued solicitor general tried to force the young woman to change her mind. He called his good friend Rex Lee to ask him to intercede. Brooks received phone calls late at night and early in the morning from conservative groups pressuring her to let Fried join in the oral argument. She in turn talked to a lot of people she knew in Washington, and nearly all of them told her the same thing: keep Charles Fried out. A federal appeals judge whom she knew told her that she could cross Justice Stevens's vote off if Fried appeared.[23] While she agonized over the decision, in the end she stuck to her guns, and Fried had to be content with filing an *amicus* brief.

There the solicitor general argued one main point, that the county had failed to justify its discriminatory actions against Johnson because its affirmative action plan did not result from a clear record of prior discrimination. Moreover, even legitimate affirmative action plans had to be narrowly tailored in order to protect the interests of innocent persons. But Fried did not claim that there had been absolutely no prior discrimination; rather, he suggested, the issue had not been investigated properly by the lower courts.

This ploy would give the judges, if they wanted it, an opportunity to remand the case to the district court for a new hearing to determine if, in fact, the numerical disparities actually showed prior discrimination. A remand would be a victory for the government, because it would seem to support the Reagan Administration's view of affirmative action, and nearly everyone admitted that whatever the numbers, the county had never committed deliberate discrimination. Moreover, a new trial would have to take account of *Wygant*, and introduce the higher standards of equal protection into the equation.[24]

A few days before the hearing, Woodside flew back to Washington, accompanied by Ann Ravel, his colleague from the county counsel's office. (Dave Rosenfeld, who had wanted to have part of the oral argument, and had unsuccessfully tried to have the union pressure the county into this arrangement, decided to stay in San Francisco and not waste his client's money on a useless trip.)[25] Suzanne Wilson and Zoe Lofgren from the Board of Supervisors came to hear the case, and they arranged for Diane Joyce and her pregnant daughter, Donna, to be there as well. Kristy Sermersheim, still assigned to keep Diane calm, represented the union.

On Tuesday, November 11, Woodside went through one last moot court arranged by the League of Cities. The league had a fairly sophisticated arrangement, with videotape facilities, and a panel made up of former Supreme Court law clerks, each of whom would ask the type of questions that one might expect from their respective judges. This last session went well, with only one hitch. At the start of the hearing, each attorney stands up and identifies himself or herself to the Court, and whom he or she is representing. In the practice session at the League of Cities, Woodside had said he represented the respondents, Santa Clara County and Local 715 of the Service Employees' International Union. Several of the critics immediately urged him not to say that. "Don't rub it in that you're here for the union to Justice Scalia, or to these other folks," they warned. "Just say you're here for the county."

Woodside went over to confer with Kristy Sermersheim and Diane Joyce. "They're telling us that I need to not say that we're here together. Is that okay? It's really up to you."

Sermersheim later recalled how much this frightened her. She thought, "If we don't get credit for this, there goes all the work we've done. But if Diane loses, this would be awful, too." She and Diane spoke together for a few minutes, and then told Steve, "Just go ahead and win it."

Steve nodded, and returned to the practice session. "May it please the Court, my name is Steven Woodside, and I represent the respondent, Transportation Agency of Santa Clara County, California." After the session, he went back to his hotel to rest and to wait. A few blocks away, Connie Brooks did the same.

8

Before the Bar

At ten o'clock on Wednesday morning, November 12, 1986, the marshal of the Supreme Court of the United States, formally dressed as always, stood and called out "All rise!" As the audience clambered to their feet, the nine members of the nation's highest tribunal filed in through the red velvet curtain in back of the bench and stood behind their chairs as the marshal called out the traditional opening.

"Oyez, oyez, oyez. The honorable, the Chief Justice and the Associate Justices of the Supreme Court of the United States. All persons having business before the honorable, the Supreme Court of the United States, are admonished to draw near and give their attention, for the Court is now sitting. God save the United States and this honorable court."

All the months and years of litigation, of planning and research, now came to fruition. The Court had allotted one hour for oral argument, and then would take the case under advisement. If Paul Johnson lost here, he had no other legal avenues to pursue; even if he did not lose, he might not necessarily win. Rather than affirming or striking down the Santa Clara plan, the justices might take the advice of the solicitor general and remand to the district court with orders to rehear the suit. In that case, it would be starting over at square one.

Johnson and his wife, Betty, had come to Washington to hear the case argued. Diane Joyce and her daughter, Donna, were there as guests of the county. For all of them, this was the first time they had been in the Marble Palace, and they looked carefully at the eight men and one woman, all clad in black robes, who now settled down in their large chairs to hear the case. Connie Brooks and Jim Dawson, sitting at the petitioner's counsel table, and Steve Woodside and Ann Ravel at the respondent's table, also studied the people sitting at the slightly curved and elevated bench before them. They all thought it too close to call, and both expected that, whoever won, it would be by a 5–4 vote.[1]

By tradition, the justices sit according to their seniority on the Court, with the Chief Justice in the middle, the most senior judge to his right, the next most senior to his left, and then alternating so that the most junior justice sits at the far end of the bench on the Chief's left.

In the center chair sat William Hubbs Rehnquist, whom President Reagan had named the preceding spring as the sixteenth Chief Justice of the United States. Rehnquist had originally been appointed to the Court by Richard Nixon in 1971, and in his fifteen terms as an associate justice has earned a reputation as perhaps the best legal mind on the bench, and certainly its most conservative. But while his opinions can be devastating in their logic, and his dissents especially sarcastic regarding the alleged mushiness of majority liberal opinions, Rehnquist gets on well with all his colleagues. The man has a sense of humor; he likes to laugh and has a reputation as a practical joker within the Court. He and Thurgood Marshall, another man who likes to laugh, once kept up a mock feud for weeks while their clerks grew increasingly anxious.

Woodside had no illusions that he might win over the Chief Justice. Ever since *Bakke*, Rehnquist had been a firm opponent of affirmative action, and had voted against preferential hiring plans in every case the Court had decided. Rehnquist believed that if the country meant to put racial and gender discrimination behind it, then it should do so; preferential hiring plans merely substituted one form of bias for another. The Chief Justice had voted against gender discrimination, and in fact had written the opinion holding that sexual harassment constituted a form of gender discrimination.[2] But in this case, without a record of clear discrimination, Rehnquist would see the Santa Clara plan as another example of muddle-headed liberal social engineering.

To the Chief's immediate right sat the most senior and most liberal member of the Court, William J. Brennan, Jr., whom Dwight Eisenhower had named to the bench in 1956. On almost any issue, Brennan could be expected to vote exactly the opposite of Rehnquist, but like the Chief, Brennan enjoyed good collegial relations thanks to his warmth and buoyant optimism. Almost from the time he joined the Court, Brennan had been the political strategist of the liberal wing. During the fifties and sixties, he had been Earl Warren's closest adviser, and the two would meet prior to the weekly conferences to plan strategy. The former Chief Justice, Warren Burger, had found Brennan a judicial pain through most of his tenure, as the senior justice had easily outmaneuvered Burger, cobbling together majorities on a variety of issues ranging from freedom of speech to rights of the accused.

Brennan strongly endorsed affirmative action, and had written the Court's opinion in *Weber* and other cases. He also opposed gender discrimination in any form and, although he had been unable to convince a majority of his colleagues, had tried to elevate sex to the same status as race in equal-protection cases. There seemed no question that Brennan would support the Santa Clara plan.

To Rehnquist's left sat Byron R. White, former All-American athlete, Rhodes scholar, and professional football player. He had been a deputy attorney general in the Kennedy Administration, and the President, a longtime friend, had named him to the Court in 1962. Some commentators have labeled White as Kennedy's Warren, in that just as Dwight Eisenhower proved disappointed in the path Earl Warren took, so Kennedy would have been disappointed in White, who over the years has gravitated to the conservative side of the Court. This would be only partially true. Kennedy's liberalism was relative; in some areas, such as civil rights, he did lead the fight, while in others he had little interest.

White's record on the Court shows him a strong defender of minority rights and an opponent of school segregation. But White has been very tough-minded on issues such as rights of the accused and freedom of the press, and in general he is perhaps best described as a tough-minded pragmatist and a centrist, even if he tends to lean right of center. His record on affirmative action gave hope to neither Woodside nor Brooks; he had supported preferential plans, but had usually demanded that they be narrowly tailored to remedy prior discrimination. How he voted in this case might well depend on the oral argument, for White had a reputation as a tough, relentless questioner.

Next to Brennan sat Thurgood Marshall, the Court's first and only black member. Marshall had been the chief architect of the NAACP's long and ultimately successful campaign to overturn racial segregation in the nation's schools; Marshall had himself argued *Brown* before the High Court. Kennedy had named Marshall as a federal appeals judge, and then Lyndon Johnson had called him to Washington to be the solicitor general, the nation's lawyer, before nominating him to the Supreme Court in 1967.

On the bench, Marshall had remained a strong opponent of discrimination in any form, but he had never carved out his own jurisprudential niche. A liberal, he invariably voted the way Brennan did, leading some Court-watchers to claim that Brennan had two votes on any issue. Certainly in affirmative action, Marshall could be counted upon to support the county plan.

On the other side of the bench sat Harry A. Blackmun of Minnesota, named to the Court by Nixon in 1970. Blackmun had tended to vote with the conservatives in the early seventies, especially with his good friend, Chief Justice Warren Burger. By the end of the decade, however, Blackmun had traversed considerable jurisprudential ground, and more often than not would be found voting along with Brennan and Marshall. Best known as the author of the abortion decision, *Roe* v. *Wade*, Blackmun had been a consistent defender of women's equality and had generally supported affirmative action. Both Woodside and Brooks assumed he would be a vote for the county.

Next in seniority came one of the most influential members of the Court, Lewis F. Powell, Jr., of Virginia. Appointed to the bench in 1972 after a distinguished career as a practicing attorney, Powell had emerged as the leader of the Court's centrist bloc. He could be tough on criminal procedure questions, but he had helped expand the reach of the First Amendment's speech clause and, like his fellow Virginians Thomas Jefferson and James Madison, believed in full separation of church and state.

Powell's record on both affirmative action and women's issues made it clear that neither side could take his vote for granted. He had written the Court's opinion in *Bakke* that essentially said one could have race-conscious preferential plans, but only sometimes, depending on the circumstances, and circumstances usually, but not always, required a showing of prior discrimination. Powell had also followed a centrist path on women's issues; he had helped elevate scrutiny of gender discrimination claims to a so-called intermediate level, but had been unwilling to accord gender the same constitutional status as race. Both sides knew that if they were to win, they would have to secure Lewis Powell's vote.

John Paul Stevens, appointed in 1975, had a reputation as the Court's ultimate independent, a man who eschewed legal dogmatism in favor of a case-by-case pragmatism. In many ways, Stevens reminded one of Potter Stewart, who in his tenure on the bench had also been very much of a common-law judge, one who looked at the results as well as the reasoning behind a case. Stevens's record on affirmative action had been mixed, as befitted a member of the centrist bloc. Brooks believed he would vote for the county, based on his dissent in the *Wygant* case; Woodside considered him a question mark.

At the far end of the bench on the Chief's right sat Sandra Day O'Connor, the first woman appointed to the Court. Ronald Reagan had promised in his 1980 campaign to name a woman, but he wanted one who would be a conservative, tough on criminal procedure and opposed to social engineering schemes, such as affirmative action. When he named O'Connor to the bench in 1981, he thought he had found just the right person. In her first few terms, O'Connor had tended to keep a low profile and for the most part voted along with her former law school classmate, Bill Rehnquist.

But as she gained confidence on the bench, O'Connor started displaying a strong streak of independence, a development that came as no surprise to those who had known her for years. By the 1986 term, while still voting with the conservatives on many issues, she had moved closer to the centrists, and in some cases began to play a Powell-like role, seeking an acceptable consensus between liberals and conservatives. As the only woman on the Court, she also proved particularly sensitive to so-called women's issues. While not totally comfortable with *Roe*, she did not necessarily oppose the right of a woman to gain an abortion. And her own experience made her especially receptive to questions of gender discrimination.

After graduating second in her class to Rehnquist at Stanford Law, O'Connor had had difficulty in getting a job. One firm did offer to hire her, but as a legal secretary. None of the firms to which she applied had ever hired a woman as a lawyer, she later recalled, and they were still not prepared to do so. Eventually she found jobs as a deputy county attorney and as a civilian lawyer for the army, but the experience remained with her; when questions of job discrimination came before the Court, Sandra O'Connor could identify with the plaintiff in ways that none of her white male colleagues could. Both Brooks and Woodside recognized the importance of O'Connor's vote; both had targeted her and Powell as key to their winning.

At the other end of the bench sat the Court's most junior member, Antonin Scalia, whom Reagan had just named to take Rehnquist's place as associate justice. Scalia, both as an appeals judge and as a law school professor, had shown himself to be literate, very bright, and very conservative. Scalia believed in a strict separation of powers, and disdained extensive governmental remedies for social problems. Everyone knew where he stood on affirmative action—against it. In a caustic critique of affirmative action, he had once proposed the "R.J.H.S." plan, the Restorative Justice Handicapping System, where individuals would get points based on their ethnic and racial backgrounds to determine how much they owed society, or society owed them.

Brooks figured she could rely only on Rehnquist and Scalia, with White a wild card; Brennan, Marshall, Blackmun, and Stevens would vote for the affirmative action plan. In order to win, then, she needed to convince White, Powell, and O'Connor; the loss of even one would mean defeat. Woodside's head count looked similar to Brooks's. Rehnquist, Scalia, and White would vote for Paul

Johnson; Brennan, Marshall, and Blackmun would support the county plan. Stevens might, after *Wygant*, stay with the liberals, but not definitely. Powell and O'Connor would be the swing votes; he had to win at least one of them.

Johnson was the second case the Court heard that morning, and at 11:03 A.M., Chief Justice Rehnquist turned to Constance Brooks, standing at the lectern, and nodded that she could proceed.

"Thank you, Mr. Chief Justice, and may it please the Court."

There is a great deal of debate over how much, if at all, the oral argument affects the decisions of the Court. William O. Douglas believed it made no difference, and rarely participated in any questioning. He would answer his mail and write his opinions while listening with half an ear to the discussion. Oliver Wendell Holmes also used the time during oral argument to write letters, complaining that "one has to listen to discourses dragging slowly along after one has seen the point and made up one's mind."[3]

Most justices, however, believe it does make a difference. Brennan has said that "often my idea of how a case shapes up is changed by oral argument." Chief Justice Rehnquist agrees, and notes that in a "significant minority" of cases, oral argument swayed his opinion. Moreover, there is the symbolic value of oral argument in our democratic system. It is the only public part of the Supreme Court's work, the only time the people can see the nation's highest tribunal in operation.[4]

In oral argument, what the justices do not want to hear is a repetition of the brief, and they do not want to have an attorney read to them. In fact, in 1980 the Court revised its rules to include this admonishment: "The Court looks with disfavor on any oral argument that is read from a prepared brief."

What the justices are seeking is illumination. If the briefs failed, in their opinion, to cover a point of law adequately, they may look to the oral argument to elucidate a point. They may also want to know what effect a particular decision will have. Court decisions are normally prospective—that is, they only affect future conditions, and will not remedy current or past grievances. But if, for example, the Court rules that the state must provide lawyers at the first-appeals stage, what impact will that have on crowded court calendars or on the administrative costs of the criminal justice system? They may also want to know how, in this particular fact situation, a change in the law will serve a useful purpose.

These questions may arise from the counsel's argument, but a justice can ask any question he or she wants at any time, and some justices have been known to press their questions with fierce determination. Felix Frankfurter in one case interrupted a lawyer ninety-three times during two hours of oral argument. In the midst of one exchange William O. Douglas intervened to help the hard-pressed attorney. An annoyed Frankfurter said to the lawyer, "I thought *you* were arguing this case." "I am," came the reply, "but I can use all the help I can get."[5] Such hectoring of counsel often annoys the other members of the bench, but it is one of the prerogatives of a justice to ask whatever he or she pleases, and very often the counsel's valuable half-hour dwindles away in response to questions that may, or may not, further one's case.

As a strategy, therefore, one tries to get one's major points in as quickly as possible, and Connie Brooks did just that.[6] She wanted the Court to apply the *Wygant* criteria, so that a public employer could not have a preferential hiring program that did not address a specific record of discrimination. Moreover, such a plan had to be tailored narrowly, and not trammel unnecessarily on the rights of innocent parties. Santa Clara County had never gone through the process of establishing a record of discrimination that needed remedial action, while the district court had heard evidence of a clear case of discrimination against Paul Johnson.

A minute and a half went by, and then came the first question.

"If a statistical imbalance in the work force is evident," Justice Stevens asked, "and they adopt an affirmative action plan, isn't it apparent on its face that it's remedial in the sense they're trying to remedy the imbalance?"

Brooks had anticipated this question, and had an answer: imbalances are not always the result of discrimination.

"So you say just statistical imbalance will never justify by itself an affirmative action?"

"I don't believe that it should," she responded, "and let me explain why." She started to say something about good intentions not being enough under Title VII criteria, when Justice White interrupted.

"What about *Weber*? [Do] you think in *Weber* the plan adopted was to remedy past discrimination?"

Yes, she agreed, but similar evidence of discrimination did not exist here; all the county had was a single statistic—no women in the skilled-craft category—and that by itself should have no bearing on promotion decisions.

Justice O'Connor wanted to hear more about this, and began pressing Brooks on just what level of evidence she believed necessary to establish a case for discrimination. After all, you had a category of 238 skilled positions and not one woman in any of them. "And you think this is not enough for the employer to think that there might be a firm basis here?"

Not in this case, Brooks replied, because the record established that societal and attitudinal reasons,[7] not discrimination, caused the statistical imbalance.

Justice Stevens joined O'Connor in pressing Brooks for just what criteria should be applied, and whether the agency's work force could legitimately be compared to the area labor pool, in which qualified women certainly existed.

Yes, Brooks agreed, the relevant labor market had to be one consideration, but statistics by themselves could not justify a preferential hiring plan. There had to be clear evidence that discrimination existed, and equally clear guidelines on how a public employer could go about remedying actual discrimination.

The justices did not interrupt, so Brooks pressed on, reiterating the points she wanted the Court to remember. The plan had not been narrowly tailored, the aims had been too vague, the plan had no limits, only indefinite goals that too easily coerced particular divisions to make them into attainable quotas, no protection for innocent white males like Paul Johnson.

The Court, however, could not seem to shake itself of the statistical imbalance. Let's suppose, Stevens said, that the plan identified a substantial work pool, such as 238 skilled-craft positions, in which there were absolutely no women, and said that as an objective, the agency should hire the first qualified woman that applies for the job, just to break the pattern and get some representation. Would that be invalid?

Brooks cleverly rephrased the question to make it less abstract, and said that it would be invalid, because in the instant case, the county already had women actively in the work force who would be in line for promotion.

"You're saying promotions always have to be made on merit, then?"

"I think that once you've opened the doors and provided for equal opportunity, it's appropriate to have these employees moving up through the work force based on the merit system."

"I agree it's appropriate. Do you think the statute requires that all promotions be made on merit . . . in the absence of any proof of past discrimination?"

"Convincing evidence, yes, Your Honor."

Justice White wanted to know whether Brooks thought that the *Weber* decision required proof of past discrimination, and she said it did, while in Santa Clara there had been no proof. Moreover, the plan would have been defective even if there had been evidence because it failed to meet the other *Weber* criteria.

Justice Blackmun at this point wanted to know why the Court should not make this just a straightforward application of *Weber*. Because that case had dealt with hiring, Brooks explained, which diffused the burden of the remedy, whereas the Santa Clara plan denied Paul Johnson a promotion he had already earned; he, and only he, bore the burden of the plan.

Justice Scalia had been pondering the evidentiary question, and the fact that the Court had previously recognized that an employer did not have to openly admit past discrimination in order to establish a remedial plan. Brooks seemed to be saying that there had to be a clear record of past bias; the employer would have to admit that it had discriminated, and thus open itself to endless lawsuits. How would Brooks get an employer out of this dilemma—of having to admit to discrimination in order to justify the affirmative action plan, and thus be vulnerable to suit, or denying any bias, avoiding lawsuits, but leaving the discriminatory procedures in place?

It was a good question, and one that had bedeviled the county and other employers considering preferential plans. Brooks did not have a clear answer—all the employer needs to show, she said, is "some" evidence, "some" proof that he at least went through a process to examine the situation. "The employer is not necessarily required to prove to a certainty that he's discriminated."

You mean, Scalia continued, that all he has to show is that he *may* have been discriminating?

"Exactly."

"But no employer's going to like to do that. I mean, you're just developing evidence for somebody else to use in a later suit against you."

Perhaps, Brooks replied, but Title VII says you cannot discriminate against your employees. A preferential plan discriminates, and so to justify it you have to prove there's a problem that needs remediation of this form. Brooks tried to show what would constitute minimal evidence that would not get an employer in trouble. Statistics would be the starting point, but they needed more than just evidence of a statistical imbalance.

Justice White had been listening to this exchange, and it troubled him. Suppose you have a Title VII case, he asked. "The plaintiff gets through with his case or her case and the only proof is racial imbalance, and there's a motion to dismiss."

That motion should be denied, Brooks said, "because statistical imbalances, if there's no explanation, do establish a case."

"Well," White pressed, "if that makes out a prima facie case in a Title VII case, just racial imbalance, what's the employer do then—how can he win the case? Proving there isn't racial imbalance or proving that, what, there is no racial discrimination?"

"The employer can come forward with a number of explanations . . . to explain the statistical imbalance by reasons other than discrimination."

The response did not satisfy White, who wanted a real nuts-and-bolts answer. Look, he said, an employer has a racially imbalanced work force, and he goes to his attorney. If there is a suit under Title VII, the very fact of the imbalance means that the suit will survive a motion to dismiss. What the employer wants to know is,

"Should I do something about it?" And if the employer does nothing, what will that mean in a Title VII suit?

"And that's exactly why having the employer consider statistical imbalances and look for explanations and then take a remedy before he gets sued would solve the problem."

Connie Brooks looked at her watch; she had used up twenty-five minutes, and, as the petitioner, had the right to save some time for rebuttal. She informed the Court that she wanted to reserve the rest of her time, but Justice White had not finished.

"Did you just give away your case or not?" he asked. After all, Santa Clara County had evidently done just what Brooks had said it should do—consider the statistical imbalance, looked for an explanation, and then imposed a remedy to head off lawsuits.

No, we did not give away our case, she responded, because the county never went through the process; they never tried to find out why the statistical imbalance existed. If they had, the facts would have showed them that the cause was attitudinal, and not a result of discrimination.

Rehnquist, recognizing that Brooks wanted to keep some time, brought the exchange to a close. He turned to the respondent's table. "We'll hear now from you, Mr. Woodside."

A benefit of being respondent's counsel is that one can listen to the Court's questions, pick out what issues seem to concern the justices most, and then play to those issues. Woodside had prepared some points to start with, but when he heard White ask Brooks what the employer should do, and what the employer's attorney should advise, he decided to take advantage of that opening. He also knew that by picking up on the question, he was taking a gamble, since White had a reputation of engaging counsel in long discussions which would not leave enough time to make all the necessary points. Hiding his nervousness under a patina of calm, Steven Woodside walked to the lectern.

"May it please the Court, I'd like to begin by answering the questions that Justice White just posed. With no women out of 238 skilled-craft workers . . . I think there would be a prima facie case."

White immediately picked up, and wanted to know if a suit would survive a motion for dismissal on the basis of the statistical disparity alone.

"Absolutely, Your Honor."

"But it would not mean that the employer would necessarily lose the case?"

No, Woodside responded, not necessarily. "We would have the burden of articulating nondiscriminatory reasons for this particular imbalance. And I think on the facts of this case which are in the record, we would not have been able to meet that burden."

Six years after the initial complaint, four years after Judge Ingram heard the original suit, Santa Clara County finally came as close it would to admitting that there had been discrimination against women.

The pragmatic White pondered Woodside's answer for a moment, and then returned to the practical consequences of what he had said. In other words, the justice asked, if there is a statistical imbalance, must the employer then consider whether to take remedial steps?

That would be right, Woodside agreed.

But shouldn't the employer go on and say, "Well, I can think I can still win because I have a neutral explanation"?

"As I tried to make clear with the facts of this case—"

"Forget these facts," White interrupted. "Do you think the employer need not go on and say that I do or I don't have a neutral explanation?"

Yes, Woodside said, the employer should act immediately on the imbalance alone, because, as Justice Scalia had said earlier, to fail to act puts the employer between the rock and the hard place.

White seemed dissatisfied with the answer, and pressed on for a few more questions until the Chief Justice asked if this did not constitute a disagreement over whether the burden of proof should be on the plaintiff or the defendant. Woodside agreed, but before he could explain, Justice Powell caught his attention.

According to the record, the district court had found that there never had been any discrimination against women by the Transportation Agency. In fact, none was occurring at the time of the trial.

Woodside saw "Danger" written all over this question, and tried to evade it.

"That, Your Honor, was not a litigated issue in the case."

Powell would not be put off. "It did make that finding?"

Yes, Woodside conceded, it had.

"Did the Court of Appeals hold it clearly erroneous?"

No, it had not, but the question should not be whether the agency had discriminated. "The relevant inquiry," Woodside explained, using language taken from earlier decisions by Powell and O'Connor, "should be whether or not the employer believed and had a firm basis to conclude that it may have discriminated against women, based on its own knowledge of the statistics."

Justice O'Connor, the other critical swing vote, wanted Woodside to explain a bit more about the affirmative action plan, about how the goals had been determined. Did the county go to the percentage of women in the local labor market, or just to the number of women who had the requisite skills?

This, of course, had been one of the weak points of the county plan, in that it had never clearly articulated these standards. Woodside explained that the plan had a mix of both plans.

"So," O'Connor interjected, "you concede that this employer affirmative action plan was not geared to the number of qualified women in the pool of labor?"

"No, Your Honor, I don't concede that," he responded quickly, recognizing that if the Court believed there had been no rational relationship between the plan and the local work force demography, it would find against the county. There was a relationship, a goal set of three women out of fifty-five expected new skilled hires in 1983, and that reflected the available work force.

O'Connor wanted to know where she could find that.

In the joint appendix, he said. A few seconds later, a page handed O'Connor the appendix, and she spent much of the rest of the hour looking through it, while listening to the argument.

Justice Scalia had pushed Connie Brooks on the dilemma of an employer faced with a statistical imbalance and subject to suit, and now he put Woodside through his paces.

Long-term goals are very nice, but how did they relate to this case? "We're not trying somebody else who came up after there was a three-out-of-fifty-five requirement. . . . This is Mr. Johnson's case, I thought, and he's complaining about being denied a promotion." The plan had a long-term requirement of 36.4 percent of women in the skilled crafts. Didn't that deny Johnson his promotion?

No, Woodside explained, it did not. The plan did not set a quota; it set long-term goals, and merely said that when making promotion decisions, the director of the agency should give consideration to the existence of an imbalance. Woodside took the opportunity to deny an assertion that Connie Brooks had made earlier, that in such a situation a woman would always be hired over a man. "There is no evidence," Woodside explained, "to indicate that in every case women would get the promotion. Indeed, the facts are to the contrary."

Scalia then returned to the issue O'Connor had raised earlier, whether the plan related to the number of women in the local labor pool or just to the percentage of skilled women. "Is it your position that the county as an employer can set an affirmative action plan goal that is geared to the number of women in the labor force in the county generally, as opposed to the number of qualified women in the available pool?"

"Yes, Your Honor," he replied, because "one would ordinarily expect in jobs throughout an agency that [women] would be comprised, absent discrimination, of roughly their numbers that exist in the general labor pool."

A seemingly astounded Scalia leaned forward to make sure he had heard right. Do you mean, he asked, "it is statistically reasonable to expect as many women to be working on road crews and to believe that if there aren't that proportion there must be discrimination?"

Yes, Woodside agreed, there would be an inference of discrimination.

"What is that based on? Human experience or some governmental policy?"

"I think it is based on both human experience and governmental policy."

"On human experience?"

"Yes, Your Honor. I think women do seek these jobs—"

"In this country?"

"Yes."

At this exchange, Diane Joyce had to struggle to keep from bursting out laughing. She thought Scalia was joking, that he was just trying to help Steve along by pointing out the absurdity of the situation. Later, when Kristy Sermersheim and Suzanne Wilson explained that Scalia had not been kidding, that he did not believe that women wanted to work on road crews, Diane began worrying that the case would be lost.[8]

Before Scalia could push this much further, Justice Stevens began asking a series of questions that Woodside interpreted as trying to be helpful. Tell us, Stevens said, how you think your plan accords with previous cases decided by the Court, and how you can justify giving relief to a nonvictim.

If an employer had a firm basis to believe that its practices had been discriminatory, Woodside said, "then the employer could voluntarily take affirmative action which is not victim-specific."

"Do you think our cases said that the circumstances must evidence particularly egregious instances of discrimination?"

No, Woodside said, they didn't have to be particularly egregious. If a prima facie case can be made out, then the employer can act.

There was no finding of egregious discrimination in this case, was there?

No, Woodside agreed, but he reminded the Court that in addition to the statistical imbalance, the trial had produced evidence of the agency's own practices that had been overtly discriminatory.

Stevens now tried to sum up Woodside's argument, to be sure that he understood it correctly.

"You're asserting that a government always has the right to institute a plan that permits discrimination in hiring and in promotion on the basis of race or sex whenever its work force does not contain the same proportion of race, minority race, or that sex, as the work force at large. . . . that statistical disparity is enough to justify an affirmative action plan, that is to say discrimination by the government on the basis of race?"

Woodside did not like the way Stevens had phrased it, and started to hedge on how large a statistical disparity would be required and whether there were any other explanations, when Scalia interrupted.

"Well, now you sound like the other side. Now you're saying that it isn't enough to just have a statistical disparity, that the employer has to have some reason to believe that the statistical disparity is the result of discrimination."

No, that's not what he meant, Woodside said. The statistical disparity is the starting point. When you have additional facts, as you do in this case, then you know you have a discrimination problem and have to act. Moreover, in response to another question by Stevens, Woodside insisted that Diane Joyce had not gotten the job just because she was a woman. It had not been automatic; she had met the qualifications, and under the plan her gender had been an important, but not the only, consideration. Women did not get an automatic preference under the plan.

This got Scalia going again and he pressed Woodside, noting that Johnson had had his eye on the job, had taken a demotion to obtain better qualifications, and had scored higher than Joyce in the tests. "He was selected and would have gotten the job but for the fact of the affirmative action program. . . . Isn't that the facts of the case?"

Had Scalia asked this earlier, before Woodside had overcome his initial nervousness, the blunt hostility might have thrown him. But so far he had been able to hold his own on the questioning, and he knew that he could not let Scalia characterize the case in this way. He reminded the Court that Joyce had also competed for the job, that she also had worked on the road crews, that she had achieved a qualifying score. Given this situation, as well as the statistical imbalance, the Court should allow local authorities to make decisions, based on local circumstances and the employer's knowledge of the facts, that would be best and as fair as possible to all concerned.

The last few minutes of the respondent's time turned into a colloquy among Woodside, Stevens, and Scalia, about what an employer had to take into account to be fair to the work force, to minorities, and to avoid the rock-and-hard-place situation. Stevens put forward a hypothetical situation in which there are no women in the work force of 238 people. The employer knows that, but also knows that no woman has ever applied, so he has never discriminated. He knows he has never discriminated. Would he be able to adopt an affirmative action program?

No, Woodside replied, "I don't think he could—"

Before he could finish the sentence, Scalia jumped in. "Even though that would make out a prima facie case of employment discrimination?"

"That's the difficulty," Woodside said. "Given Justice Stevens's hypothetical, there is no prima facie case because—"

No, Scalia said. Given what you told us before, all the employer had to do was show an imbalance.

But Justice Stevens, Woodside continued, was suggesting that there was a legitimate explanation for the imbalance.

Would that be a defense to the prima facie case?

Yes, Woodside agreed.

Scalia pounced. "He has a prima facie case, and I thought you had been saying that so long as there is a prima facie case he can institute an affirmative action plan."

Well, yes, Woodside admitted, and I tried to—

"So maybe," Scalia said with a big grin, "you should have given a different answer to Justice Stevens."

"I'm sorry," Woodside said, but Scalia's grin was infectious, and although there is supposed to be little or no levity in the nation's highest court, laughter swept across the courtroom, a welcome break from the tension for the audience, the attorneys, and above all the justices.

A smiling Stevens ventured that "I should have asked Justice Scalia," and the audience continued to chuckle.

Woodside saw the amber warning signal on the lectern, and decided to take advantage of the situation.

"I have nothing further to add. Thank you."

The Chief Justice informed Constance Brooks that she had four minutes left of her time for rebuttal.

Brooks wanted to use those minutes to press home her main points, especially that an employer needs more than a prima facie case to institute an affirmative action plan, that it had to explore the reasons for the statistical discrepancies.

Before she had gotten very far on this, Justice O'Connor, who had been trying to figure out the proportional goals from the joint appendix, decided to press Brooks on this issue.

"What difference does it make whether the proper proportion in this particular labor pool, if we're playing statistics, was 30 percent or 5 percent? What difference does it make, inasmuch as there were no women in this job category at the time anyway?"

Because, Brooks replied, unless the numbers bore some relationship to the relevant pool, in this case the number of women qualified for the job, then the plan was arbitrary and trammeled the interests of innocent people like Paul Johnson. You could not just allow the employer to slip in whatever figures it wanted.

What if the employer had used the right percentages, would that have made this an acceptable plan?

No, it would not, said Brooks, and without any further interruptions she went on to reiterate all the points she had made earlier about the defects in the plan. There were women in the work force, and in nontraditional jobs, so that the county had not discriminated; it had not investigated the situation to determine whether there had been discrimination. She wanted to remind the Court of another consideration.

"I think there's another factor here," she began, when the amber light on the lectern switched to red, the signal that her time had expired. It is the responsibility of the Chief Justice to make sure that counsel do not exceed their allotted time. It was said that when Charles Evans Hughes sat in the center chair, he would interrupt an attorney in the middle of the word "if" when the right light flashed. The gentler Rehnquist would never snap that quickly, but neither would he allow her to continue.

"Your time has expired, Ms. Brooks."

Connie Brooks thanked the Court and sat down, and at three minutes past noon, the Chief Justice announced that the case was submitted.

*   *   *

After the Court recessed for lunch, the Santa Clara crew went down the street and crowded around a table in an Italian restaurant—Steve Woodside, Ann Ravel, Suzanne Wilson, Zoe Lofgren, Kristy Sermersheim, Diane and Donna Joyce. They all congratulated Steve, and then began analyzing the case. Suzanne Wilson thought that Scalia had behaved rudely in hectoring Steve, but a very relieved assistant county counsel said no, that had not been rudeness; it showed that the justices were really interested in the case. He felt certain they had grasped what he had to say. Suzanne Wilson, unfamiliar with the customs of oral argument, silently prayed that Steve was right.

"It was a scary, heady experience," she later recalled, "to have your affirmative action plan held in the hands of nine people who don't know your county, who don't know who we are and what we're about, and how the people in this county like this and keep electing the people who do these kinds of things."[9]

All they could do now, however, was wait.

9

The Court Decides

The actual decision of a case takes place within a few days after oral argument, at the Court's next conference. Cases argued on Monday are discussed at the Wednesday afternoon conference; those argued on Tuesday and Wednesday are decided at the Friday morning session. A buzzer sounds in each justice's chambers five minutes before the meeting is scheduled to begin, calling them to the large conference room next to the Chief Justice's chambers, where, after shaking hands with each other, they take their seats. The Chief Justice sits at one end of the large rectangular table, and the senior associate justice, then William Brennan, sits at the other. On one side are the next three most senior members, White, Marshall, and Blackmun; across from them the four junior members, at the time Powell, Stevens, O'Connor, and Scalia. Each justice will have some papers relating to the cases under discussion, such as notes taken during the oral argument or memoranda prepared by one of the clerks. A full set of briefs is available on a cart near the table. No law clerks, no secretaries, no one but the justices themselves takes part in the conference; if there is a message for one of the justices, a member of the marshal's office will knock on the door, and the most junior member of the Court goes to get it, and then hands it to the justice to whom it is addressed.[1]

The Chief Justice sets the agenda. Cases already heard in oral argument automatically are on the table, as well as petitions for certiorari and other business ready for decision. An individual justice may, as a matter of personal privilege, ask that an item be put off until the next meeting, but because of the Court's heavy work-load, its members try to stick to the regular schedule as closely as possible.

The Chief Justice will introduce each case by briefly reviewing the facts and the lower-court decision, and then indicate his understanding of the applicable law and how he intends to vote. The discussion then moves down the line of seniority, with each justice stating his or her view and vote; if someone is not sure, and wants to hear the other opinions first, he or she may abstain, and vote at the end. There is no separate ballot; each justice votes by indicating his or her stance.

The length of discussion, the acrimony or lack of it, depends on many circumstances aside from the actual issues in the case. Charles Evans Hughes ran a tight ship, and his ability to state succinctly all the issues in a case meant that the ensuing discussion rarely involved more than an indication of the vote. His successor, Harlan Fiske Stone, wanted to encourage more give-and-take, and soon lost control of the conference; debate over cases could drag on for hours, especially when Felix Frankfurter felt moved to lecture the brethren. Despite the controversial nature of many of the cases during his tenure, Earl Warren's political skills kept conferences on an even and peaceful keel. Warren Burger's personal kindness and warmth made him well liked by the brethren outside the conference; inside, he managed to alienate several of the justices by his clumsy attempts to control votes and writing assignments.

After the discussion and vote, if the Chief Justice is in the majority, he assigns responsibility for the Court's opinion, and keeps a tally of all the assignments to make sure the workload is equitably distributed. In very important cases, the Chief will usually take the opinion himself, to emphasize the Court's decision. On those occasions when the Chief Justice is in the minority, the senior justice in the majority assigns the opinion.

From all indications, most justices enter the conference knowing how they will vote. The ensuing discussion rarely wins converts, although in some very close cases a justice torn two ways may not actually decide which way to vote until he or she has heard the discussion. But if the conference is not critical to the vote, it is crucial in determining the substance of the Court's opinion. Five or more justices may agree in a particular case that the lower-court decision should be overturned; they may not agree on the grounds for reversal. The conference discussion will indicate to whoever writes the opinion the jurisprudential parameters in which he or she must operate. Stay within those lines, and keep the majority; stray beyond them, and risk losing the majority on the decision, on its grounds, or both.

The *form* of the conference is well known, but the actual *contents* are not. This is where the justices decide cases, and in two hundred years they have remained very close-mouthed about what transpires in the conference room. We can piece together some stories because in recent years the papers of some justices have become available to scholars, and William O. Douglas, for example, kept very careful notes of conference discussions. In *Johnson*, we can see clearly each justice's views on the case and how those views shaped the different opinions that the Court handed down.[2]

Docket number 85–1129, *Johnson* v. *Transportation Agency*, had been argued on a Wednesday morning, and the justices discussed it at their Friday morning conference on November 14, 1986. Chief Justice Rehnquist began the discussion with a brief précis of the facts. There had been a promotional opportunity; Diane Joyce had scored lower than Paul Johnson in the screening process; the district court had found the county's action in violation of Title VII; the Court of Appeals had reversed on the basis of *Weber*. Rehnquist found the county's plan flawed, because it did not seem to have any end date; it would just always be there. Moreover, unlike *Weber*, which involved hiring and thus spread the burden, Johnson had been rejected for a promotion on the grounds of gender alone, and thus had to bear the entire burden by himself. No question existed that the county had instituted a gender-conscious plan, and the Court's previous cases held that before a public employer could adopt a race-conscious, or in this instance a gender-conscious, plan, it had to make a prima facie case that the minority had actually been discriminated against. While statistics will sometimes be sufficient to make the prima facie case, there are occasions when more evidence is necessary. He believed the record in *Johnson*, by itself, did not establish the prima facie case, although the statistic of no women in 238 positions certainly hinted at it. The Chief Justice believed that the solicitor general's proposal made sense, and he recommended sending the case back for reconsideration, to see whether there had been sufficient discrimination to warrant the plan.

When Rehnquist finished, William Brennan took the floor, and as the most consistent champion of affirmative action on the bench, it came as no surprise that he supported affirming the Court of Appeals. Brennan had had a memo prepared by one of his clerks indicating the main points of law that he believed governed the case. Although Connie Brooks had wanted the Court to take *Wygant* as its standard, Brennan insisted that the county's plan accorded with the Title VII criteria set out in *Weber*. The Court, he argued, should not decide this case on an equal-protection analysis because that claim had neither been raised nor argued in the courts below; it had started as a Title VII case, and should be decided as much.[3]

Under the *Weber* criteria, employers did not have to admit past discrimination, but only show "imbalances in traditionally segregated job categories." The county had demonstrated such an imbalance, and in several previous cases the Court had held that statistical disparities by themselves establish a prima facie case. If that were not enough, testimony at the trial confirmed the existence of past employment practices that disadvantaged women.

What about Paul Johnson? Did the plan unnecessarily trammel his rights, contrary to *Weber*'s imperative? Brennan did not believe it did. No specific positions had been set aside for women; rather, gender became just one more factor to consider on a case-by-case basis. It is true that Johnson had not gotten the job, but he had not lost anything he already had, such as seniority and salary. In a growing department, it would be reasonable to expect there would be other promotional opportunities for him.

Brennan disagreed with the Chief Justice over the duration of the county plan. It would not operate indefinitely, he insisted, but would be reviewed annually and continuously adjusted to measure progress toward its goal. Summing up, Brennan believed that Santa

Clara's plan "was adopted on the basis of even more striking evidence than put forth in *Weber*, and has a far less intrusive impact on nonprotected employees than the plan upheld in that case."

For Justice White, who spoke next, the significant fact seemed to be that the case involved a public rather than a private employer; this made it more like *Wygant* than *Weber*, and imposed a higher standard of review. A public employer had to show some evidence of egregious discrimination, and he did not believe that Diane Joyce had ever faced that experience. In order for an employer to establish a plan, White believed that the standard of proof should be that the employer would lose a Title VII case, and he found very little evidence in the record to meet that standard.

The Chief Justice looked next at Thurgood Marshall, who grumbled "Affirm." Harry Blackmun, sitting beside Marshall, agreed with Brennan that the Court should not take up Brooks's invitation to apply an equal-protection claim. Moreover, it really did not matter whether one started out under the equal-protection clause or the Civil Rights Act; one still had to demonstrate that discrimination had existed, and statistical evidence of a racial or gender imbalance established the prima facie case. Under Title VII, he thought the record straightforward enough to justify the plan, and he voted to affirm.

Across the table, Lewis Powell looked up from his notes and agreed that the case had to be decided on Title VII, not constitutional grounds. There had not been purposeful discrimination, but the record certainly showed a numerical imbalance. Powell believed the county plan resembled thousands across the country, and while the numbers could have been more reflective of the available work force, he believed the plan set goals, not quotas. He would vote to affirm.

John Paul Stevens agreed with Powell that the record did not show purposeful discrimination. Stevens, who had not participated in the *Weber* case, had on more than one occasion indicated that he believed it had been wrongly decided. But, he said, *Weber* was the law for Title VII cases and therefore controlled here; he agreed that the county plan met its criteria.

At the oral argument, Sandra Day O'Connor had given every indication that she thought the plan defective because the numbers did not match the percentage of qualified women in the work force, but she did not pursue this idea at the conference. The employer had decided it was just not right to have no qualified women in one of the skilled-job categories, and under perfectly proper personnel procedures, it had chosen Diane Joyce for the job. O'Connor disagreed with White that Joyce had not faced discrimination; this lady had filed grievances before, and could well have scared the employer with an implicit threat to sue.

Even before O'Connor spoke, it had become clear that a majority supported affirming the Court of Appeals and upholding the county plan. But the Court's junior justice, Antonin Scalia, wanted to tell his colleagues that he thought this was a terrible plan, and it would be awful to make employers institute preferential plans on the basis of numbers alone.

Connie Brooks and Steve Woodside had thought it would be very close, probably 5–4; in fact, six of the justices—Brennan, Marshall, Blackmun, Powell, Stevens, and O'Connor—voted to endorse the plan, while Rehnquist, White, and Scalia wanted to overturn it. Both key center votes, Powell and O'Connor, votes that Brooks and Woodside recognized as crucial, had come down in favor of affirmative action.

With the Chief Justice in the minority, the senior justice, William Brennan, would determine who wrote the opinion for the Court. Later that afternoon he dropped a note to Rehnquist that he would try his hand at the two affirmative action suits decided that morning, *Johnson* and *Paradise*, the Alabama state trooper case.

While ultimately each justice is responsible for opinions in his or her name, nearly all of them rely on clerks to write at least a first draft. The normal practice is for justices, immediately following conference, to meet with their clerks to go over the cases. They then assign the cases to specific clerks, with instructions on what approach the justice wants to take.

Up until World War II, most justices had only one clerk. Following the war, the number of clerks began to increase, so that by the October 1986 term, each chamber had four clerks.[4] On the positive side of this proliferation, each member of the Court could handle more paperwork, go through the ever-increasing number of cert and pauper petitions, and have better staff work in preparation for oral argument and conference. On the downside, it has led to a geometric expansion of opinions, as well as the size of opinions. As late as the 1940s and early 1950s, justices in general agreement with a draft of the majority opinion would swallow their qualms about particular sections. Now, with three or four clerks for assistance, it is no trouble at all to have one of them draft a concurrence or a dissent focusing on a very limited question of fact or law.

In William Brennan's chambers, the justice left a fair amount of organizational responsibility to his staff. The four clerks divided up incoming cases, and then did all the necessary work on them, such as preparing bench memoranda prior to the oral argument or conference. The *Johnson* case wound up on the desk of Mitt Regan, Jr., a native of Houston who had originally gone into urban planning and had worked for the city of Alexandria, Virginia, as a planner before deciding on law school. He had done well at the Georgetown Law Center in Washington, and then had clerked for a year for Judge Ruth Bader Ginsburg in the D.C. Circuit, a place from which Brennan drew many of his clerks.

Shortly after Brennan returned from the conference, he sat down with Regan to go over his notes, indicating how the justices in favor of affirming the lower court differed in their view. Regan already knew much of this, since a prime form of communication, and often of negotiation in the Court, takes place among the clerks, who put forth their justice's view, and in turn learn the special concerns of other chambers. Regan set about drafting an opinion for Brennan, and throughout the weeks and months that followed, he paid special attention to what the clerks in Lewis Powell's office said to him.[5]

Within two weeks, Regan had a draft in Brennan's hands, and after a minor editing, Brennan circulated the eighteen-page first iteration to his colleagues for their inspection.

Court opinions for the most part follow a set pattern. The first paragraph summarizes the specific question, notes the lower-court decisions, and indicates whether the Court affirms, reverses, or remands. Next comes a fairly detailed statement of the facts, with copious references to the record. Finally, the opinion deals with the one or more issues of law which the justices have decided.

After relating the story of Joyce's promotion under the affirmative action plan and Johnson's suit, Brennan first dealt with whether or not Johnson had carried his burden of proving the plan invalid. In *Wygant* the previous term, the Court had held that an employer's plan would have the benefit of assumed validity by the courts; those claiming discrimination under the plan would have to prove that it had either violated equal-protection claims or the criteria established in *Weber*. If a plaintiff could prove that race or sex had been taken into account in an employment decision, then the employer had to provide a nondiscriminatory rationale, and the existence of an affirmative action plan provided such a rationale. Contrary to what Connie Brooks had argued, Brennan held that an employer did not have to justify the plan; those attacking it had to prove it invalid. In this case, the gender imbalances provided a sufficient rationale for the county to establish an affirmative action plan, and no evidence produced by Johnson showed the plan as defective under *Weber*.

How would one assess the legality of the county's plan? *Weber* provided the criteria—it had to address the problem of racial (or gender) segregation and hierarchy, it could not unnecessarily trammel the interests of white (or male) employees, and it had to be narrowly tailored and of limited duration. Moreover, in his concurrence in *Weber*, Justice Blackmun had made clear that the decision did not require an employer to admit to prior discriminatory practices, but need only point to a "conspicuous . . . imbalance in traditionally segregated job categories." The record here supported that claim by the county that it had addressed the problem, that it had not unnecessarily trammeled white male interests, and that the plan had a limited duration with narrowly drawn goals. The justification for instituting the plan lay in the numbers—no females in the 238 skilled-craft positions. Brennan then spent several pages showing how the Transportation Agency plan met the *Weber* criteria, and concluded that

substantial evidence shows that the Agency has sought to take a moderate, gradual approach to eliminating the imbalance in its work force, one which establishes realistic guidance for employment decisions, and which visits minimal intrusion on the legitimate expectations of other employees. . . .

We therefore hold that the Agency appropriately took into account as one factor the sex of Diane Joyce in determining that she should be promoted to the road dispatcher position. The decision to do so was made pursuant to an affirmative action plan that represents a moderate, flexible, case-by-case approach to effecting a gradual improvement in the representation of minorities and women in the Agency's work force. Such a plan is fully consistent with Title VII, for it embodies the contribution that voluntary employer action can make in eliminating the vestiges of discrimination in the workplace. Accordingly, the judgment of the Court of Appeals is *Affirmed.*

Although the opinion would go through five iterations, in substance the holding and rationale remained consistent throughout. Brennan distributed this first draft on the morning of December 1. That afternoon he had his first two responses. Thurgood Marshall wrote, "Dear Bill: Please join me," indicating he fully subscribed to the opinion.

Byron White had voted on the other side in conference, but because he had in the past supported some affirmative action plans, Brennan hoped that by emphasizing that the Santa Clara proposal met the *Weber* criteria, he might win White over. But White had been unconvinced, and told Brennan that he would wait to see what the dissent might say.

The next day, John Paul Stevens signed on, while Antonin Scalia informed Brennan that he would be preparing a dissent, no great surprise following Scalia's comments in conference. And Brennan might also have anticipated the two-page memo he received from Sandra Day O'Connor. While in agreement with "substantial portions" of the opinion and with the judgment, she found it troubling that the draft did not address the question of what precise evidence would be necessary to justify an affirmative action plan, the same issue that had concerned her during oral argument.

Brennan had interpreted *Weber* to mean that an employer only had to show a "manifest . . . imbalance in traditionally segregated job categories." While O'Connor agreed that *Weber* could be read that way, she believed more should be required, some "firm basis for believing that remedial action is required." Citing the ten-year-old *Hazelwood* decision,[6] she suggested that a prima facie case under Title VII needed at the least some comparison of the women in the work force with those in the local demographic area having the relevant qualifications. She believed this did not contradict *Weber*, since that case dealt with *unskilled* workers, whereas *Hazelwood* and *Johnson* involved skilled categories.

O'Connor indicated that Brennan's opinion already headed in this direction in his discussion of statistics as a justification for a preferential hiring plan, and she believed that in this case the Transportation Agency had a firm basis, according to her criteria, for establishing the plan. But she wanted this spelled out more specifically, and promised to circulate a partial concurrence as promptly as possible.

The entire tone of O'Connor's letter is friendly, and there is no question of her changing votes on the result. No judge, however, wants to write an opinion for the Court where he or she cannot even get a majority to go along. O'Connor wanted a higher level of proof than Brennan, and her letter implied that if Brennan would adopt her standard, she would be glad to go along fully.

On Wednesday, December 3, Harry Blackmun joined the opinion. Brennan now had four votes, including his own, in full support of his draft, and O'Connor concurring in all but one section. With one more added, all he would have to do was some stylistic editing. That Friday, however, Lewis Powell informed him that he shared O'Connor's concern that the adoption and implementation of a voluntary affirmative action plan should be based on a "reasonable comparison" of the percentages of the protected group in the available labor pool and in the employer's work force.[7] He suggested modifying a paragraph in Brennan's draft to make this explicit, and also suggested adding a footnote to the effect that "where the issue is properly raised, public employers must justify the adoption and implementation of a voluntary affirmative action plan under the Equal Protection Clause. See *Wygant* . . ."

"If you prefer not to make these changes I will of course understand," Powell concluded. "I will join your judgment in any event, and will say in whatever I write that I agree for the most part with your opinion."

Brennan had his majority, but barely. O'Connor and Powell had both raised the issue of numbers, but with differing emphasis. For O'Connor, numbers provided the evidence supporting affirmative action; numbers also indicated the fairness and relevancy of the plan, that a direct link existed between the problem and the solution. Powell, on the other hand, saw the numbers as one more piece of the puzzle, an important piece to be sure, but one viewed in the light of other historical and societal factors. Brennan had no problem incorporating Powell's suggested changes, practically word for word, in the second draft of his opinion, which he circulated on December 9.[8] That afternoon, Powell informed Brennan that he would join the opinion.

Although Justice Stevens had indicated he would join Brennan's opinion, on December 18 he circulated the first draft of a concurrence. He still signed on to both the reasoning and result in Brennan's draft, but the changes that Brennan had put in to meet Powell's suggestions seemed to Stevens to narrow the opinion more than necessary. He wanted to emphasize that "the opinion does not establish the permissible outer limits of voluntary programs undertaken by employers to benefit disadvantaged groups."

Stevens first reviewed the Court's decisions interpreting how race-conscious affirmative action plans fit into Title VII's seemingly absolute prohibition against any preferment by race or gender. Had the Court adhered to a strict interpretation of the statute, Paul Johnson would win this case. But in *Bakke* and in *Weber*, a majority "interpreted the antidiscriminatory strategy of the statute in a fundamentally different way," allowing race to be taken into account. The two cases "are now an important part of the fabric of our law, and so must be taken into account in order to provide stability."

The "logic" of Title VII, Stevens believed, required that the courts leave "breathing room" for employer initiatives designed to benefit minority groups. As such, employers ought not to be required to justify their behavior in terms of past conduct. The question should not be whether a particular employer had or had not discriminated in the past, but whether an affirmative action plan would benefit it in the future. Quoting from a recent law review article,[9] Stevens pointed out that a school board might institute a plan not because of past discrimination, but to improve the quality of education. Businesses might establish preferential programs to improve their services to black constituencies or to avert racial tension or to increase the diversity of their work forces. Stevens saw all these as legitimate rationales, which, he wanted to emphasize, constituted as strong a reason for establishing affirmative action plans as the proof of past discrimination. Because Brennan's opinion did not foreclose these options, Stevens still joined it.[10]

Brennan had been waiting to see whether Sandra Day O'Connor would join the majority and, like Stevens, write a concurrence that emphasized her special understanding of one point, or whether she would concur only in the result. When he returned from the New Year's break, Brennan found O'Connor's draft. Quickly skimming through it, he found exactly what he had hoped for—she had signed on to both the result and the reasoning, and had written on the particular point that troubled her, the need by a public (as opposed to private) employer to show evidence of an imbalance in the work force.

Relying on her concurring opinion in *Wygant*, O'Connor noted that the Court had agreed that evidence of past discrimination by the employer—not societal discrimination in general—provided sufficient justification for a race- or gender-conscious hiring plan. But although the employer did not have to point to "contemporaneous findings of actual discrimination," there had to be a firm basis for concluding that remedial action was necessary, and that this evidentiary test could be met by showings of a statistical imbalance.

This had been, at least for her, the primary holding in *Wygant*, and although Brennan did not say so explicitly, she concluded that his opinion followed those principles. The fact that no woman— "the inexorable zero"—occupied a skilled-craft position, although women constituted 5 percent of the local labor pool of skilled workers, provided the necessary evidence of a prima facie Title VII case. Moreover, she agreed that the rights of male workers had not been unnecessarily trammeled, and the plan also fit the *Weber* requirement of narrow tailoring. She would, therefore, join the Court's opinion.[11]

Although both Stevens and O'Connor still joined in Brennan's opinion, their interpretations of the predicates for a preferential hiring plan seemed diametrically opposed. Stevens wanted to allow employers great latitude in their justification, while O'Connor did not. In fact, in her concurrence she had specifically attacked the Stevens view as contrary to the Court's earlier holdings. Brennan leaned somewhat toward the Stevens view, and did not want to force employers to show previous or present discrimination in order to institute affirmative action plans.

So on January 8, 1987, he circulated the third draft of his opinion, in which he added a paragraph and a footnote directly responding to O'Connor:

> A manifest imbalance need not be such that it would support a prima facie case against the employer, as suggested in JUSTICE O'CONNOR's concurrence, since we do not regard as identical the constraints of Title VII and the federal constitution on voluntarily adopted affirmative action plans. Application of the "prima facie" standard in Title VII cases would be inconsistent with *Weber*'s focus on statistical imbalance, and could inappropriately create a significant disincentive for employers to adopt an affirmative action plan. . . . A corporation concerned with maximizing return on investment, for instance, is hardly likely to adopt a plan if in order to do so it must compile evidence that could be used to subject it to a colorable Title VII suit.

In an accompanying footnote, Brennan explained that if the Court had applied O'Connor's suggested test in *Weber*, it would not have found evidence of past discrimination, because in terms of *skilled* workers, there would have been no statistical imbalance: the lack of skilled minority workers in the employer's work force reflected their absence in the available labor pool. But that condition had resulted from years of prior discrimination in which blacks had been excluded from training programs. *Weber*, according to Brennan, thus stood for a more flexible approach to evaluating justifications for preferential plans.

With these alterations, Brennan lost O'Connor from his majority. That same day, she wrote that his additions "compel me to change my concurrence to an opinion concurring in the judgment. Apparently, you interpret *Weber* in a way I would not." She promised to make the necessary changes as soon as possible so as not to delay announcement of the decision. The next day she circulated a third draft, concurring in the judgment, but not the reasoning, of the majority.

She wished to emphasize that, in her view, the same evidentiary standards applied to a public employer under Title VII as under the equal-protection clause, and this did not include, as Stevens seemed to suggest in his concurrence, evidence only of a general societal discrimination. She interpreted the Court's prior decisions, especially in *Weber* and *Wygant*, as requiring "a firm basis for believing that remedial action is required, and that a statistical imbalance sufficient for a Title VII prima facie case would satisfy this firm basis requirement." Unfortunately, she wrote,

> the Court today gives little guidance for what statistical imbalance is sufficient to support an affirmative action plan. Although the Court denies that a statistical imbalance need be sufficient for a prima facie case, the Court fails to suggest an alternative standard. Because both *Wygant* and *Weber* attempt to reconcile the same competing concerns, I see no justification for the adoption of different standards for affirmative action under Title VII and the Equal Protection Clause.

Brennan pondered what changes, if any, he should make either to answer O'Connor's charge or to try to win her back to the majority. Before he circulated another draft, however, he wanted to see what the dissent would say. Whatever the reason for the delay, weeks went by with no further action on the case. Then on February 24, Antonin Scalia circulated the first draft of his dissent to the Court.

If there is any single document that can be said to epitomize conservative opposition to affirmative action, it could well be Justice Scalia's dissent in the *Johnson* case. He began with an appeal to read the plain language of Title VII, language "with a clarity which, had it not proven so unavailing, one might well recommend as a model of statutory draftsmanship." He then quoted from the section which prohibited the use of race or sex for employment decisions, and charged the majority with converting it into a guarantee that race or sex *will be used*, a process, he claimed, that had been going on for over a decade. "We effectively replace the goal of a discrimination-free society with the quite incompatible goal of proportionate representation by race and by sex in the workplace."

Scalia's well-written and well-organized opinion could leave no one in doubt of the intellectual power he would bring to bear on the conservative side of the bench. In three parts he first described the plan and its effect on Paul Johnson. He then explored those prior holdings of the Court which, he claimed, the majority had tacitly overruled. In the third part, he turned to what he called "the engine of discrimination we have finally completed."

A chief, perhaps the chief, conservative argument against affirmative action is that while the actual victims of discrimination should certainly be compensated and given some preference to make them whole, people who had not suffered from discrimination should not benefit from preferential plans. The Santa Clara plan, Scalia charged, did not remedy prior discrimination because there had been no prior sex discrimination to remedy. Rather its stated goal had been all along to "mirror the racial and sexual composition of the entire county labor force," a statistical situation that would never occur in a truly discrimination-free world. To achieve that goal, the plan expected concrete results from its managers, and only through quotas could they achieve those results.

And who would pay for this plan? People like the petitioner, Paul Johnson, who had clearly and unfairly been discriminated against, and denied a promotion he had fairly won. The majority, Scalia charged, glossed over the plain facts of the record that showed Johnson had had the better qualifications, and ignored the testimony of Graebner, as well as the finding of the district court, that gender had been the determining factor. Since the Court of Appeals had not rejected this finding as clearly erroneous, then under the federal rules he and the other justices had to accept them as true, and not ignore them as the majority had done.

Scalia then accused the majority of ignoring the Court's earlier rulings, including the major case decided in the previous term, *Wygant* v. *Jackson Board of Education*. That case had made crystal clear that efforts to remedy societal discrimination could not violate the equal-protection clause. Even though this case came up under Title VII, Scalia could not believe that Congress had intended to place a lesser restraint on discrimination by public agencies under the statute than existed under the Constitution. Only Justice O'Connor, in her concurrence, had attempted to explain away this incongruity, an effort which, however, had failed to convince him.

Scalia roamed over the entire gamut of the Court's earlier pronouncements, and indicted the majority for its willful distortion of previous holdings or for ignoring them completely. Those cases had made plain that preferential programs had to be addressed to specific and egregious past or present discrimination, and that certainly had not been the case here. Instead, he charged, the majority had given its approval to a rank form of social engineering which had as its unrealistic and unattainable goal the reshaping of every work force to mirror the overall population. "It is absurd to think that the nationwide failure of road maintenance crews, for example, to achieve the Agency's ambition of 36.4 percent female representation is attributable primarily, if even substantially, to systematic exclusion of women eager to shoulder pick and shovel."

Scalia noted that social attitudes which caused women to choose certain jobs and avoid others could be "as nefarious as conscious, exclusionary discrimination." But whatever the truth or falsity of that assumption, no national consensus existed that even remotely compared to the general antipathy to conscious discrimination. The majority, he charged, had manipulated the law in an attempt to alter societal attitudes, a direction sanctioned neither by statute nor the Constitution.

In the last part of his eighteen-page draft, Scalia turned his guns on what he considered the chief culprit of the Court's consistent weakening of both Title VII and the equal-protection clause, the *Weber* opinion, and called for its reconsideration and overruling. *Weber*, he claimed, had completely rewritten the original intention of Title VII, and distorted its true purpose of doing away with any and all forms of discrimination. In doing this, the Court had ignored the intent of Congress and had engaged in the most blatant form of judicial policy-making.

In effect, *Weber* held that the legality of intentional discrimination by private employers against certain disfavored groups or individuals is to be judged not by Title VII but by a judicially crafted code of conduct, the contours of which are determined by no discernible standard, aside from . . . the divination of congressional "purposes" belied by the face of the statute and by its legislative history. We have been recasting that self-promulgated code of conduct ever since—and what it has led us to today adds to the reasons for abandoning it.

The latest decision of the Court, according to Scalia, went further than any previous decision, and not just in extending the *Weber* doctrine to public as well as private employers. In effect, the majority opinion had taken the original meaning of Title VII, which forbade taking race or gender into account, and now required employers to do so. After today, he predicted, it would be "economic folly" for an employer not to engage in reverse discrimination, lest it be sued for failure to give preference to one minority or the other. Thus "a statute designed to establish a color-blind and gender-blind workplace has thus been converted into a powerful engine of racism and sexism, not merely *permitting* intentional race- and sex-based discrimination, but often making it, through operation of the legal system, practically compelled." And who suffers? Innocent victims like Paul Johnson, "predominantly unknown, unaffluent, unorganized."

It was a powerful indictment, all the more so for the clarity in which Scalia had framed the issue. One could, of course, argue with Scalia's basic premises, that the Court had distorted the original meaning of Title VII, since in the Civil Rights Act of 1964 Congress had recognized the need for affirmative action programs to remedy past discrimination. And while some sections of the bill did seem to have been written with remarkable directness, other sections left a great deal to the imagination. Moreover, evidence—strong evidence—existed that the Court's interpretation of the "spirit" of Title VII, so derided by Scalia, had been right on target, that the Court had in fact gotten it right.

Statutory construction, that is, the Court's interpretation of a congressional law, is always open to review and revision by the Congress. On more than one occasion, Congress has revised a law in response to what it saw as judicial misinterpretation. If *Weber* and its progeny had been misguided, Congress could easily have stepped in and revised Title VII, in essence telling the Court "You guys got it wrong. *This* is what we meant." The failure of Congress to do so can, and should, be taken as an endorsement of the *Weber* position.[12]

Brennan recognized that at least some of Scalia's charges had to be refuted, lest he lose O'Connor, Powell, or both, and with them his majority. Two days after receiving the draft dissent, he circulated proposed revisions to his own opinion answering the more important points Scalia had raised. Most of the response he cast in the form of footnotes, both to downplay their importance and to keep his opinion on a positive track, rather than having it appear defensive.

He argued that Scalia had mistakenly equated Title VII and equal-protection obligations. The Court had examined that issue, and rejected the notion in *Weber*, because the two derived from different portions of the Constitution. Title VII, which originally focused on private employers, derived its authority from the commerce clause, and when Congress added public employers in 1972 it subjected them to the same criteria as it had originally applied to private firms. While a public employer also had to satisfy the Constitution, that constituted a separate issue from Title VII, and involved different standards.

Brennan also took issue with the charge that the Court had rewritten Title VII. The legislative history of the Civil Rights Act showed clearly, he claimed, that Congress had in fact wanted to give employers flexibility to devise programs aimed at remedying discrimination. He went on to remind the reader of the circumstances surrounding passage of the bill, the widespread racial unrest of the time to which businesses had begun to respond through early affirmative action plans.

Scalia had raised one issue that Brennan knew greatly bothered Sandra O'Connor, the predicate necessary to justify an affirmative action program. Scalia (and the Reagan Administration) believed that an employer could institute a plan only to redress its own past discrimination. According to Brennan, the Court had specifically rejected that view, because it placed the employer on the horns of a cruel dilemma. Admit discrimination to justify affirmative action and be open to Title VII lawsuits, or deny past discrimination and be foreclosed from instituting affirmative action plans that might be wholly justified by the record. To buttress his argument, he quoted from O'Connor's concurrence in *Wygant* that made just this point.

Finally, Brennan dismissed Scalia's dire prediction that the ruling would loose a flood of "less qualified" minorities and women upon the work force, as employers sought to forestall possible Title VII liability, as well as Scalia's claim that Joyce had been less qualified than Johnson. Brennan defended the county's plan as consistent with standard personnel practices, in which the person with the highest score is not always chosen, since there has to be flexibility to take other factors into account.

Only Lewis Powell responded to this memorandum, and gently suggested that Brennan delete some of the references to the racial disorders at the time when Congress had been debating the 1964 Civil Rights Act. The discussion, Powell said, "based as it is on newspaper references, seems unnecessary and I think it may detract from the strength and persuasiveness of your excellent Court opinion."

He also wanted to have the opinion make clear that *Johnson* did not override the *Wygant* holding that societal discrimination by itself justified a plan utilizing racial (or gender) classification. In response to Scalia's argument that nondiscriminatory reasons might account for women not working on road crews, Brennan, who had himself written quite eloquently on the prejudicial effects that stereotypes had on women, had again quoted from an O'Connor opinion. Discrimination, she had argued, creates assumptions about the "proper" employment for women, and the acceptance of these assumptions by women themselves produces a "self-fulfilling prophecy."[13] To Powell, this ran too close to allowing general societal discrimination as a rationale for a preferential plan. The always courteous Virginian concluded with a note of appreciation for

Brennan's work: "Thank you so much, Bill, for your attention to my concerns. This is another 'landmark' decision. You can well be proud of both this case and *Paradise*."[14]

Brennan recognized that Powell's suggestions made good sense; while he himself might be willing to permit an affirmative action plan in response to societal discrimination, the key centrist votes on the Court shied away from such a stance. So he decided to eliminate the footnote completely, and avoid the issue. He wrote to Powell the next day, February 28, to tell him he would accede to both requests. He also took the opportunity to express his appreciation.

"This letter," wrote Brennan, "is another opportunity to reiterate my pleasure in being able to work with you in this case to achieve a majority opinion for the Court. Thank you again, Lewis, for your comments and your patience."

Justice O'Connor, apparently stung by the bitterness in the Scalia dissent, revised her concurrence two more times, and in doing so edged closer to the dissenters, although in the end she still concurred in the result. O'Connor hinted that if the issue of overruling *Weber* had been raised, and if the case in the lower courts had involved equal-protection claims, she might have voted differently. But in the end the statistical disparity, that "inexorable zero," convinced her that the county had sufficient justification to institute an affirmative action program. Scalia also made some revisions to his dissent, responding in part to Brennan's new points as well as some of O'Connor's arguments.

On March 5, the Reporter of Decisions prepared a syllabus, or headnote, to be released with the opinion, summarizing the main points of the majority decision, and sent it to Brennan for his approval. The end was now rapidly approaching. On March 16, Brennan circulated his fifth and final draft; he still had a firm majority of five, with Sandra Day O'Connor concurring in the result. Chief Justice Rehnquist joined Scalia's dissent, and White subscribed to most of it.[15]

Until 1971, many of the justices actually read their full opinions on decision days, although since the late 1930s some justices had adopted the practice of announcing the result and summarizing the reasoning. Chief Justice Burger finally convinced his colleagues that with the proliferation of opinions, the Court spent too much of its time reading aloud. Although individual justices may still, on occasion, read their dissents in order to draw attention, the general practice now is for the author of the majority opinion to announce the result, briefly summarize the reasoning, and note which justices have filed separate concurring or dissenting opinions. Full copies of all the opinions are available at the clerk's office on the day the decision is announced, but no advance notice is given of when a particular decision will be handed down.

Shortly after ten o'clock on Wednesday morning, March 25, 1987, six years after Paul Johnson had first filed his complaint in federal district court, Chief Justice Rehnquist announced that Justice Brennan would announce the Court's decision in No. 85–1129, *Johnson* v. *Transportation Agency, Santa Clara County, California.* Briefly and emotionlessly, Brennan informed those in the courtroom that an affirmative action plan instituted by a public employer to remedy a statistical imbalance of women in its work force, even without a showing of prior discrimination, did not violate Title VII of the Civil Rights Act. The Santa Clara plan, therefore, remained in place. Diane Joyce had won.

10

High Tide and Ebb

Following the Court's decision in *Johnson*, both friends and foes of preferential hiring plans interpreted it as a victory for affirmative action. The case, along with the *Paradise* decision handed down a few weeks earlier, seemed to cap a nine-year cycle, beginning with *Bakke*, that legitimized the use of race and gender to compensate for past discrimination. While the Court had set some limits on preferential hiring, the central idea of affirmative action apparently had come through the ordeal of judicial scrutiny intact. Yet within a relatively short time, the certainty that had accompanied *Johnson* had all but disappeared.

On hearing the decision, an elated Diane Joyce initially responded with uncharacteristic restraint. "I knew I could do the job from the beginning," she told the Associated Press. "I knew I could do it very well. The case will have an impact on all women, and I'm very happy for them." A few days later, when the news had sunk in, she crowed with victory. "There was never any doubt in my mind that I was going to bury the sucker." But, she added, "I'm not a heroine. I'm not a pioneer. I went in for the money. It was pure greed. I'm more a rugged individualist than a feminist." When someone asked whether she felt bad for Paul Johnson, Joyce remembered all the times she had been turned down for no other reason than that she was female. "Why should I feel guilty now?" she retorted. "I've already given up thirty years of big bucks."[1]

Paul Johnson called the decision "a gross miscarriage of justice" and said he could not understand how "people with intelligence could rule this way." Two years later, interviewed at his home, he remained very bitter. "It's pretty damn sad," he said. "These people are up there and the first thing they're supposed to do is defend the Constitution of the United States. I have lost a lot of respect for that Court."[2]

"All the broad questions have now been answered," a joyful Richard Seymour announced. The head of the Lawyers' Committee for Civil Rights Under Law, which had filed an *amicus* brief on behalf of the county plan, believed the most important aspect of the decision was that "the kind of affirmative action that has been practiced by most employers in this country over the last decade has been upheld by the Supreme Court." *Business Week* agreed. "The great affirmative action debate of the 1980s is over," the journal declared. The decision "ended a nightmare that has been plaguing companies since the Reagan Administration began trying to rein in affirmative action. . . .With the key legal issues settled, companies can view affirmative action as an opportunity rather than a burden." The U.S. Chamber of Commerce also breathed an audible sigh of relief. The Chamber's counsel, Stephen Bokat, noted that employers could now be assured of the legality of their plans, and he hoped the Reagan Administration would finally give up its efforts to undo affirmative action.[3]

The Administration, however, refused to concede defeat. Terry Eastland, the spokesman for the Justice Department, expressed disappointment "that the Court has departed from the moral principle of nondiscrimination for all citizens that is the basis of our civil rights laws." Bruce Fein of the conservative Heritage Foundation also questioned the wisdom of the decision, but called the ruling "the most significant . . . doctrinally since the Court started to confront things in *Bakke*."

Some liberals suggested that the extreme view pushed by the Adminstration may have backfired. William Goldstein of the NAACP Legal Defense Fund, with tongue partially in cheek, gave credit to the Assistant Attorney General, William Bradford Reynolds, who had been a vociferous critic of affirmative action. Reynolds "really helped us develop the law. I don't think it would be as strong today if it were not for the extreme actions taken by the Justice Department."[4]

In magazines and law journals, commentators praised or damned the *Johnson* decision according to their views on affirmative action.[5] The conservative *National Review* still considered affirmative action against the law, and "there being no National Association for the Protection of White Males, white males will bear the brunt of this discrimination, with the Court's blessing." As if in response, the *New Republic* columnist "TRB" declared "it's hard to feel any terrible injustice was done to Paul Johnson because he 'scored' two points higher on his interview." While Scalia's dissent on the face of it seemed to make some sense, in the call for a color-blind, gender-blind legal standard, a closer reading showed that Scalia and other conservatives had a different agenda. "They want less civil rights, not more civil rights," TRB charged, "and should stop pretending otherwise."[6]

Some feminist scholars charged that both the majority and its critics had failed to understand the issue. Giving Diane Joyce an edge over Paul Johnson, Chicago law professor Mary Becker wrote, would be affirmative action only if the two had been similarly situated. But, she claimed:

> The notion that they might have been similarly situated is fanciful. Their prior employment experiences were not similar even when they had identical titles. For Joyce, work as the only female road maintenance worker would have involved a constant struggle, including dealing with hazing and harassment. Johnson was one of the boys. It is, however, likely that many male decision makers would neither see what Joyce went through nor appreciate that her unique experiences might be qualifications for promotion.[7]

In fact, Professor Becker claimed, men would probably see Johnson as more qualified because as a road dispatcher, Joyce would continue to have problems operating in a male world.

From a legal standpoint, the *Johnson* decision extended doctrines that the Court had been developing for nearly a decade. Most important, it gave public employers the same opportunity to institute affirmative action plans as private employers had, and held them to the same standards under Title VII. Because the equal-protection claim had not been litigated in the lower courts, the question remained whether an affirmative action plan by a public employer, challenged explicitly under the Fourteenth Amendment, would survive a legal challenge.

Second, the Court for the first time included women as a group eligible for affirmative action. Although it seemed logical to extend to women the reasoning that had informed all of the Court's previous decisions on race-based preferential programs, no one had been sure if in fact the Court itself would take that step. Some feminists also worried that because race and gender discrimination derived from different causes, a simple extension of *Bakke* might actually work against women.[8] *Johnson* not only explicitly allowed a gender-based plan; it also gave the employer a great deal of flexibility in determining the need for such a plan and its details.

The third important aspect of the decision involved the factual predicate which the majority had adopted. For Justice O'Connor, the "inexorable zero" provided sufficient proof that women had been kept out of the job category, and statistics, without proof of actual prior discrimination, seemed sufficient to justify instituting a plan.

The approval of public employer plans, the extension of the legal concept justifying affirmative action to women, and the flexibility in fashioning the program certainly seemed to warrant optimistic claims that affirmative action had finally been fully accepted, by the courts as well as by the business community.

Not everyone, of course, shared this euphoric outlook. Conservatives still opposed what they labeled as "quotas" and "reverse discrimination," and demanded that if the United States wanted to do away with bias in employment, then it should apply the same color-blind and gender-blind standards to everyone. Feminist legal scholars pointed out that women still did not share the same protected position as blacks, and programs that either implicitly or explicitly discriminated against women did not face the same strict scrutiny barriers as those involving race.[9]

Moreover, the Court's decisions on affirmative action really said little more than Justice Powell had said in *Bakke*, that under certain circumstances, it might be legitimate to take race, and now gender, into account in employment decisions in an effort to remedy past discrimination. While the Court's approval obviously meant a great deal, especially to employers seeking to protect themselves from future lawsuits, these decisions have not resolved many of the truly difficult questions surrounding affirmative action.[10]

It is one thing to say that blacks or women have been discriminated against, but what other classes should come under the umbrella? And how does one define the class of "innocent victims" whose interests, according to *Johnson* as well as *Weber*, are not to be "needlessly trammeled upon"? How, also, especially in promotion decisions, can one define with any clarity the "best qualified" standard? In Paul Johnson's case, the two-point spread in the test score certainly did not make him better qualified than Diane Joyce, but what about the judgment of his superiors? While one cannot objectify such documents, they are certainly important, and from the supervisory point of view they are critical in promotion decisions.[11]

While these are unresolved *legal* questions, they are also unresolved issues of public policy. A quarter-century after Lyndon Johnson called for affirmative action, the country seems no closer to agreeing on whether there should be such plans, and if so, what criteria should be applied. Who should be helped? How much should they be helped? And, in an era of limited resources, who will pay? Paul Johnson put the issue succinctly: "If they're going to make a change, why should I be the goat? If they want to do it, let them compensate me."[12]

Both critics and champions of the Court's decisions also noted that the justices had not been unanimous in a single affirmative action case. Many had been decided by a 5–4 vote, and even the 6–3 tally in *Johnson* did not indicate that great a consensus. Sandra Day O'Connor had concurred in the result, not in the reasoning, and had indicated that if faced by an equal-protection claim and a direct challenge to *Weber*, she might well vote the other way. That left a bare majority of five, and one of them, Lewis Powell, did not support all affirmative action plans. So only four members of the Court—the four oldest members—could be counted on in future cases.

Then, at the close of the term, Lewis Powell resigned after a distinguished fifteen-year career on the bench. He had had some serious health problems, and while apparently recovered, he worried about how a recurrent illness or even death might affect the Court. Moreover, if he waited another year, the President would be naming a successor in the middle of an election campaign, and Powell did not want to see the Court embroiled in campaign politics. Ronald Reagan's nomination of Court of Appeals Judge Robert Bork, however, touched off the most bitter confirmation struggle of this century, and triggered an extensive public debate of many of the Court's recent doctrines, such as affirmative action. Although liberals managed to defeat Bork, the man who ultimately took Lewis Powell's seat on the Court, Ninth Circuit Judge Anthony Kennedy, stood firmly aligned with the conservative bloc.

The October 1987 term did not have any significant affirmative action cases on the docket. Moreover, in a case that might have implications for future affirmative action suits, a unanimous bench held that a former bank employee could use statistics to prove she had been the victim of racial discrimination in the bank's promotion practices. The Court brushed aside a brief by the Reagan Administration opposing the use of statistics to prove racial or gender discrimination, and cleared the way for plaintiffs in employment discrimination suits to introduce the number of blacks or women at management levels as evidence of bias.[13]

Then, in the 1988 term, the roof seemed to fall in on affirmative action in the High Court. First the Court backtracked on nearly two decades of precedent regarding the use of statistics to demonstrate bias. Ever since the *Griggs* case in 1971,[14] the Court had permitted statistical evidence of a racial imbalance—the same types of statistics involved in the *Johnson* case—to support a charge of discrimination under Title VII, even if the hiring practices appeared facially neutral. Given an imbalance, the employer then had the burden of proving that the practices which had created the imbalance were justified by the circumstances of the business.

By a 5–4 vote (*Wards Cove* v. *Antonio*), the Court now gave companies accused of discrimination an important procedural victory by shifting the burden of proof from the employer to the employee alleging discrimination. Moreover, in the opinion written by Justice White, employees could no longer use statistics of racial disparity in the workplace to support charges of discrimination. In a biting dissent, Justice Blackmun questioned whether the majority "still believes that race discrimination . . . is a problem in our society, or even remembers that it ever was."[15]

The Court further restricted Title VII suits when it narrowly construed the law's time limitations. The majority held that suits charging racially neutral seniority systems with discriminatory impact had to be filed at the time the system is adopted, not when its operation subsequently has allegedly discriminatory effects. Since it might be impossible to know how a system would operate at its inception, this ruling could all but eliminate Title VII suits against seniority plans.[16]

The Court dealt two potentially devastating blows against affirmative plans. The first involved an archetypical consent decree in Birmingham, Alabama. In response to a discrimination suit by blacks against the city, a federal district court had approved two consent decrees in which the city agreed to hire more black firefighters, and to arrange promotion goals for blacks. The court also ruled efforts by a white firefighters' union as well as some individual white firemen to intervene in the case as untimely.

A group of other white firemen, who had not been involved in the earlier suit, then sued the city under Title VII, claiming that they had been denied promotions in favor of less qualified blacks. The city admitted that it had made race-conscious decisions, but argued as a defense that such decisions had been permitted, indeed required, as part of the consent decree, and were therefore immune to this type of attack.

The Court of Appeals for the Eighth Circuit, as well as a majority of the Supreme Court, disagreed. Justice Rehnquist rejected the idea of an "impermissible collateral attack" that would protect consent decrees from suits by persons not party to the agreement. A person, the Chief Justice declared, cannot be deprived of his legal rights in a proceeding to which he is not a party.[17]

The decision raised alarms all over the nation in cities which had signed consent decrees in response to antidiscrimination suits. In nearly all such agreements, there are many people who are not parties to the agreement who may be affected by its terms. Under this ruling, any such person could attack the decrees as impinging on his or her rights, and then tie up the municipal government for years in expensive and time-consuming litigation.[18]

The decision that posed the greatest threat to affirmative action came in a case challenging a minority set-aside program adopted by the city of Richmond, Virginia. Congress had first adopted set-aside programs in 1980, when it had determined the existence of long-term and widespread discrimination in the construction industry. It had therefore required that prime contractors subcontract 10 percent of federally financed construction projects to minority business enterprises (MBEs), which it statutorily defined as any business at least 51 percent owned by blacks, Spanish speakers, Asians, Indians, Eskimos, or Aleuts. The Court had upheld the federal set-aside in *Fullilove* v. *Klutznik* (1980),[19] ruling that Congress had sufficient evidence to support its findings of discrimination and ample power under the Fourteenth Amendment to enact such remedial legislation.

Following that decision, many state and local governments enacted similar set-aside measures designed to support MBEs. In 1983, Richmond, Virginia, which is 50 percent black, approved a program calling for at least 30 percent of all city-financed prime contracts to go to MBEs, and adopted the same definitions used by Congress. The city council developed no evidence that discrimination existed in the area construction industry other than noting that few blacks belonged to the local employer trade groups. The one bit of hard evidence showed that over the previous five years, MBEs had received only 0.67 percent of the city's prime contracts.

The J. A. Croson Company, attempting to bid on a city contract to install new plumbing fixtures in the jail, could not find an MBE willing and able to enter a bid for the subcontract. When the city rejected all bids and announced it would rebid the contract, the Croson Company sued under §1983, charging reverse discrimination.

Justice O'Connor, for a 6–3 majority, held that the city had not proven its case that prior discrimination existed, and that its 30 percent figure bore no relation to any of the facts submitted in support of the set-aside. "An amorphous claim that there has been past discrimination in a particular industry cannot justify the use of an unyielding racial quota." She also held that such programs, when undertaken by state or local agencies, are subject to a strict scrutiny standard, the highest criterion used by the courts in racial classification cases.

The majority opinion distinguished between the power of Congress in this area, which derives directly from the Fourteenth Amendment, and that of lesser governmental agencies, which do not enjoy such constitutional grants. O'Connor did not hold that state and local governments can never establish set-aside programs; she carefully spelled out what proofs they had to offer and what standards they had to meet. One had to establish the existence of prior discrimination, and then narrowly tailor the program to meet the specific situation. The Richmond program failed to meet any of these criteria.[20]

The National League of Cities found the ruling "troubling in what it says about the capacity of states and cities to govern at all in some matters." The decision did not, however, nullify congressional set-aside measures, nor those voluntarily undertaken by private firms. Moreover, while it might be more difficult in the future for cities and states to establish the evidentiary threshold, it would not be impossible. Parren Mitchell, chairman of the Minority Business Enterprise Legal Defense Fund, believes evidence exists to support findings of extensive discrimination in construction and other industries, and that is the starting point for future successful programs. By this interpretation, the Court did not attack set-asides; Richmond merely failed to set up its program properly.[21]

What all this means is still too early to determine. In some ways, these cases do no more than tighten up some of the protections the Court had set in place earlier; in others, they seem clear evidence

183

of a definite turn to the right. Conservatives quickly grasped at the latter interpretation. "For the first time in thirty years," exclaimed Bruce Fein, "the Court has a working five-member majority saying that the goal is color-blindness and gender-blindness." Walter Burns of the American Enterprise Institute noted that the civil rights community had launched its campaign against Robert Bork because it had feared he would champion just such a path. "Now they are getting what they feared, without him on the Court."[22]

Affirmative action has been debated in this country for well over a quarter century. There are those who believe that only preferential plans will abolish the legacy of racism and sexism in this country; others take just the opposite view, that affirmative action in fact perpetuates race and gender bias and stereotypes. Probably the large majority of Americans believe that there ought to be some help given to those directly affected by discrimination, and even to blacks and women in general. The consensus breaks down when one begins to look at specific issues, such as goals versus quotas, recruitment versus promotion, and who "pays" for the program in terms of lost or closed opportunities.

There is also a question of whether, aside from some individual success stories, affirmative action has been an effective policy. There is a dearth of statistics to prove the case one way or the other. On the one hand, the black middle class seems larger than ever, and one can find blacks, women, and Hispanics in many middle-management and professional positions. On the other hand, some studies indicate that the top jobs remain disproportionately in the hands of white males, and during the Reagan years, blacks and women apparently suffered significant slippage. In a study of affluent Westchester County, New York, white males held two out of every three of the 487 county government jobs paying $43,000 or more, although they made up barely a third of the total work force of 8,500 people. In 1984, women had held 30 percent of those jobs, and blacks 8.7 percent; four years later their respective numbers had slipped to 25.5 and 7.1 percent.[23] Another study, involving blacks in journalism, showed not only that blacks were underrepresented in proportion to their numbers in the general population,

but that the number of blacks working in televised news had declined 13 percent from 1979 to 1986.[24] The most recent survey of
the status of blacks in America reached this conclusion: "The status
of black Americans today can be characterized as a glass that is half
full—if measured by the progress since 1939—or as a glass that is
half empty—if measured by the persisting disparities between black
and white Americans since the early 1970s. . . . Since the early
1970s, the economic status of blacks relative to whites has, on
average, stagnated or deteriorated."

In a section devoted to affirmative action, the report documents
not only the continuing discrimination faced by blacks, but also
the failure of affirmative action. In 1984, the last year for which
figures are available, the average yearly earnings of black male
college graduates, a group most likely to benefit from affirmative
action, amounted to only 74 percent of their white counterparts.
Between 1970 and 1986, the proportion of black families with in-
flation-adjusted incomes of $35,000 or more increased only 4 per-
cent, from 18 to 22 percent. A worse story exists when one looks
at blue-collar black workers, where in some categories real income
decreased by 20 percent in the affluent eighties. All in all, black per
capita income stood at 57 percent of the white level in 1984, exactly
the same percentage it had been in 1971.[25]

The story is somewhat different, and better, for women, especially white women who have sought to enter the professions. In
some law schools, for example, recent classes have run at almost
an identical gender mix as that of society at large. It is clear that
there are more women doctors, lawyers, judges, and business ex-
ecutives. Today over 15 percent of doctors and lawyers are women,
as compared with less than 3 percent in 1970. During the Reagan
years, despite the Administration's opposition to affirmative action,
women's wages did increase; in 1987, for the first time, the hourly
earnings of women employed full-time exceeded 75 percent of the
earnings of men working full-time and with the same amount of
schooling, up from the 60 percent figure that held fairly steady
throughout the 1970s. Some economists suggest that unless and
until the United States adopts either a comprehensive family support system or imposes wage controls, it is unlikely that women

overall will ever earn as much as men, because of the time they drop out of the labor market to have families.[26]

Like their black counterparts, women in blue-collar or so-called pink collar clerical jobs have shared least in the economic good times. While some estimates place women at nearly half of the professional work force (including business management), they are still for the most part excluded from skilled crafts. Only 8.6 percent of precision, production, craft, and repair jobs are held by women; only 3 percent of mechanics and 1.5 percent of construction workers are female. Despite Scalia's assumption that women do not want to go into these traditional male domains, the evidence shows that they do, but recognize the barriers. When Santa Clara County surveyed one hundred of its female employees in 1984, it found that eighty-five of them did in fact want to work in the skilled-craft categories, which paid twice or three times a secretary's wages. Ninety of them said they knew they would not be able to get those jobs because of discrimination![27]

The story started with Paul Johnson, Diane Joyce, and the Santa Clara County Transportation Agency, and ends with them as well. Johnson, bitter after the Ninth Circuit reversed Judge Ingram, took early retirement at the end of 1984. He and his wife, Betty, moved to the small seaside town of Sequim, on Washington's Olympic Peninsula. He feels, with some justification, that the press made him the "heavy" of this story, and several times during our interview said how tired he was of all the distortions, and only wanted to see the facts set out clearly. He frequently gets calls from other people who are involved in reverse-discrimination suits, and in 1989 sent out an "Open Letter to the White Males of America," suggesting that they should somehow organize before any more of their rights were taken away.

James Dawson, who argued Johnson's case in the district and appeals courts, left the office where Johnson met him, and formed his own law partnership, which later merged with another to form a larger firm. Dawson continues to practice law in San Jose.

Constance Brooks left Mountain States about a year after the case, and is now a partner in the Portland, Oregon, law firm of

Lindsay, Hart, Neil & Weigler. A good part of her practice involves public interest questions.

With the end of the Reagan Administration, Charles Fried returned to the Harvard Law School, from which he occasionally sallies forth to argue cases, as a private lawyer, before the Supreme Court.

Steven Woodside has remained with Santa Clara County, but has been promoted; he is now chief county counsel. David Rosenfeld, who represented the union, continues to practice in San Francisco.

In July 1990, William Brennan, Jr., the Court's most effective champion of affirmative action, retired after a distinguished career of thirty-four years on the nation's highest tribunal.

Michael Baratz, who served as director for Local 715 of the Service Employees International Union and who had championed Diane's cause, is now in Washington, the director of field services and bargaining for the international union. His place in San Jose has been taken by Kristy Sermersheim, who spoke up for Diane Joyce and had the task of keeping her calm during the protracted legal proceedings.

Has anything really changed in the Transportation Agency because of the suit and the affirmative action plan that caused it? On this there seems to be general agreement: things are pretty much the same as they were a decade ago. There are a few more minorities, a few more women, but as Michael Baratz said, "the guys are still the same today; by and large the same culture exists." Kristy Sermersheim agrees: things have not changed; the road department remains predominantly white, predominantly male.

Suzanne Wilson is still a supervisor, and she takes a far more optimistic view. Reforms take time, she says, but the longer the affirmative action plan is in place, the more things will open up. There have been some incremental changes, and as the old-guard managers retire or move on, they will be replaced, sometimes by women or minorities, but certainly by people sensitive to the problems faced by women and minorities.

Diane Joyce has the dispatcher's mike, but still feels the resentment of many of her male coworkers. She does not really expect that she will see revolutionary changes in her lifetime, but she hopes for the future. There are now other women—a few—working on the road crews, including her daughter, Donna.

A year or so ago she applied for but did not get a job as assistant road district superintendent in neighboring Monterey County. "They accepted my application," she noted, "and they didn't say they wanted a man. Now, for me, that's progress."

Appendix

SUPREME COURT
OF THE UNITED STATES

No. 85–1129

PAUL E. JOHNSON, PETITIONER *v.*
TRANSPORTATION AGENCY,
SANTA CLARA COUNTY,
CALIFORNIA, ET AL.

[March 25, 1987]

480 U.S. 616 (1987).

Justice BRENNAN delivered the opinion of the Court.

Respondent, Transportation Agency of Santa Clara County, California, unilaterally promulgated an Affirmative Action Plan applicable, *inter alia*, to promotions of employees. In selecting applicants for the promotional position of road dispatcher, the Agency, pursuant to the Plan, passed over petitioner Paul Johnson, a male employee, and promoted a female employee applicant, Diane Joyce. The question for decision is whether in making the promotion the Agency impermissibly took into account the sex of the applicants in violation of Title VII of the Civil Rights Act of 1964,

42 U.S.C. § 2000e *et seq.*[1] The District Court for the Northern District of California, in an action filed by petitioner following receipt of a right-to-sue letter from the Equal Employment Opportunity Commission (EEOC), held that respondent had violated Title VII. App. to Pet. for Cert. 1a. The Court of Appeals for the Ninth Circuit reversed. 748 F.2d 1308 (1984); modified, 770 F.2d 752 (1985). We granted certiorari, 478 U.S. 1019 (1986). We affirm.[2]

I

A

In December 1978, the Santa Clara County Transit District Board of Supervisors adopted an Affirmative Action Plan (Plan) for the County Transportation Agency. The Plan implemented a County Affirmative Action Plan, which had been adopted, declared the County, because "mere prohibition of discriminatory practices is not enough to remedy the effects of past practices and to permit attainment of an equitable representation of minorities, women and handicapped persons." App. 31.[3] Relevant to this case, the Agency

1. Section 703(a) of the Act, 78 Stat. 255, as amended, 86 Stat. 109, 42 U.S.C. § 2000e–2(a), provides that it "shall be an unlawful employment practice for an employer—

    "(1) to fail or refuse to hire or to discharge any individual, or otherwise to discriminate against any individual with respect to his compensation, terms, conditions, or privileges of employment, because of such individual's race, color, religion, sex, or national origin; or

    "(2) to limit, segregate, or classify his employees or applicants for employment in any way which would deprive or tend to deprive any individual of employment opportunities or otherwise adversely affect his status as an employee, because of such individual's race, color, religion, sex, or national origin."

2. No constitutional issue was either raised or addressed in the litigation below. See 748 F.2d 1308, 1310, n. 1 (1984). We therefore decide in this case only the issue of the prohibitory scope of Title VII. Of course, where the issue is properly raised, public employers must justify the adoption and implementation of a voluntary affirmative action plan under the Equal Protection Clause. See *Wygant v. Jackson Board of Education*, 476 U.S. 267 (1986).

3. The Plan reaffirmed earlier County and Agency efforts to address the issue of employment discrimination, dating back to the County's adoption in 1971 of an Equal Employment Opportunity Policy. App. 37–40.

Plan provides that, in making promotions to positions within a traditionally segregated job classification in which women have been significantly underrepresented, the Agency is authorized to consider as one factor the sex of a qualified applicant.

In reviewing the composition of its work force, the Agency noted in its Plan that women were represented in numbers far less than their proportion of the county labor force in both the Agency as a whole and in five of seven job categories. Specifically, while women constituted 36.4% of the area labor market, they composed only 22.4% of Agency employees. Furthermore, women working at the Agency were concentrated largely in EEOC job categories traditionally held by women: women made up 76% of Office and Clerical Workers, but only 7.1% of Agency Officials and Administrators, 8.6% of Professionals, 9.7% of Technicians, and 22% of Service and Maintenance workers. As for the job classification relevant to this case, none of the 238 Skilled Craft Worker positions was held by a woman. *Id.*, at 49. The Plan noted that this underrepresentation of women in part reflected the fact that women had not traditionally been employed in these positions, and that they had not been strongly motivated to seek training or employment in them "because of the limited opportunities that have existed in the past for them to work in such classifications." *Id.*, at 57. The Plan also observed that, while the proportion of ethnic minorities in the Agency as a whole exceeded the proportion of such minorities in the county work force, a smaller percentage of minority employees held management, professional, and technical positions.[4]

The Agency stated that its Plan was intended to achieve "a statistically measurable yearly improvement in hiring, training and promotion of minorities and women throughout the Agency in all major job classifications where they are underrepresented." *Id.*, at 43. As a benchmark by which to evaluate progress, the Agency stated that its long-term goal was to attain a work force whose composition reflected the proportion of minorities and women in

---

4. While minorities constituted 19.7% of the county labor force, they represented 7.1% of the Agency's Officials and Administrators, 19% of its Professionals, and 16.9% of its Technicians. *Id.*, at 48.

the area labor force. *Id.*, at 54. Thus, for the Skilled Craft category in which the road dispatcher position at issue here was classified, the Agency's aspiration was that eventually about 36% of the jobs would be occupied by women.

The Plan acknowledged that a number of factors might make it unrealistic to rely on the Agency's long-term goals in evaluating the Agency's progress in expanding job opportunities for minorities and women. Among the factors identified were low turnover rates in some classifications, the fact that some jobs involved heavy labor, the small number of positions within some job categories, the limited number of entry positions leading to the Technical and Skilled Craft classifications, and the limited number of minorities and women qualified for positions requiring specialized training and experience. *Id.*, at 56–57. As a result, the Plan counselled that short-range goals be established and annually adjusted to serve as the most realistic guide for actual employment decisions. Among the tasks identified as important in establishing such short-term goals was the acquisition of data "reflecting the ratio of minorities, women and handicapped persons who are working in the local area in major job classifications relating to those utilized by the County Administration," so as to determine the availability of members of such groups who "possess the desired qualifications or potential for placement." *Id.*, at 64. These data on qualified group members, along with predictions of position vacancies, were to serve as the basis for "realistic yearly employment goals for women, minorities and handicapped persons in each EEOC job category and major job classification." *Ibid.*

The Agency's Plan thus set aside no specific number of positions for minorities or women, but authorized the consideration of ethnicity or sex as a factor when evaluating qualified candidates for jobs in which members of such groups were poorly represented. One such job was the road dispatcher position that is the subject of the dispute in this case.

B

On December 12, 1979, the Agency announced a vacancy for the promotional position of road dispatcher in the Agency's Roads

Division. Dispatchers assign road crews, equipment, and materials, and maintain records pertaining to road maintenance jobs. *Id.*, at 23–24. The position requires at minimum four years of dispatch or road maintenance work experience for Santa Clara County. The EEOC job classification scheme designates a road dispatcher as a Skilled Craft worker.

Twelve County employees applied for the promotion, including Joyce and Johnson. Joyce had worked for the County since 1970, serving as an account clerk until 1975. She had applied for a road dispatcher position in 1974, but was deemed ineligible because she had not served as a road maintenance worker. In 1975, Joyce transferred from a senior account clerk position to a road maintenance worker position, becoming the first woman to fill such a job. Tr. 83–84. During her four years in that position, she occasionally worked out of class as a road dispatcher.

Petitioner Johnson began with the county in 1967 as a road yard clerk, after private employment that included working as a supervisor and dispatcher. He had also unsuccessfully applied for the road dispatcher opening in 1974. In 1977, his clerical position was downgraded, and he sought and received a transfer to the position of road maintenance worker. *Id.*, at 127. He also occasionally worked out of class as a dispatcher while performing that job.

Nine of the applicants, including Joyce and Johnson, were deemed qualified for the job, and were interviewed by a two-person board. Seven of the applicants scored above 70 on this interview, which meant that they were certified as eligible for selection by the appointing authority. The scores awarded ranged from 70 to 80. Johnson was tied for second with score of 75, while Joyce ranked next with a score of 73. A second interview was conducted by three Agency supervisors, who ultimately recommended that Johnson be promoted. Prior to the second interview, Joyce had contacted the County's Affirmative Action Office because she feared that her application might not receive disinterested review.[5] The Office in

5. Joyce testified that she had had disagreements with two of the three members of the second interview panel. One had been her first supervisor when she began work as a road maintenance worker. In performing arduous work in this job, she had not been issued coveralls, although her male coworkers had received them. After ruining her pants, she complained to her supervisor, to no avail.

turn contacted the Agency's Affirmative Action Coordinator, whom the Agency's Plan makes responsible for, *inter alia*, keeping the Director informed of opportunities for the Agency to accomplish its objectives under the Plan. At the time, the Agency employed no women in any Skilled Craft position, and had never employed a woman as a road dispatcher. The Coordinator recommended to the Director of the Agency, James Graebner, that Joyce be promoted.

Graebner, authorized to choose any of the seven persons deemed eligible, thus had the benefit of suggestions by the second interview panel and by the Agency Coordinator in arriving at his decision. After deliberation, Graebner concluded that the promotion should be given to Joyce. As he testified: "I tried to look at the whole picture, the combination of her qualifications and Mr. Johnson's qualifications, their test scores, their expertise, their background, affirmative action matters, things like that . . . I believe it was a combination of all those." *Id.*, at 68.

The certification form naming Joyce as the person promoted to the dispatcher position stated that both she and Johnson were rated as well-qualified for the job. The evaluation of Joyce read: "Well qualified by virtue of 18 years of past clerical experience including 3½ years at West Yard plus almost 5 years as a [road maintenance worker]." App. 27. The evaluation of Johnson was as follows: "Well qualified applicant; two years of [road maintence worker] experience plus 11 years of Road Yard Clerk. Has had previous outside Dispatch experience but was 13 years ago." *Ibid.* Graebner testified

After three other similar incidents, ruining clothes on each occasion, she filed a grievance, and was issued four pair of coveralls the next day. Tr. 89–90. Joyce had dealt with a second member of the panel for a year and a half in her capacity as chair of the Roads Operations Safety Committee, where she and he "had several differences of opinion on how safety should be implemented." *Id.*, at 90–91. In addition, Joyce testified that she had informed the person responsible for arranging her second interview that she had a disaster preparedness class on a certain day the following week. By this time about ten days had passed since she had notified this person of her availability, and no date had yet been set for the interview. Within a day or two after this conversation, however, she received a notice setting her interview at a time directly in the middle of her disaster preparedness class. *Id.*, at 94–95. This same panel member had earlier described Joyce as a "rebel-rousing, skirt-wearing person," Tr. 153.

that he did not regard as significant the fact that Johnson scored 75 and Joyce 73 when interviewed by the two-person board. Tr. 57–58.

Petitioner Johnson filed a complaint with the EEOC alleging that he had been denied promotion on the basis of sex in violation of Title VII. He received a right-to-sue letter from the agency on March 10, 1981, and on March 20, 1981, filed suit in the United States District Court for the Northern District of California. The District Court found that Johnson was more qualified for the dispatcher position than Joyce, and that the sex of Joyce was the "*determining factor* in her selection." App. to Pet. for Cert. 4a (emphasis in original). The court acknowledged that, since the Agency justified its decision on the basis of its Affirmative Action Plan, the criteria announced in *Steelworkers v. Weber*, 443 U.S. (1979), should be applied in evaluating the validity of the plan. App. to Pet. for Cert. 5a. It then found the Agency's Plan invalid on the ground that the evidence did not satisfy *Weber*'s criterion that the Plan be temporary. *Id.*, at 6a. The Court of Appeals for the Ninth Circuit reversed, holding that the absence of an express termination date in the Plan was not dispositive, since the Plan repeatedly expressed its objective as the attainment, rather than the maintenance, of a work force mirroring the labor force in the county. 748 F.2d, at 1312, modified, 770 F.2d 752 (1985). The Court of Appeals added that the fact that the Plan established no fixed percentage of positions for minorities or women made it less essential that the Plan contain a relatively explicit deadline. 748 F.2d, at 1312. The Court held further that the Agency's consideration of Joyce's sex in filling the road dispatcher position was lawful. The Agency Plan had been adopted, the court said, to address a conspicuous imbalance in the Agency's work force, and neither unnecessarily trammeled the rights of other employees, nor created an absolute bar to their advancement. *Id.*, at 1313–1314.

II

As a preliminary matter, we note that petitioner bears the burden of establishing the invalidity of the Agency's Plan. Only last term in *Wygant v. Jackson Board of Education*, 476 U.S. 267, 277–278 (1986), we held that "[t]he ultimate burden remains with the employees to demonstrate the unconstitutionality of an affirmative-action program," and we see no basis for a different rule regarding a plan's alleged violation of Title VII. This case also fits readily within the analytical framework set forth in *McDonnell Douglas Corp. v. Green*, 411 U.S. 792 (1973). Once a plaintiff establishes a prima facie case that race or sex has been taken into account in an employer's employment decision, the burden shifts to the employer to articulate a nondiscriminatory rationale for its decision. The existence of an affirmative action plan provides such a rationale. If such a plan is articulated as the basis for the employer's decision, the burden shifts to the plaintiff to prove that the employer's justification is pretextual and the plan is invalid. As a practical matter, of course, an employer will generally seek to avoid a charge of pretext by presenting evidence in support of its plan. That does not mean, however, as petitioner suggests, that reliance on an affirmative action plan is to be treated as an affirmative defense requiring the employer to carry the burden of proving the validity of the plan. The burden of proving its invalidity remains on the plaintiff.

The assessment of the legality of the Agency Plan must be guided by our decision in *Webster, supra*.[6] In that case, the Court addressed

6. The dissent maintains that the obligations of a public employer under Title VII must be identical to its obligations under the Constitution, and that a public employer's adoption of an affirmative action plan therefore should be governed by *Wygant*. This rests on the following logic: Title VI embodies the same constraints as the Constitution; Title VI and Title VII have the same prohibitory scope; therefore, Title VII and the Constitution are coterminous for purposes of this case. The flaw is with the second step of the analysis, for it advances a proposition that we explicitly considered and rejected in *Weber*. As we noted in that case, Title VI was an exercise of federal power "over a matter in which the Federal Government was already directly involved," since Congress "was legislating to assure federal funds would not be used in an improper manner." 443 U.S., at 206 n. 6. "Title VII, by contrast, was enacted pursuant to the commerce power to regulate purely private decisionmaking and was not intended to incorporate and particularize the commands of the Fifth and Fourteenth Amendments. Title VII and Title VI, therefore, cannot be read *in pari materia*." *Ibid*. This point is underscored by Congress' concern that the receipt of any form of financial assistance might render an employer subject to the commands

the question whether the employer violated Title VII by adopting a voluntary affirmative action plan designed to "eliminate manifest racial imbalances in traditionally segregated job categories." *Id.*, 443 U.S., at 197. The respondent employee in that case challenged the employer's denial of his application for a position in a newly established craft training program, contending that the employer's selection process impermissibly took into account the race of the applicants. The selection process was guided by an affirmative action plan, which provided that 50% of the new trainees were to be black until the percentage of black skilled craftworkers in the employer's plant approximated the percentage of blacks in the local labor force. Adoption of the plan had been prompted by the fact that only 5 of 273, or 1.83%, of skilled craftworkers at the plant were black, even though the work force in the area was approximately 39% black. Because of the historical exclusion of blacks from craft positions, the employer regarded its former policy of hiring trained outsiders as inadequate to redress the imbalance in its work force.

We upheld the employer's decision to select less senior black applicants over the white respondent, for we found that taking race into account was consistent with Title VII's objective of "break[ing]

of Title VI rather than Title VII. As a result, Congress added § 604 to Title VI, 42 U.S.C. § 2000d–3, which provides:

"Nothing contained in this subchapter shall be construed to authorize action under this subchapter by any department or agency with respect to any employment practice or any employer, employment agency, or labor organization except where a primary objective of the Federal financial assistance is to provide employment."

The sponsor of this section, Senator Cooper, stated that it was designed to clarify that "it was not intended that [T]itle VI would impinge on [T]itle VII." 110 Cong.Rec. 11615 (1964).

While public employers were not added to the definition of "employer" in Title VII until 1972, there is no evidence that this mere addition to the definitional section of the statute was intended to transform the substantive standard governing employer conduct. Indeed, "Congress expressly indicated the intent that the same Title VII principles be applied to governmental and private employers alike." *Dothard v. Rawlinson*, 433 U.S. 321, 332 n. 14 (1977). The fact that a public employer must also satisfy the Constitution does not negate the fact that the *statutory* prohibition with which that employer must contend was not intended to extend as far as that of the Constitution.

down old patterns of racial segregation and hierarchy." *Id.*, at 208. As we stated:

> "It would be ironic indeed if a law triggered by a Nation's concern over centuries of racial injustice and intended to improve the lot of those who had 'been excluded from the American dream for so long' constituted the first legislative prohibition of all voluntary, private, race-conscious efforts to abolish traditional patterns of racial segregation and hierarchy." *Id.*, at 204 (quoting remarks of Sen. Humphrey, 110 Cong. Rec. 6552 (1964)).[7]

7. The dissent maintains that *Weber*'s conclusion that Title VII does not prohibit voluntary affirmative action programs "rewrote the statute it purported to construe." *Post*, at 670. *Weber*'s decisive rejection of the argument that the "plain language" of the statute prohibits affirmative action rested on (1) legislative history indicating Congress' clear intention that employers play a major role in eliminating the vestiges of discrimination, 443 U.S., at 201–204, and (2) the language and legislative history of § 703(j) of the statute, which reflect a strong desire to preserve managerial prerogatives so that they might be utilized for this purpose. *Id.*, at 204–207. As Justice BLACKMUN said in his concurrence in *Weber*, "[I]f the Court has misperceived the political will, it has the assurance that because the question is statutory Congress may set a different course if it so chooses." *Id.*, at 216. Congress has not amended the statute to reject our construction, nor have any such amendments even been proposed, and we therefore may assume that our interpretation was correct.

Justice SCALIA's dissent faults the fact that we take note of the absence of Congressional efforts to amend the statute to nullify *Weber*. It suggests that Congressional inaction cannot be regarded as acquiescence under all circumstances, but then draws from that unexceptional point the conclusion that *any* reliance on Congressional failure to act is necessarily a "canard." *Post*, at 672. The fact that inaction may not always provide crystalline revelation, however, should not obscure the fact that it may be probative to varying degrees. *Weber*, for instance, was a widely-publicized decision that addressed a prominent issue of public debate. Legislative inattention thus is not a plausible explanation for Congressional inaction. Furthermore, Congress not only passed no contrary legislation in the wake of *Weber*, but not one legislator even proposed a bill to do so. The barriers of the legislative process therefore also seem a poor explanation for failure to act. By contrast, when Congress has been displeased with our interpretation of Title VII, it has not hesitated to amend the statute to tell us so. For instance, when Congress passed the Pregnancy Discrimination Act of 1978, 42 U.S.C. § 2000e(k), "it unambiguously expressed its disapproval of both the holding and the reasoning of the Court in [*General Electric v. Gilbert*, 429 U.S. 125 (1976)]." *Newport News Shipbuilding & Dry Dock v. EEOC*, 462 U.S. 669 (1983). Surely, it is appropriate to find some probative value in such radically different Congressional reactions to this Court's interpretations of the same statute.

As one scholar has put it, "When a court says to a legislature: 'You (or

We noted that the plan did not "unnecessarily trammel the interests of the white employees," since it did not require "the discharge of white workers and their replacement with new black hirees." *Ibid.* Nor did the plan create "an absolute bar to the advancement of white employees," since half of those trained in the new program were to be white. *Ibid.* Finally, we observed that the plan was a temporary measure, not designed to maintain racial balance, but to "eliminate a manifest racial imbalance." *Ibid.* As Justice BLACKMUN's concurrence made clear, *Weber* held that an employer seeking to justify the adoption of a plan need not point to its own prior discriminatory practices, nor even to evidence of an "arguable violation" on its part. *Id.*, at 212. Rather, it need point only to a "conspicuous . . . imbalance in traditionally segregated job categories." *Id.*, at 209. Our decision was grounded in the recognition that voluntary employer action can play a crucial role in furthering Title VII's purpose of eliminating the effects of discrimination in the workplace, and that Title VII should not be read to thwart such efforts. *Id.*, at 204.[8]

your predecessor) mean X,' it almost invites the legislature to answer: 'We did not.' " G. Calabresi, A Common Law for the Age of Statutes 31–32 (1982). Any belief in the notion of a dialogue between the judiciary and the legislature must acknowledge that on occasion an invitation declined is as significant as one accepted.

8. See also *Firefighters v. Cleveland*, 478 U.S. 501, 515 (1986) ("We have on numerous occasions recognized that Congress intended for voluntary compliance to be the preferred means of achieving the objectives of Title VII"); *Alexander v. Gardner-Denver*, 415 U.S. 36, 44 (1974) ("Cooperation and voluntary compliance were selected as the preferred means for achieving [Title VII's] goal"). The dissent's suggestion that an affirmative action program may be adopted only to redress an employer's past discrimination, see *post*, at 664–665, was rejected in *Steelworkers v. Weber*, 443 U.S. 193 (1979), because the prospect of liability created by such an admission would create a significant disincentive for voluntary action. As Justice BLACKMUN's concurrence in that case pointed out, such a standard would "plac[e] voluntary compliance with Title VII in profound jeopardy. The only way for the employer and the union to keep their footing on the 'tightrope' it creates would be to eschew all forms of voluntary affirmative action." 443 U.S., at 210. Similarly, Justice O'CONNOR has observed in the constitutional context that "[t]he imposition of a requirement that public employers make findings that they have engaged in illegal discrimination before they engage in affirmative action programs would severely undermine public employers' incentive to meet voluntarily their civil rights obligations."

In reviewing the employment decision at issue in this case, we must first examine whether that decision was made pursuant to a plan prompted by concerns similar to those of the employer in *Weber*. Next, we must determine whether the effect of the plan on males and non-minorities is comparable to the effect of the plan in that case.

The first issue is therefore whether consideration of the sex of applicants for skilled craft jobs was justified by the existence of a "manifest imbalance" that reflected underrepresentation of women in "traditionally segregated job categories." *Id.*, at 197. In determining whether an imbalance exists that would justify taking sex or race into account, a comparison of the percentage of minorities or women in the employer's work force with the percentage in the area labor market or general population is appropriate in analyzing jobs that require no special expertise, see *Teamsters v. United States*, 431 U.S. 324 (1977) (comparison between percentage of blacks in employer's work force and in general population proper in determining extent of imbalance in truck driving positions), or training programs designed to provide expertise, see *Weber, supra* (comparison between proportion of blacks working at plant and proportion of blacks in area labor force appropriate in calculating imbalance for purpose of establishing preferential admission to craft training program). Where a job requires special training, however, the com-

---

Wygant, *supra*, at 290 (O'CONNOR, J., concurring in part and concurring in the judgment).

Contrary to the dissent's contention, *post*, at 664–668, our decisions last term in *Firefighters, supra,* and *Sheet Metal Workers v. EEOC*, 478 U.S. 501 (1986), provide no support for a standard more restrictive than that enunciated in *Weber*. *Firefighters* raised the issue of the conditions under which parties could enter into a consent decree providing for explicit numerical quotas. By contrast, the affirmative action plan in this case sets aside no positions for minorities or women. See *infra*, at 635. In *Sheet Metal Workers*, the issue we addressed was the scope of judicial remedial authority under Title VII, authority that has not been exercised in this case. The dissent's suggestion that employers should be able to do no more voluntarily than courts can order as remedies, *post*, at 664–668, ignores the fundamental difference between volitional private behavior and the exercise of coercion by the state. Plainly, "Congress' concern that federal courts not impose unwanted obligations on employers and unions," *Firefighters, supra*, 478 U.S., at 524, reflects a desire to preserve a relatively large domain for voluntary employer action.

parison should be with those in the labor force who possess the relevant qualifications. See *Hazelwood School District v. United States*, 433 U.S. 299 (1977) (must compare percentage of blacks in employer's work ranks with percentage of qualified black teachers in area labor force in determining underrepresentation in teaching positions). The requirement that the "manifest imbalance" relate to a "traditionally segregated job category" provides assurance both that sex or race will be taken into account in a manner consistent with Title VII's purpose of eliminating the effects of employment discrimination, and that the interests of those employees not benefitting from the plan will not be unduly infringed.

A manifest imbalance need not be such that it would support a prima facie case against the employer, as suggested in Justice O'CONNOR's concurrence, *post* at 649, since we do not regard as identical the constraints of Title VII and the federal constitution on voluntarily adopted affirmative action plans.[9] Application of the "prima facie" standard in Title VII cases would be inconsistent with *Weber*'s focus on statistical imbalance,[10] and could inappro-

---

9. See *supra*, n. 6.
10. The difference between the "manifest imbalance" and "prima facie" standards is illuminated by *Weber*. Had the Court in that case been concerned with past discrimination by the employer, it would have focused on discrimination in hiring skilled, not unskilled, workers, since only the scarcity of the former in Kaiser's work force would have made it vulnerable to a Title VII suit. In order to make out a prima facie case on such a claim, a plaintiff would be required to compare the percentage of black skilled workers in the Kaiser work force with the percentage of black skilled workers in the area labor market.

Weber obviously did not make such a comparison. Instead, it focused on the disparity between the percentage of black skilled craft workers in Kaiser's ranks and the percentage of blacks in the area labor force. 443 U.S., at 198–199. Such an approach reflected a recognition that the proportion of black craft-workers in the local labor force was likely as minuscule as the proportion in Kaiser's work force. The Court realized that the lack of imbalance between these figures would mean that employers in precisely those industries in which discrimination has been most effective would be precluded from adopting training programs to increase the percentage of qualified minorities. Thus, in cases such as *Weber*, where the employment decision at issue involves the selection of unskilled persons for a training program, the "manifest imbalance" standard permits comparison with the general labor force. By contrast, the "prima facie" standard would require comparison with the percentage of minorities or women

priately create a significant disincentive for employers to adopt an affirmative action plan. See *Weber, supra*, 443 U.S., at 204 (Title VII intended as a "catalyst" for employer efforts to eliminate vestiges of discrimination). A corporation concerned with maximizing return on investment, for instance, is hardly likely to adopt a plan if in order to do so it must compile evidence that could be used to subject it to a colorable Title VII suit.[11]

It is clear that the decision to hire Joyce was made pursuant to an Agency plan that directed that sex or race be taken into account for the purpose of remedying underrepresentation. The Agency Plan acknowledged the "limited opportunities that have existed in the past," App. 57, for women to find employment in certain job classifications "where women have not been traditionally employed in significant numbers." *Id.*, at 51.[12] As a result, observed the Plan, women were concentrated in traditionally female jobs in the Agency, and represented a lower percentage in other job classifi-

qualified for the job for which the trainees are being trained, a standard that would have invalidated the plan in *Weber* itself.

11. In some cases, of course, the manifest imbalance may be sufficiently egregious to establish a prima facie case. However, as long as there is a manifest imbalance, an employer may adopt a plan even where the disparity is not so striking, without being required to introduce the non-statistical evidence of past discrimination that would be demanded by the "prima facie" standard. See, *e.g.*, *Teamsters v. United States*, 431 U.S. 324, 339 (1977) (statistics in pattern and practice case supplemented by testimony regarding employment practices). Of course, when there is sufficient evidence to meet the more stringent "prima facie" standard, be it statistical, non-statistical, or a combination of the two, the employer is free to adopt an affirmative action plan.

12. For instance, the description of the Skilled Craft Worker category, in which the road dispatcher position is located, is as follows:

"Occupations in which workers perform jobs which require special manual skill and a thorough and comprehensive knowledge of the process involved in the work which is acquired through on-the-job training and experience or through apprenticeship or other formal training programs. Includes: mechanics and repairmen; electricians, heavy equipment operators, stationary engineers, skilled machining occupations, carpenters, compositors and typesetters and kindred workers." App. 108.

As the Court of Appeals said in its decision below, "A plethora of proof is hardly necessary to show that women are generally underrepresented in such positions and that strong social pressures weigh against their participation." 748 F.2d, at 1313.

cations than would be expected if such traditional segregation had not occurred. Specifically, 9 of the 10 Para-Professionals and 110 of the 145 Office and Clerical Workers were women. By contrast, women were only 2 of the 28 Officials and Administrators, 5 of the 58 Professionals, 12 of the 124 Technicians, none of the Skilled Craft Workers, and 1—who was Joyce—of the 110 Road Maintenance Workers. *Id.*, at 51–52. The Plan sought to remedy these imbalances through "hiring, training and promotion of . . . women throughout the Agency in all major job classifications where they are underrepresented." *Id.*, at 43.

As an initial matter, the Agency adopted as a benchmark for measuring progress in eliminating underrepresentation the long-term goal of a work force that mirrored in its major job classifications the percentage of women in the area labor market.[13] Even as it did so, however, the Agency acknowledged that such a figure could not by itself necessarily justify taking into account the sex of applicants for positions in all job categories. For positions requiring specialized training and experience, the Plan observed that the number of minorities and women "who possess the qualifications required for entry into such job classifications is limited." *Id.*, at 56. The Plan therefore directed that annual short-term goals be formulated that would provide a more realistic indication of the degree to which sex should be taken into account in filling particular positions. *Id.*, at 61–64. The Plan stressed that such goals "should not be construed as 'quotas' that must be met," but as reasonable aspirations in correcting the imbalance in the Agency's work force. *Id.*, at 64. These goals were to take into account factors such as "turnover, layoffs, lateral transfers, new job openings, retirements and availability of minorities, women and handicapped persons in the area work force who possess the desired qualifications or potential for placement." *Ibid.* The Plan specifically directed that, in establishing such goals, the Agency work with the County Planning Department and other sources in attempting to compile data on the

13. Because of the employment decision at issue in this case, our discussion henceforth refers primarily to the Plan's provisions to remedy the underrepresentation of women. Our analysis could apply as well, however, to the provisions of the plan pertaining to minorities.

percentage of minorities and women in the local labor force that were actually working in the job classifications comprising the Agency work force. *Id.*, at 63–64. From the outset, therefore, the Plan sought annually to develop even more refined measures of the underrepresentation in each job category that required attention.

As the Agency Plan recognized, women were most egregiously underrepresented in the Skilled Craft job category, since *none* of the 238 positions was occupied by a woman. In mid-1980, when Joyce was selected for the road dispatcher position, the Agency was still in the process of refining its short-term goals for Skilled Craft Workers in accordance with the directive of the Plan. This process did not reach fruition until 1982, when the Agency established a short-term goal for that year of three women for the 55 expected openings in that job category—a modest goal of about 6% for that category.

We reject petitioner's argument that, since only the long-term goal was in place for Skilled Craft positions at the time of Joyce's promotion, it was inappropriate for the Director to take into account affirmative action considerations in filling the road dispatcher position. The Agency's Plan emphasized that the long-term goals were not to be taken as guides for actual hiring decisions, but that supervisors were to consider a host of practical factors in seeking to meet affirmative action objectives, including the fact that in some job categories women were not qualified in numbers comparable to their representation in the labor force.

By contrast, had the Plan simply calculated imbalances in all categories according to the proportion of women in the area labor pool, and then directed that hiring be governed solely by those figures, its validity fairly could be called into question. This is because analysis of a more specialized labor pool normally is necessary in determining underrepresentation in some positions. If a plan failed to take distinctions in qualifications into account in providing guidance for actual employment decisions, it would dictate mere blind hiring by the numbers, for it would hold supervisors to "achievement of a particular percentage of minority employment or membership . . . regardless of circumstances such as economic

conditions or the number of qualified minority applicants . . . "
Sheet Metal Workers' v. EEOC, 478 U.S. 421, 495 (1986) (O'CON-NOR, J., concurring in part and dissenting in part).

The Agency's Plan emphatically did *not* authorize such blind hiring. It expressly directed that numerous factors be taken into account in making hiring decisions, including specifically the qualifications of female applicants for particular jobs. Thus, despite the fact that no precise short-term goal was yet in place for the Skilled Craft category in mid-1980, the Agency's management nevertheless had been clearly instructed that they were not to hire solely by reference to statistics. The fact that only the long-term goal had been established for this category posed no danger that personnel decisions would be made by reflexive adherence to a numerical standard.

Furthermore, in considering the candidates for the road dispatcher position in 1980, the Agency hardly needed to rely on a refined short-term goal to realize that it had a significant problem of underrepresentation that required attention. Given the obvious imbalance in the Skilled Craft category, and given the Agency's commitment to eliminating such imbalances, it was plainly not unreasonable for the Agency to determine that it was appropriate to consider as one factor the sex of Ms. Joyce in making its decision.[14] The promotion of Joyce thus satisfies the first requirement enunciated in *Weber*, since it was undertaken to further an affirmative action plan designed to eliminate Agency work force imbalances in traditionally segregated job categories.

We next consider whether the Agency Plan unnecessarily trammeled the rights of male employees or created an absolute bar to their advancement. In contrast to the plan in *Weber*, which provided that 50% of the positions in the craft training program were exclu-

---

14. In addition, the Agency was mindful of the importance of finally hiring a woman in a job category that had formerly been all-male. The Director testified that, while the promotion of Joyce "made a small dent, for sure, in the numbers," nonetheless "philosophically it made a larger impact in that it probably has encouraged other females and minorities to look at the possibility of so-called 'non-traditional' jobs as areas where they and the agency both have samples of a success story." Tr. 64.

sively for blacks, and to the consent decree upheld last term in *Firefighters v. Cleveland*, 478 U.S. 501 (1986), which required the promotion of specific numbers of minorities, the Plan sets aside no positions for women. The Plan expressly states that "[t]he 'goals' established for each Division should not be construed as 'quotas' that must be met." App. 64. Rather, the Plan merely authorizes that consideration be given to affirmative action concerns when evaluating qualified applicants. As the Agency Director testified, the sex of Joyce was but one of numerous factors he took into account in arriving at his decision. Tr. 68. The Plan thus resembles the "Harvard Plan" approvingly noted by Justice POWELL in *University of California Regents v. Bakke*, 438 U.S. 265, 316–319 (1978), which considers race along with other criteria in determining admission to the college. As Justice POWELL observed, "In such an admissions program, race or ethnic background may be deemed a 'plus' in a particular applicant's file, yet it does not insulate the individual from comparison with all other candidates for the available seats." *Id.*, at 317. Similarly, the Agency Plan requires women to compete with all other qualified applicants. *No* persons are automatically excluded from consideration; *all* are able to have their qualifications weighed against those of other applicants.

In addition, petitioner had no absolute entitlement to the road dispatcher position. Seven of the applicants were classified as qualified and eligible, and the Agency Director was authorized to promote any of the seven. Thus, denial of the promotion unsettled no legitimate firmly rooted expectation of the part of the petitioner. Furthermore, while the petitioner in this case was denied a promotion, he retained his employment with the Agency, at the same salary and with the same seniority, and remained eligible for other promotions.[15]

15. Furthermore, from 1978 to 1982 Skilled Craft jobs in the Agency increased from 238 to 349. The Agency's personnel figures indicate that the Agency fully expected most of these positions to be filled by men. Of the 111 new Skilled Craft jobs during this period, 105, or almost 95%, went to men. As previously noted, the Agency's 1982 Plan set a goal of hiring only three women out of the 55 new Skilled Craft positions projected for that year, a figure of about 6%. While this degree of employment expansion by an employer is by no

Finally, the Agency's Plan was intended to *attain* a balanced work force, not to maintain one. The Plan contains ten references to the Agency's desire to "attain" such a balance, but no reference whatsoever to a goal of maintaining it. The Director testified that, while the "broader goal" of affirmative action, defined as "the desire to hire, to promote, to give opportunity and training on an equitable, non-discriminatory basis," is something that is "a permanent part" of "the Agency's operating philosophy," that broader goal "is divorced, if you will, from specific number of percentages." Tr. 48–49.

The Agency acknowledged the difficulties that it would confront in remedying the imbalance in its work force, and it anticipated only gradual increases in the representation of minorities and women.[16] It is thus unsurprising that the Plan contains no explicit end date, for the Agency's flexible, case-by-case approach was not expected to yield success in a brief period of time. Express assurance that a program is only temporary may be necessary if the program actually sets aside positions according to specific numbers. See, *e.g.*, *Firefighters*, *supra*, 478 U.S., at 510, (four-year duration for consent decree providing for promotion of particular number of minorities); *Weber*, 443 U.S., at 199 (plan requiring that blacks constitute 50% of new trainees in effect until percentage of employer

---

means essential to a plan's validity, it underscores the fact that the Plan in this case in no way significantly restricts the employment prospects of such persons. Illustrative of this is the fact that an additional road dispatcher position was created in 1983, and petitioner was awarded the job. Brief for Respondent Transportation Agency 36, n. 35.

16. As the Agency Plan stated, after noting the limited number of minorities and women qualified in certain categories, as well as other difficulties in remedying underrepresentation:

"As indicated by the above factors, it will be much easier to attain the Agency's employment goals in some job categories than in others. It is particularly evident that it will be extremely difficult to significantly increase the representation of women in technical and skilled craft job classifications where they have traditionally been greatly underrepresented. Similarly, only gradual increases in the representation of women, minorities or handicapped persons in management and professional positions can realistically be expected due to the low turnover that exists in these positions and the small numbers of persons who can be expected to compete for available openings." App. 58.

work force equal to percentage in local labor force). This is necessary both to minimize the effect of the program on other employees, and to ensure that the plan's goals "[are] not being used simply to achieve and maintain . . . balance, but rather as a benchmark against which" the employer may measure its progress in eliminating the underrepresentation of minorities and women. *Sheet Metal Workers, supra*, 478 U.S., at 477–478. In this case, however, substantial evidence shows that the Agency has sought to take a moderate, gradual approach to eliminating the imbalance in its work force, one which establishes realistic guidance for employment decisions, and which visits minimal intrusion on the legitimate expectations of other employees. Given this fact, as well as the Agency's express commitment to "attain" a balanced work force, there is ample assurance that the Agency does not seek to use its Plan to maintain a permanent racial and sexual balance.

III

In evaluating the compliance of an affirmative action plan with Title VII's prohibition on discrimination, we must be mindful of "this Court's and Congress' consistent emphasis on 'the value of voluntary efforts to further the objectives of the law.' " *Wygant*, 476 U.S., at 290 (O'CONNOR, J., concurring in part and concurring in judgment) (quoting *Bakke, supra*, 438 U.S., at 364.) The Agency in the case before us has undertaken such a voluntary effort, and has done so in full recognition of both the difficulties and the potential for intrusion on males and non-minorities. The Agency has identified a conspicuous imbalance in job categories traditionally segregated by race and sex. It has made clear from the outset, however, that employment decisions may not be justified solely by reference to this imbalance, but must rest on a multitude of practical, realistic factors. It has therefore committed itself to annual adjustment of goals so as to provide a reasonable guide for actual hiring and promotion decisions. The Agency earmarks no positions for anyone; sex is but one of several factors that may be taken into account in evaluating qualified applicants for a position.[17] As both

17.   The dissent predicts that today's decision will loose a flood of "less qualified"

the Plan's language and its manner of operation attest, the Agency has no intention of establishing a work force whose permanent composition is dictated by rigid numerical standards.

We therefore hold that the Agency appropriately took into account as one factor the sex of Diane Joyce in determining that she should be promoted to the road dispatcher position. The decision to do so was made pursuant to an affirmative action plan that represents a moderate, flexible, case-by-case approach to effecting a gradual improvement in the representation of minorities and women in the Agency's work force. Such a plan is fully consistent with Title VII, for it embodies the contribution that voluntary employer action can make in eliminating the vestiges of discrimination in the workplace. Accordingly, the judgment of the Court of Appeals is
Affirmed.

Justice STEVENS, concurring.
While I join the Court's opinion, I write separately to explain

minorities and women upon the workforce, as employers seek to forestall possible Title VII liability. *Post*, at 673–677. The first problem with this projection is that it is by no means certain that employers could in every case necessarily avoid liability for discrimination merely by adopting an affirmative action plan. Indeed, our unwillingness to require an admission of discrimination as the price of adopting a plan has been premised on concern that the potential liability to which such an admission would expose an employer would serve as a disincentive for creating an affirmative action program. See *supra*, n. 6.

A second, and more fundamental, problem with the dissent's speculation is that it ignores the fact that
"[i]t is a standard tenet of personnel administration that there is rarely a single, 'best qualified' person for a job. An effective personnel system will bring before the selecting official several fully-qualified candidates who each may possess different attributes which recommend them for selection. Especially where the job is an unexceptional, middle-level craft position, without the need for unique work experience or educational attainment and for which several well-qualified candidates are available, final determinations as to which candidate is 'best qualified' are at best subjective." Brief for American Society for Personnel Administration as *Amicus Curiae* 9.

This case provides an example of precisely this point. Any differences in qualifications between Johnson and Joyce were minimal, to say the least. See *supra*, at 1447–1449. The selection of Joyce thus belies the dissent's contention that the beneficiaries of affirmative action programs will be those employees who are merely not "utterly unqualified." *Post*, at 675.

209

my view of this case's position in our evolving antidiscrimination law and to emphasize that the opinion does not establish the permissible outer limits of voluntary programs undertaken by employers to benefit disadvantaged groups.

I

Antidiscrimation measures may benefit protected groups in two distinct ways. As a sword, such measures may confer benefits by specifying that a person's membership in a disadvantaged group must be a neutral, irrelevant factor in governmental or private decisionmaking or, alternatively, by compelling decisionmakers to give favorable consideration to disadvantaged group status. As a shield, an antidiscrimination statute can also help a member of a protected class by assuring decisionmakers in some instances that, when they elect for good reasons of their own to grant a preference of some sort to a minority citizen, they will not violate the law. The Court properly holds that the statutory shield allowed respondent to take Diane Joyce's sex into account in promoting her to the road dispatcher position.

Prior to 1978 the Court construed the Civil Rights Act of 1964 as an absolute blanket prohibition against discrimination which neither required nor permitted discriminatory preferences for any group, minority or majority. The Court unambiguously endorsed the neutral approach, first in the context of gender discrimination[1] and then in the context of racial discrimination against a white person.[2] As I explained in my separate opinion in *University of*

1. "Discriminatory preference for any group, minority or majority, is precisely and only what Congress has proscribed. What is required by Congress is the removal of artificial, arbitrary, and unnecessary barriers to employment when the barriers operate invidiously to discriminate on the basis of racial or other impermissible classification." *Griggs v. Duke Power Co.*, 401 U.S. 424, 431 (1971).
2. "Similarly the EEOC, whose interpretations are entitled to great deference, [401 U.S.,] at 433–434, 91 S.Ct., at 854–55, has consistently interpreted Title VII to proscribe racial discrimination in private employment against whites on the same terms as racial discrimination against nonwhites, holding that to proceed otherwise would
'constitute a derogation of the Commission's Congressional mandate to eliminate

California Regents v. Bakke, 438 U.S. 265, 412–418 (1978), and the Court forcefully stated in *McDonald v. Santa Fe Trail Transportation Co.*, 427 U.S. 273, 280 (1976), Congress intended " 'to eliminate all practices which operate to disadvantage the employment opportunities of any group protected by Title VII including Caucasians.' " (citations omitted). If the Court had adhered to that construction of the Act, petitioner would unquestionably prevail in this case. But it has not done so.

In the *Bakke* case in 1978 and again in *Steelworkers v. Weber*, 443 U.S. 193 (1979), a majority of the Court interpreted the antidiscriminatory strategy of the statute in a fundamentally different way. The Court held in the *Weber* case that an employer's program designed to increase the number of black craftworkers in an aluminum plant did not violate Title VII.[3] It remains clear that the Act does not *require* any employer to grant preferential treatment on the basis of race or gender, but since 1978 the Court has unambiguously interpreted the statute to *permit* the voluntary adoption of special programs to benefit members of the minority groups for whose protection the statute was enacted. Neither the "same standards" language used in *McDonald*, nor the "color blind" rhetoric used by the Senators and Congressmen who enacted the bill, is now controlling. Thus, as was true in *Runyon v. McCrary*, 427 U.S. 160,

---

all practices which operate to disadvantage the employment opportunities of any group protected by Title VII, including Caucasians.' EEOC Decision No. 74–31, 7 FEP Cases 1326, 1328, CCH EEOC Decisions ¶ 6404, p. 4084 (1973)."

"This conclusion is in accord with uncontradicted legislative history to the effect that Title VII was intended to 'cover white men and white women and all Americans,' 110 Cong.Rec. 2578 (1964) (remarks of Rep. Celler), and create an 'obligation not to discriminate against whites,' *id.*, at 7218 (memorandum of Sen. Clark). See also *id.*, at 7213 (memorandum of Sens. Clark and Case); *id.*, at 8912 (remarks of Sen. Williams). We therefore hold today that Title VII prohibits racial discrimination against the white petitioners in this case upon the same standards as would be applicable were they Negroes and Jackson white." *McDonald v. Santa Fe Trail Transportation Co.*, 427 U.S. 273, 279–280 (1976) (footnotes omitted).

3. Toward the end of its opinion, the Court mentioned certain reasons why the plan did not impose a special hardship on white employees or white applicants for employment. *Steelworkers v. Weber*, 443 U.S. 193, 208 (1979). I have never understood those comments to constitute a set of conditions that every race-conscious plan must satisfy in order to comply with Title VII.

189 (1976) (STEVENS, J., concurring), the only problem for me is whether to adhere to an authoritative construction of the Act that is at odds with my understanding of the actual intent of the authors of the legislation. I conclude without hesitation that I must answer that question in the affirmative, just as I did in *Runyon*. *Id*., at 191–192.

Bakke and *Weber* have been decided and are now an important part of the fabric of our law. This consideration is sufficiently compelling for me to adhere to the basic construction of this legislation that the Court adopted in *Bakke* and in *Weber*. There is an undoubted public interest in "stability and orderly development of the law." 427 U.S., at 190.[4]

The logic of antidiscrimination legislation requires that judicial constructions of Title VII leave "breathing room" for employer initiatives to benefit members of minority groups. If Title VII had never been enacted, a private employer would be free to hire members of minority groups for any reason that might seem sensible from a business or a social point of view. The Court's opinion in *Weber* reflects the same approach; the opinion relied heavily on legislative history indicating that Congress intended that traditional management prerogatives be left undisturbed to the greatest extent possible. See 443 U.S., at 206–207. As we observed Last Term, " '[i]t would be ironic indeed if a law triggered by a Nation's concern

4. "As Mr. Justice Cardozo remarked, with respect to the routine work of the judiciary: 'The labor of judges would be increased almost to the breaking point if every past decision could be reopened in every case, and one could not lay one's own course of bricks on the secure foundation of the courses laid by others who had gone before him.' Turning to the exceptional case, Mr. Justice Cardozo noted: '[W]hen a rule, after it has been duly tested by experience, has been found to be inconsistent with the sense of justice or with the social welfare, there should be less hesitation in frank avowal and full abandonment. . . . If judges have woefully misinterpreted the *mores* of their day, or if the *mores* of their day are no longer those of ours, they ought not to tie, in helpless submission, the hands of their successors.' In this case, those admonitions favor adherence to, rather than departure from, precedent." *Id*., at 190–192, 96 S.Ct., at 2604–2605. For even while writing in dissent in the *Weber* case, Chief Justice Burger observed that the result reached by the majority was one that he "would be inclined to vote for were I a Member of Congress considering a proposed amendment of Title VII." 443 U.S., at 216.

over centuries of racial injustice and intended to improve the lot of those who had "been excluded from the American dream for so long" constituted the first legislative prohibition of all voluntary, private, race-conscious efforts to abolish traditional patterns of racial segregation and hierarchy.' " *Firefighters v. Cleveland*, 478 U.S. 501, 516 (1986) (citing *Weber*, 443 U.S., at 204). In *Firefighters*, we again acknowledged Congress' concern in Title VII to avoid "undue federal interference with managerial discretion." 478 U.S., at 519.[5]

As construed in *Weber* and in *Firefighters*, the statute does not absolutely prohibit preferential hiring in favor of minorities; it was merely intended to protect historically disadvantaged groups *against* discrimination and not to hamper managerial efforts to benefit members of disadvantaged groups that are consistent with that paramount purpose. The preference granted by respondent in this case does not violate the statute as so construed; the record amply supports the conclusion that the challenged employment decision served the legitimate purpose of creating diversity in a category of employment that had been almost an exclusive province of males in the past. Respondent's voluntary decision is surely not prohibited by Title VII as construed in *Weber*.

II

Whether a voluntary decision of the kind made by respondent would ever be prohibited by Title VII is a question we need not answer until it is squarely presented. Given the interpretation of the statute the Court adopted in *Weber*, I see no reason why the employer has any duty, prior to granting a preference to a qualified

5. As Justice BLACKMUN observed in *Weber*, 433 U.S., at 209, 214–215 (BLACKMUN, J., concurring):
"Strong considerations of equity support an interpretation of Title VII that would permit private affirmative action to reach where Title VII itself does not. The bargain struck in 1964 with the passage of Title VII guaranteed equal opportunity for white and black alike, but where Title VII provides no remedy for blacks, it should not be construed to foreclose private affirmative action from supplying relief. . . . Absent compelling evidence of legislative intent, I would not interpret Title VII itself as a means of 'locking in' the effects of discrimination for which Title VII provides no remedy."

minority employee, to determine whether his past conduct might constitute an arguable violation of Title VII. Indeed, in some instances the employer may find it more helpful to focus on the future. Instead of retroactively scrutinizing his own or society's possible exclusions of minorities in the past to determine the outer limits of a valid affirmative-action program—or indeed, any particular affirmative-action decision—in many cases the employer will find it more appropriate to consider other legitimate reasons to give preferences to members of underrepresented groups. Statutes enacted for the benefit of minority groups should not block these forward-looking considerations.

"Public and private employers might choose to implement affirmative action for many reasons other than to purge their own past sins of discrimination. The Jackson school board, for example, said it had done so in part to improve the quality of education in Jackson—whether by improving black students' performance or by dispelling for black and white students alike any idea that white supremacy governs our social institutions. Other employers might advance different forward-looking reasons for affirmative action: improving their services to black constituencies, averting racial tension over the allocation of jobs in a community, or increasing the diversity of a work force, to name but a few examples. Or they might adopt affirmative action simply to eliminate from their operations all de facto embodiment of a system of racial caste. All of these reasons aspire to a racially integrated future, but none reduces to 'racial balancing for its own sake.' " Sullivan, The Supreme Court—Comment, Sins of Discrimination: Last Term's Affirmative Action Cases, 100 Harv.L.Rev. 78, 96 (1986).

The Court today does not foreclose other voluntary decisions based in part on a qualified employee's membership in a disadvantaged group. Accordingly, I concur.

Justice O'CONNOR, concurring in the judgment.

In *Steelworkers v. Weber*, 443 U.S. 193 (1979), this Court held that § 703(d) of Title VII does not prohibit voluntary affirmative action efforts if the employer sought to remedy a "manifest . . . imbalanc[e] in traditionally segregated job categories." *Id.*, at 197. As Justice SCALIA illuminates with excruciating clarity, § 703 has been interpreted by *Weber* and succeeding cases to permit what its language read literally would prohibit. *Post*, at 669–671; see also *ante*, at 642–643 (STEVENS, J., concurring). Section 703(d) prohibits employment discrimination "against *any individual* because of his race, color, religion, sex, or national origin." 42 U.S.C. § 2000e–2(d) (emphasis added). The *Weber* Court, however, concluded that voluntary affirmative action was permissible in some circumstances because a prohibition of every type of affirmative action would " 'bring about an end completely at variance with the purpose of the statute.' " 443 U.S., at 202 (quoting *United States v. Public Utilities Comm'n*, 345 U.S. 295, 315 (1953)). This purpose, according to the Court, was to open employment opportunities for blacks in occupations that had been traditionally closed to them.

None of the parties in this case have suggested that we overrule *Weber* and that question was not raised, briefed, or argued in this Court or in the courts below. If the Court is faithful to its normal prudential restraints and to the principle of *stare decisis* we must address once again the propriety of an affirmative action plan under Title VII in light of our precedents, precedents that have upheld affirmative action in a variety of circumstances. This time the question posed is whether a public employer violated Title VII by promoting a qualified woman rather than a marginally better qualified man when there is a statistical imbalance sufficient to support a claim of a pattern or practice of discrimination against women under Title VII.

I concur in the judgment of the Court in light of our precedents. I write separately, however, because the Court has chosen to follow an expansive and ill-defined approach to voluntary affirmative action by public employers despite the limitations imposed by the Constitution and by the provisions of Title VII, and because the dissent rejects the Court's precedents and addresses the question of how Title VII should be interpreted as if the Court were writing on a clean slate. The former course of action gives insufficient guidance to courts and litigants; the latter course of action serves as a useful point of academic discussion, but fails to reckon with the reality of the course that the majority of the Court has determined to follow.

In my view, the proper initial inquiry in evaluating the legality of an affirmative action plan by a public employer under Title VII is no different from that required by the Equal Protection Clause. In either case, consistent with the congressional intent to provide some measure of protection to the interests of the employer's non-minority employees, the employer must have had a firm basis for believing that remedial action was required. An employer would have such a firm basis if it can point to a statistical disparity sufficient to support a prima facie claim under Title VII by the employee beneficiaries of the affirmative action plan of a pattern or practice claim of discrimination.

In *Weber*, this Court balanced two conflicting concerns in construing § 703(d): Congress' intent to root out invidious discrimination against *any* person on the basis of race or gender, *McDonald v. Santa Fe Transp. Co.*, 427 U.S. 273 (1976), and its goal of eliminating the lasting effects of discrimination against minorities. Given these conflicting concerns, the Court concluded that it would be inconsistent with the background and purpose of Title VII to prohibit affirmative action in all cases. As I read *Weber*, however, the Court also determined that Congress had balanced these two competing concerns by permitting affirmative action only as a remedial device to eliminate actual or apparent discrimination or the lingering effects of this discrimination.

Contrary to the intimations in Justice STEVENS' concurrence, this Court did not approve preferences for minorities "for any reason that might seem sensible from a business or a social point of view." *Ante*, at 647. Indeed, such an approach would have been wholly at odds with this Court's holding in *McDonald* that Congress intended to prohibit practices that operate to discriminate against the employment opportunities of nonminorities as well as minorities. Moreover, in *Weber* the Court was careful to consider the effects of the affirmative action plan for black employees on the employment opportunities of white employees. 443 U.S., at 208. Instead of a wholly standardless approach to affirmative action, the Court determined in *Weber* that Congress intended to permit affirmative action only if the employer could point to a "manifest . . . imbalanc[e] in traditionally segregated job categories." *Id.*, at 197. This requirement both "provides assurance that sex or race will be taken into account in a manner consistent with Title VII's purpose of eliminating the effects of employment discrimination," *ante*, at 632, and is consistent with this Court's and Congress' consistent emphasis on the value of voluntary efforts to further the antidiscrimination purposes of Title VII. *Wygant v. Jackson Board of Education*, 476 U.S. 267 (1986) (O'CONNOR, J., concurring in part and concurring in judgment).

The *Weber* view of Congress' resolution of the conflicting concerns of minority and nonminority workers in Title VII appears substantially similar to this Court's resolution of these same concerns in *Wygant v. Jackson Board of Education, supra*, which involved the claim that an affirmative action plan by a public employer violated the Equal Protection Clause. In *Wygant*, the Court was in agreement that remedying past or present racial discrimination by a state actor is a sufficiently weighty interest to warrant the remedial use of a carefully constructed affirmative action plan. The Court also concluded, however, that "[s]ocietal discrimination, without more, is too amorphous a basis for imposing a racially classified remedy." *Id.*, at 276. Instead, we determined that affirmative action was valid if it was crafted to remedy past or present discrimination by the employer. Although the employer need not point to any contemporaneous findings of actual discrimination, I concluded in *Wygant* that the employer must point to evidence sufficient to establish a firm basis for believing that remedial action is required, and that a statistical imbalance sufficient for a Title VII prima facie case against the employer would satisfy this firm basis requirement:

"Public employers are not without reliable benchmarks in making this determination. For example, demonstrable evidence of a disparity between the percentage of qualified blacks on a school's teaching staff and the percentage of qualified minorities in the relevant labor pool sufficient to support a prima facie Title VII pattern or practice claim by minority teachers would lend a compelling basis for a competent authority such as the School Board to conclude that implementation of a voluntary affirmative action plan is appropriate to remedy apparent prior employment discrimination." *Id.*, at 292.

The *Wygant* analysis is entirely consistent with *Weber*. In *Weber*, the affirmative action plan involved a training program for unskilled production workers. There was little doubt that the absence of black craftworkers was the result of the exclusion of blacks from craft unions. *Steelworkers v. Weber*, 443 U.S., at 198, n. 1 ("Judicial findings of exclusion from crafts on racial grounds are so numerous as to make such exclusion a proper subject for judicial notice"). The employer in *Weber* had previously hired as craftworkers only persons with prior craft experience, and craft unions provided the sole avenue for obtaining this experience. Because the discrimination occurred at entry into the craft union, the "manifest racial imbalance" was powerful evidence of prior race discrimination. Under our case law, the relevant comparison for a Title VII prima facie case in those circumstances—discrimination in admission to entry-level positions such as membership in craft unions—is to the total percentage of blacks in the labor force. See *Teamsters v. United States*, 431 U.S. 324 (1977); cf. *Sheet Metal Workers v. EEOC*, 478 U.S. 421, 437 (1986) (observing that lower courts had relied on comparison to general labor force in finding Title VII violation by union). Here, however, the evidence of past discrimination is more complex. The number of women with the qualifications for entry into the relevant job classification was quite small. A statistical imbalance between the percentage of women in the work force generally and the percentage of women in the particular specialized job classification, therefore, does not suggest past discrimination for purposes of proving a Title VII prima facie case. See *Hazelwood School District v. United States*, 433 U.S. 299, 308, and n. 13 (1977).

Unfortunately, the Court today gives little guidance for what statistical imbalance is sufficient to support an affirmative action plan. Although the Court denies that the statistical imbalance need be sufficient to make out a prima facie case of discrimination against women, *ante*, at 632, the Court fails to suggest an alternative standard. Because both *Wygant* and *Weber* attempt to reconcile the same competing concerns, I see little justification for the adoption of different standards for affirmative action under Title VII and the Equal Protection Clause.

While employers must have a firm basis for concluding that remedial action is necessary, neither *Wygant* nor *Weber* places a burden on employers to prove that they actually discriminated against women or minorities. Employers are "trapped between the competing hazards of liability to minorities if affirmative action is *not* taken to remedy apparent employment discrimination and liability to nonminorities if affirmative action *is* taken." *Wygant v. Jackson Board of Education*, 476 U.S., at 291 (O'CONNOR, J., concurring in part and concurring in judgment). Moreover, this Court has long emphasized the importance of voluntary efforts to eliminate discrimination. *Id.*, at 290. Thus, I concluded in *Wygant* that a contemporaneous finding of discrimination should not be required because it would discourage voluntary efforts to remedy apparent discrimination. A requirement that an employer actually prove that it had discriminated in the past would also unduly discourage voluntary efforts to remedy apparent discrimination. As I emphasized in *Wygant*, a challenge to an affirmative action plan "does not automatically impose upon the public employer the burden of convincing the court of its liability for prior unlawful discrimination; nor does it mean that the court must make an actual finding of prior discrimination based on the employer's proof before the employer's affirmative action plan will be upheld." *Id.*, at 292. Evidence sufficient for a prima facie Title VII pattern or practice claim against the employer itself suggests that the absence of women or minorities in a work force cannot be explained by general societal discrimination alone and that remedial action is appropriate.

In applying these principles to this case, it is important to pay close attention to both the affirmative action plan, and the manner in which that plan was applied to the specific promotion decision at issue in this case. In December 1978, the Santa Clara Transit District Board of Supervisors adopted an affirmative action plan for the Santa Clara County Transportation Agency (Agency). At the time the plan was adopted, not one woman was employed in respondents' 238 skilled craft positions, and the plan recognized that women "are not strongly motivated to seek employment in job classifications where they have not been traditionally employed because of the limited opportunities that have existed in the past for them to work in such classifications." App. 57. Additionally, the plan stated that respondents "recognize[d] that mere prohibition of discriminatory practices is not enough to remedy the effects of past practices and to permit attainment of an equitable representation of minorities, women and handicapped persons," *id.*, at 31, and that "the selection and appointment processes are areas where hidden discrimination frequently occurs." *Id.*, at 71. Thus, the respondents had the expectation that plan "should result in improved personnel practices that will benefit all Agency employees who may have been subjected to discriminatory personnel practices in the past." *Id.*, at 35.

The long-term goal of the plan was "to attain a work force whose composition in all job levels and major job classification approximates the distribution of women . . . in the Santa Clara County work force." *Id.*, at 54. If this long-term goal had been applied to the hiring decisions made by the Agency, in my view, the affirmative action plan would violate Title VII. "[I]t is completely unrealistic to assume that individuals of each [sex] will gravitate with mathematical exactitude to each employer . . . absent unlawful discrimination." *Sheet Metal Workers, supra,* 478 U.S., at 494 (O'CONNOR, J., concurring in part and dissenting in part). Thus, a goal that makes such an assumption, and simplistically focuses on the proportion of women and minorities in the work force without more, is not remedial. Only a goal that takes into account the number of women and minorities qualified for the relevant position could satisfy the requirement that an affirmative action plan be remedial. This long-range goal, however, was never used as a guide for actual hiring decisions. Instead, the goal was merely a statement of aspiration wholly without operational significance. The affirmative action plan itself recognized the host of reasons why this goal was extremely unrealistic, App. 56–57, and as I read the record, the long-term goal was not applied in the promotion decision challenged in this case. Instead, the plan provided for the development of short-term goals, which alone were to guide the respondents, *id.*, at 61, and the plan cautioned that even these goals "should not be construed as 'quotas' that must be met." *Id.*, at 64. Instead, these short-term goals were to be focused on remedying past apparent discrimination, and would "[p]rovide an objective standard for use in determining if the representation of minorities, women and handicapped persons in particular job classifications is at a reasonable level in comparison with estimates of the numbers of persons from these groups in the area work force who can meet the educational and experience requirements for employment." *Id.*, at 61.

At the time of the promotion at issue in this case, the short-term goals had not been fully developed. Nevertheless, the Agency had already recognized that the long-range goal was unrealistic, and had determined that the progress of the Agency should be judged by a comparison to the *qualified* women in the area work force. As I view the record, the promotion decision in this case was entirely consistent with the philosophy underlying the development of the short-term goals.

The Agency announced a vacancy for the position of road dispatcher in the Agency's Roads Division on December 12, 1979. Twelve employees applied for this position, including Diane Joyce and petitioner. Nine of these employees were interviewed for the position by a two-person board. Seven applicants—including Joyce and petitioner—scored above 70 on this interview, and were certified as eligible for selection for the promotion. Petitioner scored 75 on the interview, while Joyce scored 73. After a second interview, a committee of three agency employees recommended that petitioner be selected for the promotion to road dispatcher. The County's Affirmative Action Officer, on the other hand, urged that Joyce be selected for the position.

The ultimate decision to promote Joyce rather than petitioner was made by James Graebner, the Director of the Agency. As Justice SCALIA views the record in this case, the Agency Director made the decision to promote Joyce rather than petitioner solely on the basis of sex and with indifference to the relative merits of the two applicants. See *post*, at 662–663. In my view, however, the record simply fails to substantiate the picture painted by Justice SCALIA. The Agency Director testified that he "tried to look at the whole picture, the combination of [Joyce's] qualifications and Mr. Johnson's qualifications, their test scores, their experience, their background, affirmative action matters, things like that." Tr.

68. Contrary to Justice SCALIA's suggestion, *post*, at 663, the Agency Director knew far more than merely the sex of the candidates and that they appeared on a list of candidates eligible for the job. The Director had spoken to individuals familiar with the qualifications of both applicants for the promotion, and was aware that their scores were rather close. Moreover, he testified that over a period of weeks he had spent several hours making the promotion decision, suggesting that Joyce was not selected solely on the basis of her sex. Tr. 63. Additionally, the Director stated that had Joyce's experience been less than that of petitioner by a larger margin, petitioner might have received the promotion. *Id.*, at 69–70. As the Director summarized his decision to promote Joyce, the underrepresentation of women in skilled craft positions was only one element of a number of considerations that led to the promotion of Ms. Joyce. *Ibid.* While I agree with the dissent that an affirmative action program that automatically and blindly promotes those marginally qualified candidates falling within a preferred race or gender category, or that can be equated with a permanent plan of "proportionate representation by race and sex" would violate Title VII, I cannot agree that this is such a case. Rather, as the Court demonstrates, Joyce's sex was simply used as a "plus" factor. *Ante*, at 636–637.

In this case, I am also satisfied that the respondent had a firm basis for adopting an affirmative action program. Although the District Court found no discrimination against women in fact, at the time the affirmative action plan was adopted, there were *no* women in its skilled craft positions. The petitioner concedes that women constituted approximately 5% of the local labor pool of skilled craft workers in 1970. Reply Brief for Petitioner 9. Thus, when compared to the percentage of women in the qualified work force, the statistical disparity would have been sufficient for a prima facie Title VII case brought by unsuccessful women job applicants. See *Teamsters*, 431 U.S., at 342, n. 23 ("[F]ine tuning of the statistics could not have obscured the glaring absence of minority line drivers. . . . [T]he company's inability to rebut the inference of discrimination came not from a misuse of statistics but from 'the inexorable zero' ").

In sum, I agree that the respondents' affirmative action plan as implemented in this instance with respect to skilled craft positions satisfied the requirements of *Weber* and *Wygant*. Accordingly, I concur in the judgment of the Court.

Justice WHITE, dissenting.

I agree with Parts I and II of Justice SCALIA's dissenting opinion. Although I do not join Part III, I also would overrule *Weber*. My understanding of *Weber* was, and is, that the employer's plan did not violate Title VII because it was designed to remedy intentional and systematic exclusion of blacks by the employer and the unions from certain job categories. That is how I understood the phrase "traditionally segregated jobs" we used in that case. The Court now interprets it to mean nothing more than a manifest imbalance between one identifiable group and another in an employer's labor force. As so interpreted, that case, as well as today's decision, as Justice SCALIA so well demonstrates, is a perversion of Title VII. I would overrule *Weber* and reverse the judgment below.

Justice SCALIA, with whom THE CHIEF JUSTICE joins, and with whom Justice WHITE joins in Parts I and II, dissenting.

With a clarity which, had it not proven so unavailing, one might well recommend as a model of statutory draftsmanship, Title VII of the Civil Rights Act of 1964 declares:

"It shall be unlawful employment practice for an employer—

"(1) to fail or refuse to hire or to discharge any individual, or otherwise to discriminate against any individual with respect to his compensation, terms, conditions, or privileges of employment, because of such individual's race, color, religion, sex, or national origin; or

"(2) to limit, segregate, or classify his employees or applicants for employment in any way which would deprive or tend to deprive any individual of employment opportunities or otherwise adversely affect his status as an employee, because of such individual's race, color, religion, sex, or national origin." 42 U.S.C. § 2000e–2(a).

APPENDIX

The Court today completes the process of converting this from a guarantee that race or sex will *not* be the basis for employment determinations, to a guarantee that it often *will*. Ever so subtly, without even alluding to the last obstacles preserved by earlier opinions that we now push out of our path, we effectively replace the goal of a discrimination-free society with the quite incompatible goal of proportionate representation by race and by sex in the workplace. Part I of this dissent will describe the nature of the plan that the Court approves, and its effect upon this petitioner. Part II will discuss prior holdings that are tacitly overruled, and prior distinctions that are disregarded. Part III will describe the engine of discrimination we have finally completed.

I

On October 16, 1979, the County of Santa Clara adopted an Affirmative Action Program (County plan) which sought the "attainment of a County work force whose composition . . . includes women, disabled persons and ethnic minorities in a ratio in all job categories that reflects their distribution in the Santa Clara County area work force." App. 113. In order to comply with the County plan and various requirements imposed by federal and state agencies, the Transportation Agency adopted, effective December 18, 1978, the Equal Employment Opportunity Affirmative Action Plan (Agency plan or plan) at issue here. Its stated long-range goal was the same as the County plan's: "to attain a work force whose composition in all job levels and major job classifications approximates the distribution of women, minority and handicapped persons in the Santa Clara County work force." *Id.*, at 54. The plan called for the establishment of a procedure by which Division Directors would review the ethnic and sexual composition of their work forces whenever they sought to fill a vacancy, which procedure was expected to include "a requirement that Division Directors indicate why they did *not* select minorities, women and handicapped persons if such persons were on the list of eligibles considered and if the Division had an underrepresentation of such persons in the job classification being filled." *Id.*, at 75 (emphasis in original).

Several salient features of the plan should be noted. Most importantly, the plan's purpose was assuredly not to remedy prior sex discrimination by the Agency. It could not have been, because there was no prior sex discrimination to remedy. The majority, in cataloguing the Agency's alleged misdeeds, *ante*, at 1448, n. 5, neglects to mention the District Court's finding that the Agency "has not discriminated in the past, and does not discriminate in the present against women in regard to employment opportunities in general and promotions in particular." App. to Pet. for Cert. 13a. This finding was not disturbed by the Ninth Circuit.

Not only was the plan not directed at the results of past sex discrimination by the Agency, but its objective was not to achieve the state of affairs that this Court has dubiously assumed would result from an absence of discrimination—an overall work force "more or less representative of the racial and ethnic composition of the population in the community." *Teamsters v. United States*, 431 U.S. 324, 340, n. 20 (1977). Rather, the oft-stated goal was to mirror the racial and sexual composition of the entire county labor force, not merely in the Agency work force as a whole, but in each and every individual job category at the Agency. In a discrimination-free world, it would obviously be a statistical oddity for every job category to match the racial and sexual composition of even that portion of the county work force *qualified* for that job; it would be utterly miraculous for each of them to match, as the plan expected, the composition of the *entire* work force. Quite obviously, the plan did not seek to replicate what a lack of discrimination would produce, but rather imposed racial and sexual tailoring that would, in defiance of normal expectations and laws of probability, give each protected racial and sexual group a governmentally determined "proper" proportion of each job category.

That the plan was not directed at remedying or eliminating the effects of past discrimination is most clearly illustrated by its description of what it regarded as the *"Factors Hindering Goal Attainment"*—i.e., the existing impediments to the racially and sexually representative work force that it pursued. The plan noted that it would be "difficult," App. 55, to attain its objective of across-the-board statistical parity in at least some job categories, because:

APPENDIX

"a. Most of the positions require specialized training and experience. Until recently, relatively few minorities, women and handicapped persons sought entry into these positions. Consequently, the number of persons from these groups in the area labor force who possess the qualifications required for entry into such job classifications is limited.

.   .   .   .   .

"c. Many of the Agency positions where women are underrepresented involve heavy labor; e.g., Road Maintenance Worker. Consequently, few women seek entry into these positions.

.   .   .   .   .

"f. Many women are not strongly motivated to seek employment in job classifications where they have not been traditionally employed because of the limited opportunities that have existed in the past for them to work in such classifications." *Id.*, at 56–57.

That is, the qualifications and desires of women may fail to match the Agency's Platonic ideal of a work force. The plan concluded from this, of course, not that the ideal should be reconsidered, but that its attainment could not be immediate. *Id.*, at 58–60. It would, in any event, be rigorously pursued, by giving "special consideration to Affirmative Action requirements in every individual hiring action pertaining to positions where minorities, women and handicapped persons continue to be underrepresented." *Id.*, at 60.[1]

Finally, the one message that the plan unmistakably communicated was that concrete results were expected, and supervisory personnel would be evaluated on the basis of the affirmative-action numbers they produced. The plan's implementation was expected to "result in a statistically measurable yearly improvement in the hiring, training and promotion of minorities, women and handicapped persons in the major job classifications utilized by the Agency where these groups are underrepresented." *Id.*, at 35. Its

1. This renders utterly incomprehensible the majority's assertion that "the Agency acknowledged that [its long-term goal] could not by itself necessarily justify taking into account the sex of applicants for positions in all job categories." *Ante*, at 635.

Preface declared that "[t]he degree to which each Agency Division *attains the Plan's objectives* will provide a direct measure of that Division Director's personal commitment to the EEO Policy," *ibid.* (emphasis added), and the plan itself repeated that "[t]he degree to which each Division *attains the Agency Affirmative Action employment goals* will provide a measure of that Director's commitment and effectiveness in carrying out the Division's EEO Affirmative Action requirements." *Id.*, at 44 (emphasis added). As noted earlier, supervisors were reminded of the need to give attention to affirmative action in every employment decision, and to explain their reasons for *failing* to hire women and minorities whenever there was an opportunity to do so.

The petitioner in the present case, Paul E. Johnson, had been an employee of the Agency since 1967, coming there from a private company where he had been a road dispatcher for seventeen years. He had first applied for the position of Road Dispatcher at the Agency in 1974, coming in second. Several years later, after a reorganization resulted in a downgrading of his Road Yard Clerk II position, in which Johnson "could see no future," Tr. 127, he requested and received a voluntary demotion from Road Yard Clerk II to Road Maintenance Worker, to increase his experience and thus improve his chances for future promotion. When the Road Dispatcher job next became vacant, in 1979, he was the leading candidate—and indeed was assigned to work out of class full-time in the vacancy, from September of 1979 until June of 1980. There is no question why he did not get the job.

The fact of discrimination against Johnson is much clearer, and its degree more shocking, than the majority and Justice O'CONNOR's concurring opinion would suggest—largely because neither of them recites a single one of the District Court findings that govern this appeal, relying instead upon portions of the transcript which those findings implicitly rejected, and even upon a document (favorably comparing Joyce to Johnson), *ante*, at 625, that was prepared *after* Joyce was selected. See App. 27–28; Tr. 223–227. It is worth mentioning, for example, the trier of fact's determination that, if the Affirmative Action Coordinator had not intervened, "the decision as to whom to promote . . . would have been made by [the Road Operations Division Director]," App. to Pet. for Cert. 12a, who had recommended that Johnson be appointed to the position. *Ibid.*[2] Likewise, the even more extraordinary findings that James Graebner, the Agency Director who made the appointment, "did not inspect the applications and related examination records of either [Paul Johnson] or Diane Joyce before making his decision," *ibid.*, and indeed "did little or nothing to inquire into the results of the interview process and conclusions which [were] described as of critical importance to the selection process." *Id.*, at 3a. In light of these determinations, it is impossible to believe (or to think that the District Court believed) Graebner's self-serving statements relied upon by the majority and concurrence, such as the assertion that he "tried to look at the whole picture, the combination of [Joyce's] qualifications and Mr. Johnson's qualifications, their test scores, their expertise, their background, affirmative action matters, things like that," Tr. 68 (quoted *ante*, at 625; *ante*, at 655 (O'CONNOR, J., concurring in judgment)). It was evidently enough for Graebner to know that both candidates (in the words of Johnson's counsel, to which Graebner assented) "met the M.Q.'s, the minimum. Both were minimally qualified." Tr. 25. When asked whether he had "any basis," *ibid.*, for determining whether one of the candidates was more qualified than the other, Graebner can-

---

2. The character of this intervention, and the reasoning behind it, was described by the Agency Director in his testimony at trial:

"Q. How did you happen to become involved in this particular promotional opportunity?

"A. I . . . became aware that there was a difference of opinion between specifically the Road Operations people [Mr. Shields] and the Affirmative Action Director [Mr. Morton] as to the desirability of certain of the individuals to be promoted.

.   .   .   .   .

" . . . Mr. Shields felt that Mr. Johnson should be appointed to that position.

"Q. Mr. Morton felt that Diane Joyce should be appointed?

"A. Mr. Morton was less interested in the particular individual; he felt that this was an opportunity for us to take a step toward meeting our affirmative action goals, and because there was only one person on the [eligibility] list who was one of the protected groups, he felt that this afforded us an opportunity to meet those goals through the appointment of that member of a protected group." Tr. 16–18.

didly answered, "No. . . . As I've said, they both appeared, and my conversations with people tended to corroborate, that they were both capable of performing the work." *Ibid.*

After a two-day trial, the District Court concluded that Diane Joyce's gender was "*the determining factor*," *id.*, at 4a, in her selection for the position. Specifically, it found that "[b]ased upon the examination results and the departmental interview, [Mr. Johnson] was more qualified for the position of Road Dispatcher than Diane Joyce," *id.*, at 12a; that "[b]ut for [Mr. Johnson's] sex, male, he would have been promoted to the position of Road Dispatcher," *id.*, at 13a; and that "[b]ut for Diane Joyce's sex, female, she would not have been appointed to the position. . . ." *Ibid.* The Ninth Circuit did not reject these findings as clearly erroneous, nor could it have done so on the record before us. We are bound by those findings under Federal Rule of Civil Procedure 52(a).

II

The most significant proposition of law established by today's decision is that racial or sexual discrimination is permitted under Title VII when it is intended to overcome the effect, not of the employer's own discrimination, but of societal attitudes that have limited the entry of certain races, or of a particular sex, into certain jobs. Even if the societal attitudes in question consisted exclusively of conscious discrimination by other employers, this holding would contradict a decision of this Court rendered only last Term. *Wygant v. Jackson Board of Education*, 476 U.S. 267 (1986), held that the objective of remedying social discrimination cannot prevent remedial affirmative action from violating the Equal Protection Clause. See *id.*, at 276 (O'CONNOR, J., concurring in part and concurring in judgment); *id.*, at 295 (WHITE, J., concurring in judgment). While Mr. Johnson does not advance a constitutional claim here, it is most unlikely that Title VII was intended to place a *lesser* restraint on discrimination by public actors than is established by the Constitution. The Court has already held that the prohibitions on discrimination in Title VI, 42 U.S.C. § 2000d, are at least as stringent as those in the Constitution. See *Regents of the*

229

APPENDIX

University of California v. Bakke, 438 U.S. 265, 286–287 (1978) (opinion of POWELL, J.) (Title VI embodies constitutional restraints on discrimination); *id.*, at 329–340 (opinion of BRENNAN, WHITE, MARSHALL, and BLACKMUN, JJ.) (same); *id.*, at 416 (opinion of STEVENS, J., joined by Burger, C.J., and Stewart and REHNQUIST, JJ.) (Title VI "has independent force, with language and emphasis *in addition to* that found in the Constitution") (emphasis added). There is no good reason to think that Title VII, in this regard, is any different from Title VI.[3] Because, therefore, those justifications (*e.g.*, the remedying of past societal wrongs) that are inadequate to insulate discriminatory action from the racial discrimination prohibitions of the Constitution are also inadequate to insulate it from the racial discrimination prohibitions of Title VII; and because the portions of Title VII at issue here treat race and sex equivalently; *Wygant*, which dealt with race discrimination, is fully applicable precedent, and is squarely inconsistent with today's decision.[4]

3. To support the proposition that Title VII is more narrow than Title VI, the majority repeats the reasons for the dictum to that effect set forth in *Steelworkers v. Weber*, 443 U.S. 193, 206, n. 6 (1979)—a case which, as Justice O'CONNOR points out, *ante*, at 651–652, could reasonably be read as consistent with the constitutional standards of *Wygant*. Those reasons are unpersuasive, consisting only of the existence in Title VII of 42 U.S.C. § 2000e–2(j) (the implausibility of which, as a *restriction* upon the scope of Title VII, was demonstrated by Chief Justice REHNQUIST's literally unanswered *Weber* dissent) and the fact that Title VI pertains to recipients of federal funds while Title VII pertains to employers generally. The latter fact, while true and perhaps interesting, is not conceivably a reason for giving to virtually identical categorical language the interpretation, in one case, that intentional discrimination is forbidden, and, in the other case, that it is not. Compare 42 U.S.C. § 2000d ("No person . . . shall, on the ground of race, color, or national origin, be . . . subjected to discrimination"), with § 2000e–2(a)(1) (no employer shall "discriminate against any individual . . . because of such individual's race, color, religion, sex, or national origin").

4. Justice O'CONNOR's concurrence at least makes an attempt to bring this term into accord with last. Under her reading of Title VII, an employer may discriminate affirmatively, so to speak, if he has a "firm basis" for believing that he might be guilty of (nonaffirmative) discrimination under the Act, and if his action is designed to remedy that suspected prior discrimination. *Ante*, at 649. This is something of a half-way house between leaving employers scot-free to discriminate against disfavored groups, as the majority opinion does, and pro-

Likewise on the assumption that the societal attitudes relied upon by the majority consist of conscious discrimination by employers, today's decision also disregards the limitations carefully expressed in last Term's opinions in *Sheet Metal Workers v. EEOC*, 478 U.S. 421 (1986). While those limitations were dicta, it is remarkable to see them so readily (and so silently) swept away. The question in *Sheet Metal Workers* was whether the remedial provision of Title VII, 42 U.S.C. § 2000e–5(g), empowers courts to order race-conscious relief for persons who were not identifiable victims of discrimination. Six members of this Court concluded that it does, *under narrowly confined circumstances*. The plurality opinion for four justices found that race-conscious relief could be ordered at least when "an employer or labor union has engaged in persistent or egregious discrimination, or where necessary to dissipate the lingering effects of pervasive discrimination." 478 U.S., at 445 (opinion of BRENNAN, J., joined by MARSHALL, BLACKMUN, and STEVENS, JJ.). See also *id.*, at 476. Justice POWELL concluded that race-conscious relief can be ordered "in cases involving particularly egregious conduct," *id.* (concurring in part and concurring in judgment), and Justice WHITE similarly limited his approval of race-conscious remedies to "unusual cases." *Id.*, at 499 (dissenting). See also *Firefighters v. Cleveland*, 478 U.S., at 501, 533,

---

hibiting discrimination, as do the words of Title VII. In the present case, although the District Court found that in fact no sex discrimination existed, Justice O'CONNOR would find a "firm basis" for the agency's *belief* that sex discrimination existed in the "inexorable zero": the complete absence, prior to Diane Joyce, of any women in the Agency's skilled positions. There are two problems with this: First, even positing a "firm basis" for the Agency's belief in prior discrimination, as I have discussed above the plan was patently not *designed to remedy* that prior discrimination, but rather to establish a sexually representative work force. Second, even an absolute zero is not "inexorable." While it may inexorably provide "firm basis" for belief in the mind of an outside observer, it cannot conclusively establish such a belief *on the employer's part*, since he may be aware of the particular reasons that account for the zero. That is quite likely to be the case here, given the nature of the jobs we are talking about, and the list of *"Factors Hindering Goal Attainment"* recited by the Agency plan. See *supra*, at 661. The question is in any event one of fact, which, if it were indeed relevant to the outcome, would require a remand to the District Court rather than an affirmance.

(WHITE, J., dissenting) ("I also agree with Justice BRENNAN's opinion in *Sheet Metal Workers* . . . that in Title VII cases enjoining discriminatory practices and granting relief only to victims of past discrimination is the general rule, with relief for non-victims being reserved for particularly egregious conduct"). There is no sensible basis for construing Title VII to permit employers to engage in race- or sex-conscious employment practices that courts would be forbidden from ordering them to engage in following a judicial finding of discrimination. As Justice WHITE noted last Term:

"There is no statutory authority for concluding that if an employer desires to discriminate against a white applicant or employee on racial grounds he may do so without violating Title VII but may not be ordered to do so if he objects. In either case, the harm to the discriminatee is the same, and there is no justification for such conduct other than as a permissible remedy for prior racial discrimination practiced by the employer involved." *Id.*, at 533.

The Agency here was not seeking to remedy discrimination—much less "unusual" or "egregious" discrimination. *Firefighters*, like *Wygant*, is given only the most cursory consideration by the majority opinion.

In fact, however, today's decision goes well beyond merely allowing racial or sexual discrimination in order to eliminate the effects of prior societal *discrimination*. The majority opinion often uses the phrase "traditionally segregated job category" to describe the evil against which the plan is legitimately (according to the majority) directed. As originally used in *Steelworkers v. Weber*, 443 U.S. 193 (1979), that phrase described skilled jobs from which employers and unions had systematically and intentionally excluded black workers—traditionally segregated jobs, that is, in the sense of conscious, exclusionary discrimination. See *id.*, at 197–198. But that is assuredly not the sense in which the phrase is used here. It is absurd to think that the nationwide failure of road maintenance crews, for example, to achieve the Agency's ambition of 36.4% female representation is attributable primarily, if even substantially, to systematic exclusion of women eager to shoulder pick and shovel. It is a "traditionally segregated job category" *not* in the *Weber* sense, but in the sense that, because of longstanding social attitudes, it has not been regarded *by women themselves* as desirable work. Or as the majority opinion puts the point, quoting approvingly the Court of Appeals: " 'A plethora of proof is hardly necessary to show that women are generally underrepresented in such positions and that strong social pressures weigh against their participation.' " *Ante*, at 634, n. 12 (quoting 748 F.2d 1308, 1313 (CA9 1984)). Given this meaning of the phrase, it is patently false to say that "[t]he requirement that the 'manifest imbalance' relate to a 'traditionally segregated job category' provides assurance that sex or race will be taken into account in a manner consistent with Title VII's purpose of eliminating the effects of employment discrimination." *Ante*, at 632. There are, of course, those who believe that the social attitudes which cause women themselves to avoid certain jobs and to favor others are as nefarious as conscious, exclusionary discrimination. Whether or not that is so (and there is assuredly no consensus on the point equivalent to our national consensus against intentional discrimination), the two phenomena are certainly distinct. And it is the alteration of social attitudes, rather than the elimination of discrimination, which today's decision approves as justification for state-enforced discrimination. This is an enormous expansion, undertaken without the slightest justification or analysis.

III

I have omitted from the foregoing discussion the most obvious respect in which today's decision o'erleaps, without analysis, a barrier that was thought still to be overcome. In *Weber*, this Court held that a private-sector affirmative-action training program that overtly discriminated against white applicants did not violate Title VII. However, although the majority does not advert to the fact, until today the applicability of *Weber* to public employers remained an open question. In *Weber* itself, see 443 U.S., at 200, 204, and in later decisions, see *Firefighters v. Cleveland*, 478 U.S., at 517; *Wygant*, 476 U.S., at 282, n. 9 (opinion of POWELL, J.), this Court has repeatedly emphasized that *Weber* involved only a private employer. See *Williams v. City of New Orleans*, 729 F.2d 1554, 1565

APPENDIX

(CA5 1984) (en banc) (Gee, J., concurring) ("Writing for the Court in *Weber*, Justice Brennan went out of his way, on at least eleven different occasions, to point out that what was there before the Court was *private* affirmative action") (footnote omitted). This distinction between public and private employers has several possible justifications. *Weber* rested in part on the assertion that the 88th Congress did not wish to intrude too deeply into private employment decisions. See 443 U.S., at 206–207. See also *Firefighters v. Cleveland, supra*, at 519–521. Whatever validity that assertion may have with respect to private employers (and I think it negligible), it has none with respect to public employers or to the 92d Congress that brought them within Title VII. See Equal Employment Opportunity Act of 1972, Pub.L. 92–261, § 2, 86 Stat. 103, 42 U.S.C. § 2000e(a). Another reason for limiting *Weber* to private employers is that state agencies, unlike private actors, are subject to the Fourteenth Amendment. As noted earlier, it would be strange to construe Title VII to permit discrimination by public actors that the Constitution forbids.

In truth, however, the language of 42 U.S.C. § 2000e–2 draws no distinction between private and public employers, and the only good reason for creating such a distinction would be to limit the damage of *Weber*. It would be better, in my view, to acknowledge that case as fully applicable precedent, and to use the Fourteenth Amendment ramifications—which *Weber* did not address and which are implicated for the first time here—as the occasion for reconsidering and overruling it. It is well to keep in mind just how thoroughly *Weber* rewrote the statute it purported to construe. The language of that statute, as quoted as the outset of this dissent, is unambiguous: it is an unlawful employment practice "to fail or refuse to hire or to discharge any individual, or otherwise to discriminate against any individual with respect to his compensation, terms, conditions, or privileges of employment, because of such individual's race, color, religion, sex, or national origin." 42 U.S.C. § 2000e–2(a). *Weber* disregarded the text of the statute, invoking instead its " 'spirit,' " 443 U.S., at 201 (quoting *Holy Trinity Church v. United States*, 143 U.S. 457, 459 (1892)), and "practical and equitable [considerations] only partially perceived, if perceived at all,

234

by the 88th Congress," 443 U.S., at 209 (BLACKMUN, J., concurring). It concluded, on the basis of these intangible guides, that Title VII's prohibition of intentional discrimination on the basis of race and sex does not prohibit intentional discrimination on the basis of race and sex, so long as it is "designed to break down old patterns of racial [or sexual] segregation and hierarchy," "does not unnecessarily trammel the interests of the white [or male] employees," "does not require the discharge of white [or male] workers and their replacement with new black [or female] hirees," "does [not] create an absolute bar to the advancement of white [or male] employees," and "is a temporary measure . . . not intended to maintain racial [or sexual] balance, but simply to eliminate a manifest racial [or sexual] imbalance." *Id.*, at 208. In effect, *Weber* held that the legality of intentional discrimination by private employers against certain disfavored groups or individuals is to be judged not by Title VII but by a judicially crafted code of conduct, the contours of which are determined by no discernible standard, aside from (as the dissent convincingly demonstrated) the divination of congressional "purposes" belied by the face of the statute and by its legislative history. We have been recasting that self-promulgated code of conduct ever since—and what it has led us to today adds to the reasons for abandoning it.

The majority's response to this criticism of *Weber*, *ante*, at 629, n. 7, asserts that, since "Congress has not amended the statute to reject our construction, . . . we . . . may assume that our interpretation was correct." This assumption, which frequently haunts our opinions, should be put to rest. It is based, to begin with, on the patently false premise that the correctness of statutory construction is to be measured by what the current Congress desires, rather than by what the law as enacted meant. To make matters worse, it assays the current Congress' desires *with respect to the particular provision in isolation*, rather than (the way the provision was originally enacted) as part of a total legislative package containing many *quids pro quo*. Whereas the statute as originally proposed may have presented to the enacting Congress a question such as "Should hospitals be required to provide medical care for indigent patients, with federal subsidies to offset the cost?," the question theoretically asked of the later Congress, in order to establish the "correctness" of a judicial interpretation that the statute provides no subsidies, is simply "Should the medical care that hospitals are required to provide for indigent patients be federally subsidized?" Hardly the same question—and many of those legislators who accepted the subsidy provisions in order to gain the votes necessary for enactment of the care requirement would not vote for the subsidy in isolation, now that an unsubsidized care requirement is, thanks to the judicial opinion, safely on the books. But even accepting the flawed premise that the intent of the current Congress, with respect to the provision in isolation, is determinative, one must ignore rudimentary principles of political science to draw any conclusions regarding that intent from the *failure* to enact legislation. The "complicated check on legislation," The Federalist No. 62, p. 378 (C. Rossiter ed. 1961), erected by our Constitution creates an inertia that makes it impossible to assert with any degree of assurance that congressional failure to act represents (1) approval of the status quo, as opposed to (2) inability to agree upon how to alter the status quo, (3) unawareness of the status quo, (4) indifference to the status quo, or even (5) political cowardice. It is interesting to speculate on how the principle that congressional inaction proves judicial correctness would apply to another issue in the civil rights field, the liability of municipal corporations under § 1983. In 1961, we held that that statute did not reach municipalities. See *Monroe v. Pape*, 365 U.S. 167 (1961). Congress took no action to overturn our decision, but we ourselves did, in *Monell v. New York City Dept. of Social Services*, 436 U.S. 658, 663 (1978). On the majority's logic, *Monell* was wrongly decided, since Congress' seventeen years of silence established that *Monroe* had not "misperceived the political will," and no one could therefore "assume that [*Monroe's*] interpretation was correct." On the other hand, nine years have now gone by since *Monell*, and Congress *again* has not amended § 1983. Should we now "assume that [*Monell's*] interpretation was correct"? Rather, I think we should admit that vindication by congressional inaction is a canard.

Justice STEVENS' concurring opinion emphasizes "the underlying public interest in 'stability and orderly development of the law,' " *ante*, at 644 (citation omitted), that often requires adherence to an erroneous decision. As I have described above, however, today's decision is a demonstration not of stability and order but of the instability and unpredictable expansion which the substitution of judicial improvisation for statutory text has produced. For a number of reasons, *stare decisis* ought not to save *Weber*. First, this Court has applied the doctrine of *stare decisis* to civil rights statutes less rigorously than to other laws. See *Maine v. Thiboutot*, 448 U.S. 1, 33 (1980) (POWELL, J., dissenting); *Monroe v. Pape, supra*, 365 U.S., at 221–222 (Frankfurter, J., dissenting in part). Second, as Justice STEVENS acknowledges in his concurrence, *ante*, at 644, *Weber* was itself a dramatic departure from the Court's prior Title VII precedents, and can scarcely be said to be "so consistent with the warp and woof of civil rights law as to be beyond question." *Monell v. New York City Dept. of Social Services, supra*, 436 U.S., at 696. Third, *Weber* was decided a mere seven years ago, and has provided little guidance to persons seeking to confirm their conduct to the law, beyond the proposition that Title VII does not mean what it says. Finally, "even under the most stringent test for the propriety of overruling a statutory decision . . . —'that it appear beyond doubt . . . that [the decision] misapprehended the meaning of the controlling provision,' " 436 U.S., at 700 (quoting *Monroe v. Pape*, 365 U.S., at 192 (Harlan, J., concurring)), *Weber* should be overruled.

In addition to complying with the commands of the statute, abandoning *Weber* would have the desirable side-effect of eliminating the requirement of willing suspension of disbelief that is currently a credential for reading our opinions in the affirmative action field—from *Weber* itself, which demanded belief that the corporate employer adopted the affirmative action program "voluntarily," rather than under practical compulsion from government contracting agencies, see 443 U.S., at 204; to *Bakke*, a Title VI case cited as authority by the majority here, *ante*, at 1455, which demanded belief that the University of California took race into account as merely one of the many diversities to which it felt it was educationally important to expose its medical students, see 438 U.S., at 311–315, to today's opinion, which—in the face of a plan obviously designed to force promoting officials to prefer candidates from the favored racial and sexual classes, warning them that their "personal commitment" will be determined by how successfully they "attain" certain numerical goals, and in the face of a particular promotion awarded to the less qualified applicant by an official who "did little or nothing" to inquire into sources "critical" to determining the final candidates' relative qualifications other than their sex—in the face of all this, demands belief that we are dealing here with no more than a program that "merely authorizes that consideration be given to affirmative action concerns when evaluating qualified applicants." *Ante*, at 638. Any line of decisions rooted so firmly in naivete must be wrong.

The majority emphasizes, as though it is meaningful, that "*No* persons are automatically excluded from consideration; *all* are able to have their qualifications weighed against those of other applicants." *Ibid.* One is reminded of the exchange from Shakespeare's King Henry the Fourth, Part I: "GLENDOWER: I can call Spirits from the vasty Deep. HOTSPUR: Why, so can I, or so can any man. But will they come when you do call for them?" Act III, Scene I, lines 53–55. Johnson was indeed entitled to have his qualifications weighed against those of other applicants—but more to the point, he was virtually assured that, after the weighing, if there was any minimally qualified applicant from one of the favored groups, he would be rejected.

Similarly hollow is the Court's assurance that we would strike this plan down if it "failed to take distinctions in qualifications into account," because that "would dictate mere blind hiring by the numbers." *Ante*, at 636. For what the Court means by "taking distinctions in qualifications into account" consists of no more than eliminating from the applicant pool those who are not even *minimally qualified* for the job. Once that has been done, once the promoting officer assures himself that all the candidates before him are "M.Q.s" (minimally qualifieds), he can then ignore, as the Agency Director did here, how much better than minimally qualified some of the candidates may be, and can proceed to appoint from the pool solely on the basis of race or sex, until the affirmative action "goals" have been reached. The requirement that the employer "take distinctions in qualifications into account" thus turns out to be an assurance, not that candidates' comparative merits will always be considered, but only that none of the successful candidates selected over the others solely on the basis of their race or sex will be utterly unqualified. That may be of great comfort to those concerned with American productivity; and it is undoubtedly effective in reducing the effect of affirmative-action discrimination upon those in the upper strata of society, who (unlike road maintenance workers, for example) compete for employment in professional and semiprofessional fields where, for many reasons, including most notably the effects of past discrimination, the numbers of "M.Q." applicants from the favored groups are substantially less. But I fail to see how it has any relevance to whether selecting among final candidates solely on the basis of race or sex is permissible under Title VII, which prohibits discrimination on the basis of race or sex.[5]

Today's decision does more, however, than merely reaffirm *Weber*, and more than merely extend it to public actors. It is impossible not to be aware that the practical effect of our holding is to accomplish *de facto* what the law—in language even plainer than that ignored in *Weber*, see 42 U.S.C. § 2000e–2(j)—forbids anyone from accomplishing *de jure:* in many contexts it effectively *requires* employers, public as well as private, to engage in intentional discrimination on the basis of race or sex. This Court's prior interpretations of Title VII, especially the decision in *Griggs v. Duke Power Co.*, 401 U.S. 424 (1971), subject employers to a potential Title VII suit whenever there is a noticeable imbalance in the representation

5. In a footnote purporting to respond to this dissent's (nonexistent) "predict[ion] that today's decision will loose a flood of 'less qualified' minorities and women upon the workforce," *ante* at 641, n. 17, the majority accepts the contention of the American Society for Personnel Administration that there is no way to determine who is the best qualified candidate for a job such as Road Dispatcher. This effectively constitutes appellate reversal of a finding of fact by the District Court in the present case ("plaintiff was more qualified for the position of Road Dispatcher than Diane Joyce," App. to Pet. for Cert. 12a). More importantly, it has staggering implications for future Title VII litigation, since the most common reason advanced for failing to hire a member of a protected group is the superior qualification of the hired individual. I am confident, however, that the Court considers this argument no more enduring than I do.

of minorities or women in the employer's work force. Even the employer who is confident of ultimately prevailing in such a suit must contemplate the expense and adverse publicity of a trial, because the extent of the imbalance, and the "job relatedness" of his selection criteria, are questions of fact to be explored through rebuttal and counter-rebuttal of a "prima facie case" consisting of no more than the showing that the employer's selection process "selects those from the protected class at a 'significantly' lesser rate than their counterparts." B. Schlei & P. Grossman, Employment Discrimination Law 91 (2d ed. 1983). If, however, employers are free to discriminate through affirmative action, without fear of "reverse discrimination" suits by their nonminority or male victims, they are offered a threshold defense against Title VII liability premised on numerical disparities. Thus, after today's decision the *failure* to engage in reverse discrimination is economic folly, and arguably a breach of duty to shareholders or taxpayers, wherever the cost of anticipated Title VII litigation exceeds the cost of hiring less capable (though still minimally capable) workers. (This situation is more likely to obtain, of course, with respect to the least skilled jobs—perversely creating an incentive to discriminate against precisely those members of the nonfavored groups *least* likely to have profited from societal discrimination in the past.) It is predictable, moreover, that this incentive will be greatly magnified by economic pressures brought to bear by government contracting agencies upon employers who refuse to discriminate in the fashion we have now approved. A statute designed to establish a color-blind and gender-blind workplace has thus been converted into a powerful engine of racism and sexism, not merely *permitting* intentional race- and sex-based discrimination, but often making it, through operation of the legal system, practically compelled.

It is unlikely that today's result will be displeasing to politically elected officials, to whom it provides the means of quickly accommodating the demands of organized groups to achieve concrete, numerical improvement in the economic status of particular constituencies. Nor will it displease the world of corporate and governmental employers (many of whom have filed briefs as *amici* in the present case, all on the side of Santa Clara) for whom the cost of hiring less qualified workers is often substantially less—and infinitely more predictable—than the cost of litigating Title VII cases and of seeking to convince federal agencies by nonnumerical means that no discrimination exists. In fact, the only losers in the process are the Johnsons of the country, for whom Title VII has been not merely repealed but actually inverted. The irony is that these individuals—predominantly unknown, unaffluent, unorganized—suffer this injustice at the hands of a Court fond of thinking itself the champion of the politically impotent. I dissent.

Notes

Notes to Chapter 1

1. Interview with Paul Johnson, Sequim, Washington, 15 April 1989.
2. Interview with Diane Joyce, Morgan Hill, California, 31 July 1989.
3. *Santa Clara County Government* (San Jose, 1980), i.
4. San Jose Metropolitan Chamber of Commerce, *Membership Directory and Buyer's Guide, 1988–89* (San Jose, 1988), 22–24.
5. Interview with Suzanne Wilson, San Jose, California, 1 August 1989.
6. Chamber of Commerce, *Membership Directory*, 24.
7. Interview with Steven Woodside, San Jose, California, 31 July 1989.
8. Originally the county's transportation responsibilities had been nearly all highway-related. With the rapid population growth, however, not only did the county build more roads, it also set up public transportation, primarily buses. James Graebner, the Transportation Agency head at this time, had been hired to get a light rail system up and running. Most of the minorities working in TA worked in the public transportation units; nearly all the women worked at clerical jobs.
9. Interview with Michael H. Baratz, Washington, D.C., 7 July 1989. Suzanne Wilson, Steven Woodside, Diane Joyce, and Paul Johnson all agreed that roads constituted a closed system, although they differed on the extent to which this affected the daily operations of the department.
10. Interview with James L. Dawson, San Jose, California, 1 August 1989.
11. "The Supreme Court Puts the Mike in Diane Joyce's Hands, Giving Feminists a Major Victory," *People*, 13 April 1987, 50.
12. Interview with Paul Johnson.
13. *Reporter's Transcript of Proceedings*, Paul E. Johnson, Plaintiff, v. Transportation Agency, Santa Clara County, California, Defendant, in the United States District Court for the Northern District of California, No. C 81–1218, May 7 and 12, 1982 (hereafter cited as *Trial Transcript*), 127.
14. Interview with Paul Johnson.
15. Susan Faludi, "I Paid a Price . . . You Always Pay a Price," *West*, the magazine supplement of the (San Jose) *Mercury News*, 27 September 1987, p. 18 + ;

a shorter version also appeared under the title "Diane Joyce," *Ms.* January 1988, 62ff.

16. Interview with Diane Joyce.

17. Faludi, "I Paid a Price," 22–23.

18. For example, the men on the road crews were normally assigned coveralls; she had to file a complaint before the agency would issue coveralls to her. On the road crew, the boss would routinely assign her the dull task of handling the "Caution" paddle, and would not let her shovel or handle the equipment. One time on a short crew, she got the paddle when there were not enough men to shovel the asphalt and rake it while it was still hot and malleable. Out of necessity, the boss had to let her shovel that day.

19. Interview with Diane Joyce.

20. *Ibid.*

21. Interview with Kristina M. Sermersheim, San Jose, California, 1 August 1989.

22. Interview with Diane Joyce.

23. Testimony of James H. Graebner, *Trial Transcript*, 26, 18.

24. Michael Baratz, then the executive officer of Local 715, SEIU, described Graebner as "sort of liberal." He also believes that a woman working in the Transportation Agency personnel office at the time, Myra Beals, probably did the staff work for Morton. Interview with Michael Baratz.

25. *Trial Transcript*, 25.

26. Testimony of Paul Johnson, *Trial Transcript*, 133–34.

27. "The Supreme Court Puts the Mike in Diane Joyce's Hands," 53; interview with Paul Johnson.

28. *Trial Transcript*, 134–35; "The Supreme Court Puts the Mike in Diane Joyce's Hands," 53; interview with Paul Johnson.

29. Interview with Paul Johnson.

30. Union members could invoke one type of grievance procedure, which would be handled through the union (Local 715, SEIU); nonunion members followed a grievance procedure through the county personnel office.

31. Interview with Diane Joyce; testimony of Diane Joyce, *Trial Transcript*, 100.

32. Interview with James Dawson.

Notes to Chapter 2

1. William Gillette, *Retreat from Reconstruction, 1869–1879* (Baton Rouge: Louisiana State University Press, 1979), 191.

2. *Civil Rights Cases*, 109 U.S. 3 (1883).

3. For the FEPC, see Louis Ruchames, *Race, Jobs, and Politics* (New York: Columbia University Press, 1953).

4. The Johnson Administration worried that the Supreme Court, despite its stance in the school desegregation cases, might adhere to the precedent of the *Civil Rights Cases*. So it based the constitutional authority for the 1964 act not in the Fourteenth Amendment but in the Commerce Clause. It need not have worried; in two companion cases, *Heart of Atlanta Motel* v. *United States*, 379 U.S. 241 (1964) and *Katzenbach* v. *McClung*, 379 U.S. 294 (1964), the Court ruled that Congress "possessed ample power" to reach such discrimination.

5. *New York Times*, 5 June 1965.

6. "The Furor over 'Reverse Discrimination,' " *Newsweek*, 26 September 1977, 55.

7. A few firms, such as Reynolds Metals Corporation, voluntarily began recruiting minorities in 1964, but the Richmond-based Reynolds was the exception rather than the rule.

8. National Public Radio, "Affirmative Action: An Update 1989," ME-890619.01/01-C.

9. Douglas B. Huron, "But Government Can Help," *Washington Post*, 12 August 1984; Anthony Lewis, "Abroad at Home," *New York Times*, 19 May 1985. There were still problems, primarily in terms of promotion, but the lower courts had begun addressing this issue as well. The Supreme Court upheld a quota plan for promotions in *United States* v. *Paradise*, 480 U.S. 149 (1987).

10. Anne B. Fisher, "Businessmen Like to Hire by the Numbers," *Fortune*, 16 September 1985, 26.

11. Alan Farnham, "Holding Firm on Affirmative Action," *Fortune*, 13 March 1989, 88.

12. Fisher, "Businessmen Like to Hire by the Numbers."

13. Peggy Simpson, "Why the Big Backlash Is a Big Bust," *Working Woman*, November 1986, 165.

14. *New York Times*, 3 March 1986. In 1975, Merck's total work force was 10.1 percent minority and 23.8 percent female; among managers and professionals, the respective numbers were 5.7 and 19.5 percent. A decade later, minorities made up 15.6 percent of the work force, of which 34.1 percent were female. Managerial and professional groups now included 13.1 percent minorities and 26.7 percent women.

15. Although the Office of Federal Contract Compliance and its counterparts in fifteen government agencies supposedly monitor a quarter-million firms, in its first ten years of existence it blacklisted only nine companies. In the Department of Health, Education and Welfare in the early 1970s, Secretary Caspar Weinberger promoted a policy of conciliation rather than strict enforcement, and the U.S. Commission on Civil Rights charged HEW's attitude with frustrating the goal of the various Executive orders. However, although the power was seldom used, many contractors were well aware of its existence. As one of them put it, "It you've got the atom bomb, you don't have to drop it to make your point." *Business Week* concluded that because of its potential power, "no other antibias agency matches the OFCC in the breadth of its influence." "Acting Affirmatively to End Job Bias," *Business Week*, 27 January 1975, 94; Bernard Ortiz de Montellano, Letter, *Science*, 7 November 1975, 509.

16. Farnham, "Holding Firm on Affirmative Action," 88, reporting on a *Fortune* 500/CNN Moneyline CEO Poll.

17. *Id.*

18. Thomas Sowell, "Black Progress Can't Be Legislated," *Washington Post*, 12 August 1984.

19. Lance Morrow, "An Essay on the Unfairness of Life," *Horizon*, December 1977, 35. Glazer has written on this in *Affirmative Discrimination: Ethnic Inequality and Public Policy* (New York: Basic Books, 1975).

20. Bernard E. Anderson, "An Economic Defense of Affirmative Action," *Black Enterprise*, May 1982, 40; for similar statistics in other companies, see "Acting Affirmatively to End Job Bias."

21. *Johnson* v. *Transportation Agency, Santa Clara County, amicus* brief, National Organization of Women and other groups, 61–62. The brief has an excellent summary of job discrimination faced by women in different areas, 44ff.; see also Justice Brennan's opinion in *Frontiero* v. *Richardson*, 411 U.S. 677, 684–87 (1973).

22. "Acting Affirmatively to End Job Bias," *Business Week*, 27 January 1975, 94.

23. NOW *amicus* brief, 60.

24. Jonathan S. Leonard, *The Impact of Affirmative Action* (Washington: Government Printing Office, 1983), 25; see also Office of Federal Contract Compliance Programs, *Employment Patterns of Minorities and Women in Federal Contractor and Non-Contractor Establishments, 1974–1980* (Washington: Government Printing Office, 1984).

25. "Battle Heats Up over Sex, Race Bias in Jobs," *U.S. News & World Report*, 27 May 1985, 49; "Assault on Affirmative Action," *Time*, 25 February 1985, 20.

26. "The Women Win—Again," *U.S. News & World Report*, 6 April 1987, 18; data based on information from U.S. Department of Labor and the Census Bureau.

27. In 1970 white women made about 86 percent of white male salaries; in 1980, 83 percent. *New York Times*, 16 January 1984.

28. "Working Women Still Segregated and Underpaid," *Science*, 31 January 1986, 449.

29. McGeorge Bundy, "The Issue Before the Court: Who Gets Ahead in America," *The Atlantic* 240 (Nov. 1977): 44–45 (italics in article). Bundy was writing about the *Bakke* case, then pending before the Supreme Court (see pp. 44–46), but his argument applied to employment as well as education, women as well as blacks.

30. Anderson, "Economic Defense of Affirmative Action," 40.

31. Ralph F. Davidson, "Keep Federal Affirmative Action Strong," *New York Times*, 25 November 1985.

32. Charles Krauthammer, "In Defense of Quotas," *New Republic*, 16 & 23 September 1985, 11.

33. *New York Times*, 18 March 1977.

34. Study by Stephen N. Keith *et al.*, "Effects of Affirmative Action in Medical Schools," *New England Journal of Medicine*, 12 December 1985, 1519, 1521.

35. Dean Robert Pollack, "Farewell Letter to Columbia College Students," 8 May 1989.

36. Bundy, "Issue Before the Court," 47.

37. See the lengthy article by Andrew Hacker, "Affirmative Action: The New Look," *New York Review of Books*, 12 October 1989, 63–68.

38. Legally, courts have endorsed quotas when there has been a record of persistent discrimination against a particular group, but on the whole, as seen in Chapter Three, the general rule permits "goals" and "timetables" narrowly drawn to meet a specific situation, as in the *Johnson* case, but disallows quotas.

39. *U.S. News & World Report*, 3 October 1977, 39–40.

40. "Mr. Califano on Quotas," *Commonweal*, 13 May 1977, 292.

41. *U.S. News & World Report*, 18 August 1975, 73.

42. *New York Times*, 24 July 1984. Fleming was soon after dismissed from his post by President Reagan; in 1984, as the head of the private Citizens' Commission on Civil Rights, he denounced quotas as discriminatory.

43. Quoted in Hacker, "Affirmative Action," 63.

44. However, even treating blacks and other minorities preferentially in college admissions does not necessarily help them if they are ill-prepared to do the work. A recent study of blacks in white colleges indicates that such students face many problems that work against their success. Jacqueline Fleming, *Blacks in College: A Comparative Study of Students' Success in Black and White Institutions* (San Francisco: Jossey-Bass, 1989).

45. Daniel C. Maguire, "Unequal but Fair: The Morality of Justice by Quota," *Commonweal*, 14 October 1977, 648–49.

46. Krauthammer, "In Defense of Quotas," 10–11.

47. *U.S. News & World Report*, 27 May 1985, 50.

48. Quoted in Hacker, "Affirmative Action," 64.

49. Maguire, "Unequal but Fair," 649.

50. Paul R. Spickard, "Why I Believe in Affirmative Action," *Christianity Today*, 3 October 1986, 12. Spickard was later able to get a job in the history department of Bethel College in St. Paul, Minnesota.

51. For critics of affirmative action, the operational word is always "quotas." William Beer, for example, writes that in a series of bureaucratic and legal decisions, "affirmative action has been translated into a series of quotas (sometimes euphemistically referred to as 'goals' and 'timetables') that benefit certain groups at the cost of others." "Resolute Ignorance: Social Science and Affirmative Action," *Society*, May/June 1987, 63.

52. Sidney Hook, "Letter to Editor," *New York Times*, 7 June 1986.

53. Editorial, "Disadvantaged Groups, Individual Rights," *The New Republic*, 15 October 1977, 7.

54. *Id.*

55. Sowell, "Black Progress Can't Be Legislated."

56. *Id.*; *New York Times*, 22 May 1984.

57. George Gilder, "The Myths of Racial and Sexual Discrimination," *The National Review*, 14 November 1980, 1381, 1382. See also, Anne L. Alstott, " 'Comparable Worth' is Unfair to Women," *New York Times*, 24 May 1986, and William R. Beer, "The Wages of Discrimination," *Public Opinion*, July/August 1987, 17–20.

58. *U.S. News & World Report*, 28 March 1977, 68–69.

59. *U.S. News & World Report*, 5 December 1977, 78–80.

60. Frank Trippett, "The Sensible Limits of Non-Discrimination," *Time*, 25 July 1977, 52–63.

61. In the earlier studies, women opposed quotas, blacks favored them, and self-identified "liberals" split about evenly. Seymour Martin Lipset and William Schneider, "The Emerging National Consensus," *The New Republic*, 15 October 1977, 8–9. However, a decade later several studies showed that blacks and women both opposed quotas based on race or gender. Beer, "Resolute Ignorance," 66; *New York Times*, 24 July 1984.

62. William F. Buckley, Jr., "Racial Quotas at Medical School," *The National Review*, 5 August 1977, 904–05; for the *Bakke* case, see Chapter Three.

63. Gerald F. Kreyche, "The New McCarthyism," *USA Today*, September 1987, 9.

64. *New York Times*, 6 December 1985.

65. Stephen J. Markham, "Classifying the Races," *National Review*, 5 April 1985, 44.

66. Jonathan Kaufman, *Broken Alliance* (New York: Scribners, 1988).

67. Morris Abram, letter to editor, *The Atlantic*, January 1978, 77; interview in *U.S. News & World Report*, 27 May 1985, 50.

68. Alexander Bickel, *The Morality of Consent* (New Haven: Yale University Press, 1975), 133.

69. Carl Cohen, "Naked Racial Preference," *Commentary*, March 1986, 30; "Assault on Affirmative Action," *Time*, 25 February 1985, 19.

70. John H. Bunzel, "Affirmative Action Must Not Result in Lower Standards or Discrimination Against the Most Competent Students," *Chronicle of Higher Education*, 1 March 1989. The entry level scores for the different California schools are set by the state's Board of Regents in conjunction with the schools.

71. Hacker, "Affirmative Action," 63–64.

72. It no longer seems a problem for white women. Once professional schools opened their doors, they were able to compete with white males, since they had, for the most part, enjoyed comparable secondary and collegiate education. For the problems still faced by minorities in law schools, for example, see *New York Times*, 16 February 1985.

73. See the exchange between Charles Murray and Derek Bok in the 31 December 1984 and 4 February 1985 issues of *The New Republic*. See also, "Blacks Debate the Costs of Affirmative Action," *New York Times*, 10 June 1990; and Shelby Steele, *The Content of Our Character* (New York: St. Martin's, 1990).

74. Hacker, "Affirmative Action," 64, quoting from Thomas Sowell, *Choosing a College: A Guide for Parents and Students* (New York: Harper & Row, 1989).

75. Bunzel, "Affirmative Action."

76. "Affirmative Action at the Crossroads," *Nation's Business*, March 1986, 12; *New York Times*, 3 March 1986.

77. *Business Week*, 24 November 1980, 48.

78. *New York Times*, 18 January 1984; see also comments by Eleanor Holmes Norton, EEOC chair during the Carter administration, and J. Clay Smith, the acting director, regarding the Reagan policy in *Black Enterprise*, February 1982, 37.

79. Letter to the editor, *New York Times*, 19 February 1984.

80. *New York Times*, 16 March 1985.

81. *Business Week*, 11 March 1985, 42; *U.S. News & World Report*, 15 April 1985, 12; *New York Times*, 4 May 1985.

82. See, for example, *Newsweek*, 26 August 1985, 21.

83. Hyman Bookbinder, "Affirmative Action in Employment: We Must Not Abandon the Fight," *USA Today*, September 1986, 61.

Notes to Chapter 3

1. The law, 86 Stat. 103 (1972), also reduced to fifteen the number of employees in a firm necessary to bring it under Title VII coverage, provided additional enforcement power in the EEOC and Justice Department, and expanded the rights of private plaintiffs to pursue their cause in federal courts.

2. In addition, 94 percent of collective bargaining agreements sampled by the Bureau of National Affairs in the early 1980s had guarantees against discrimination by the employer, the union, or both. Nine out of ten of these clauses prohibited discrimination on the basis of race, sex, national origin, or age.

3. *Steele* v. *Louisville & Nashville Railroad Co.*, 323 U.S. 192, 204 (1944).

4. *Shelley* v. *Kraemer*, 334 U.S. 1 (1948).

5. In *Burton* v. *Wilmington Parking Authority*, 365 U.S. 715 (1961), the Court ruled that racial discrimination in a privately owned restaurant that rented space in a state-owned building constituted state action.

6. Robert Belton, "Title VII of the Civil Rights Act of 1964: A Decade of Private Enforcement and Judicial Developments," 20 *St. Louis L.J.* 225, 228–29 (1976).

7. See James E. Jones, Jr., William P. Murphy, and Robert Belton, *Cases and Materials on Discrimination in Employment*, 5th ed. (St. Paul: West Publishing Co., 1987).

8. *Griggs* v. *Duke Power Co.*, 401 U.S. 424 (1971); Justice Brennan did not take part in this decision.

9. Four years later, the Court deferred to the EEOC in ruling defective the validation procedures adopted by an employer to show that its tests did, in fact, relate to job skills. *Albemarle Paper Co.* v. *Moody*, 422 U.S. 405 (1975).

10. *Washington* v. *Davis*, 426 U.S. 229 (1976).

11. The Court has also addressed the question of "disparate treatment," in which an employer treats one group of people less favorably than others, and in which motive may be a critical element in the analysis. See *McDonnell Douglas Corp.* v. *Green*, 411 U.S. 792 (1973).

12. *Teamsters* v. *United States*, 431 U.S. 324, 339 (1977).

13. Alfred W. Blumrosen, "Strangers in Paradise: Griggs v. Duke Power Co., and the Concept of Employment Discrimination," 71 *Mich. L.R.* 59 (1972).

14. 215 F.Supp. 729 (E.D.Pa. 1963); aff'd, 329 F.2d 3 (3rd Cir. 1964).

15. See, for example, *Todd* v. *Joint Apprenticeship Committee*, 223 F.Supp. 12 (N.D.Ill. 1963); *Farkas* v. *Texas Instrument, Inc.*, 375 F.2d 629 (5th Cir. 1967); and *Hadnott* v. *Laird*, 463 F.2d 304 (D.C. Cir. 1972).

16. See, for example, *Balaban* v. *Rubin*, 14 N.Y. 2d 193, cert. denied, 379 U.S. 881 (1964), and *School Committee of Boston* v. *Board of Education*, 352 Mass. 693 (1967), appeal dismissed, 389 U.S. 572 (1968). See the discussion in John Kaplan, "Equal Justice in an Unequal World: Equality for the Negro—the Problem of Special Treatment," 61 *Northwestern Univ. L.R.* 363 (1966), and John Hart Ely, "The Constitutionality of Reverse Racial Discrimination," 41 *Univ. of Chicago L.R.* 723 (1974).

17. *DeFunis* v. *Odegaard*, 416 U.S. 312, 337 (1974), Douglas dissenting. The case generated a great deal of comment; see the symposia in 60 *Virginia L.R.* 917 (1974) and 75 *Columbia L.R.* 483 (1975).

18. Monrad Paulson, "DeFunis: the Road Not Taken," 60 *Virginia L.R.* 917 (1974).
19. *Regents of the University of California* v. *Bakke*, 438 U.S. 265 (1978).
20. Title VI provides: "No person in the United States shall, on the ground of race, color, or national origin, be excluded from participation in, be denied the benefits of, or be subjected to discrimination under any program or activity receiving federal financial assistance."
21. Indeed, Justice Powell, when announcing his opinion, remarked that "perhaps no case in recent memory has received so much media coverage and scholarly commentary." Allan P. Sindler, *Bakke, DeFunis, and Minority Admissions: The Quest for Equal Opportunity* (New York: Longmans, 1978), 292.
22. *U.S. News & World Report*, 28 September 1977, 39. Comments like this often seemed a rote response from civil rights leaders to any case in which the Court reviewed affirmative action; see Herbert Hill, "A Blow to Minorities," *Commonweal*, 2 September 1977, 552, in which the former NAACP labor director noted that a case upholding a seniority system that had the effect of undermining affirmative action "signifies the end of the era that began with . . . *Brown*."
23. John H. Bunzel, "Bakke vs. University of California," *Commentary*, March 1977, 63.
24. McGeorge Bundy, "The Issue Before the Court: Who Gets Ahead in America?," *Atlantic*, November 1977, 41.
25. J. Harvey Wilkinson III, *From Brown to Bakke: The Supreme Court and School Integration, 1954–1978* (New York: Oxford University Press, 1979), 301; Anthony Lewis, *New York Times*, 2 July 1978. There are literally dozens of law review articles on the opinion; for a representative sampling of the range of opinion, see the symposium in 67 *California L.R.* 1 (1979).
26. Meg Greenfield, "How to Resolve the Bakke Case," *Newsweek*, 24 October 1977.
27. 443 U.S. 193 (1979).
28. Justices Stewart, White, and Marshall joined the opinion; Blackmun concurred; Justices Powell and Stevens did not participate; and Chief Justice Burger and Justice Rehnquist dissented.
29. The due process and equal-protection clauses operate only against the state and federal governments, and do not apply to private actors. To mount a constitutional claim, therefore, a governmental employer must be involved; if a private employer is charged with discrimination, the case must be brought under Title VII or another statute.
30. The Court had held, in a non–affirmative action case, that Title VII did apply to discrimination against whites. *McDonald* v. *Santa Fe Trail Transportation Co.*, 427 U.S. 273 (1976).
31. 443 U.S. at 208.
32. The act, §103(f)(2), identified a minority-owned business (MBE) as one in which at least 51 percent of the stock is owned by "citizens of the United States who are Negroes, Spanish-speaking, Orientals, Indians, Eskimos, and Aleuts."
33. *Fullilove* v. *Klutznik*, 448 U.S. 448 (1980). Powell also entered a separate concurrence. Justices Marshall, Brennan, and Blackmun concurred in the

result, but on the more liberal basis enunciated by Marshall in his *Bakke* opinion. Justices Stewart, Rehnquist, and Stevens dissented.

34. See, for example, Judith A. Baer, *The Chains of Protection: The Judicial Response to Women's Labor Legislation* (Westport, Ct.: Greenwood Press, 1978).

35. *Bradwell* v. *Illinois*, 16 Wall. 130 (1873); see also *In re Lockwood*, 154 U.S. 116 (1894).

36. *Goesart* v. *Cleary*, 335 U.S. 464, 466 (1948). The three dissenters, Rutledge, Murphy, and Douglas, did not challenge the majority's assumptions about the proper place of women, but only the fit between the means and end desired. They, too, assumed that benign or protective legislation regarding women did not violate the Constitution.

37. *Hoyt* v. *Florida*, 368 U.S. 57 (1961).

38. Ruth Bader Ginsburg, "Women, Equality and the Bakke Case," 4 *Civil Liberties R.* 8, 9 (1977); see also her article, "Gender and the Constitution," 44 *Univ. Cincinnati L.R.* 1 (1975).

39. I have argued elsewhere that the Burger Court was never as conservative as either its critics or its defenders charged, but in fact continued and expanded many of the precedents established by its predecessor. *The Continuity of Change: The Supreme Court and Individual Liberties, 1953–1986* (Belmont: Wadsworth, 1990).

40. *Reed* v. *Reed*, 404 U.S. 71 (1971).

41. Professor Ginsburg, who wrote the appellant's brief in *Reed*, strenuously urged the Court to take this step. Even though the Court refused, Gerald Gunther, one of the nation's leading constitutional scholars, wrote: "It is difficult to understand [the result in *Reed*] without an assumption that some special sensitivity to sex as a classifying factor entered into the analysis." Gunther, "Foreword: In Search of Evolving Doctrine on a Changing Court: A Model for a Newer Equal Protection," 86 *Harvard L.R.* 1, 34 (1972).

42. 411 U.S. 677 (1973).

43. In *Stanton* v. *Stanton*, 421 U.S. 7 (1975), for example, the Court invalidated a law requiring child support for males to age twenty-one but for females only to age eighteen. *Weinberger* v. *Weisenfeld*, 420 U.S. 636 (1975), struck down a Social Security provision that provided different benefit levels to widows and widowers.

44. *Craig* v. *Boren*, 429 U.S. 190 (1976); Justice Rehnquist, joined by the Chief Justice, dissented. The difference between "intermediate" and "strict" scrutiny involves the nature of the governmental objectives—"important" as opposed to "compelling"—and the relationship of the means to the ends—"substantially related" as opposed to "necessary."

45. William John Seitz III, "Gender-Based Discrimination and a Developing Standard of Equal Protection Analysis," 46 *Univ. Cincinnati L.R.* 572, 578 (1977).

46. Nancy Gertner, "*Bakke* on Affirmative Action for Women: Pedestal or Cage?" 14 *Harvard C.R.–C.L. L.R.* 173, 214 (1979).

47. *Id.* at 205. See also Ruth Bader Ginsburg, "Women, Equality and the Bakke Case," 15.

48. See, for example, Justice Brennan's eloquent elaboration of the "long and unfortunate history of sex discrimination" in the United States in *Frontiero*, 411 U.S. at 684.

49. In *Kahn* v. *Shevin*, 416 U.S. 351 (1974), the Court upheld a state property tax relief for widows, but not for widowers, because it rested upon a recognition by the legislature that widows and widowers often had far different economic resources. *Schlesinger* v. *Ballard*, 419 U.S. 498 (1975) upheld navy regulations that gave women a longer time to earn a promotion in an "up or out" system, in recognition that women did not have certain sea duty opportunities available to men. *Califano* v. *Webster*, 430 U.S. 313 (1977) sustained a computation of benefits that favored women in an effort to compensate for past wage discrimination.
50. Ginsburg, "Women, Equality and the Bakke Case," 11.
51. *City of Los Angeles Dept. of Water* v. *Manhart*, 435 U.S. 702 (1978). See [Gordon R. Kanofsky], "Note: The End of Sex Discrimination in Employer-Operated Pension Plans: The Challenge of the *Manhart* Case," 1979 *Duke L.J.* 682.
52. *Wengler* v. *Druggists Mutual Insurance Co.*, 446 U.S. 142 (1980). See [Rosalie E. Walker], "Note: *Wengler* . . . However the discrimination is described, If Gender-Based, the Substantial Relationship Test Applies," 1981 *Utah L.R.* 431.

Notes to Chapter 4

1. Interview with Michael H. Baratz, Washington, D.C., 7 July 1989; also interviews with Paul Johnson, James Dawson, Steven Woodside, and Diane Joyce.
2. Paul Johnson, however, recalled that when Ms. Ravel was investigating the facts, she came out to the road yard and interviewed members of the second panel, and at the same time she allegedly said, "I don't know what the county's trying to do; they don't have any kind of case at all." Interview with Paul Johnson.
3. Interview with Kristina M. Sermersheim, San Jose, California, 1 August 1989.
4. Interview with Suzanne Wilson, San Jose, California, 1 August 1989.
5. As but one example, a jury in a local Florida court took only a few minutes to find an indigent drifter guilty of petty theft, a reasonable finding in a routine case. But Clarence Earl Gideon believed that the State of Florida should have provided him with counsel, and in prison he began a letter-writing campaign that ultimately brought his case to the Supreme Court, and led to what may have been the most important criminal procedure decision of this century, *Gideon* v. *Wainwright*, 372 U.S. 335 (1963). See the classic study of this case, *Gideon's Trumpet*, by Anthony Lewis (New York: Random House, 1964).
6. When the law is clear and there is no dispute over the facts, a party may propose that the evidence so plainly supports its side that the judge should render a decision in its favor without the need for further argument or sending the case to the fact-finder.
7. Interviews with Charles Fried and Steven Woodside.
8. Interview with Constance Brooks, 2 August 1989.
9. Interview with James Dawson.
10. Dawson did not know about this relationship at the time, and in fact only learned about it in our interview in August 1989.

11. This and all subsequent quotes from the trial are taken from the official report of the trial, "Paul E. Johnson, Plaintiff, vs. Transportation Agency, Santa Clara County, California, Defendant," No. C81–1218, in the U.S. District Court for the Northern District of California, May 7 and 12, 1982.
12. Interview with Steven Woodside.
13. An attorney cannot, of course, "prep" a witness so that the witness commits perjury or even distorts the evidence. But one can, especially in cases where the defendant's employees are being called to make the plaintiff's case, alert the witness to potential traps and advise on how best to present certain facts. There is, of course, a fine line to walk here, but the underlying assumption is that the defense does not have to help the plaintiff make its case.
14. Interview with James Dawson.
15. Interview with Steven Woodside.
16. This issue, which played a relatively minor role in the trial, would be a major topic in oral argument before the Supreme Court. If an employer sets goals at a percentage of women or minorities in the overall work force, one assumes that the jobs will be for the most part unskilled. If the jobs are skilled, then the realistic plan is to determine what percentage of minorities have the necessary skills. The county had classified the dispatcher as a skilled position, but its affirmative action plan seemed to rely on the total number of women in the local work force. This disjuncture bothered several of the justices; see Chapter 8.
17. Although *Weber* applied specifically to a private employer, the Ninth Circuit, which included California, had recently ruled that the *Weber* criteria applied to public employers as well. *LaRiviere* v. *EEOC*, 682 F.2d 1275 (9th Cir. 1982).
18. *Paul E. Johnson* v. *Transportation Agency, Santa Clara County, California*, C–81–1218–WAI (SJ), Judgment, 10 August 1982. A copy of the judgment, as well as Judge Ingram's findings of fact and law, are included in the petition for the writ of certiorari later filed by Mountain States Legal Foundation on behalf of Johnson.
19. Interview with James Dawson.

Notes to Chapter 5

1. Interview with Kristy Sermersheim, 1 August 1989.
2. Interview with Steven Woodside, 31 July 1989.
3. Interview with Kristy Sermersheim.
4. Interview with Michael Baratz, 7 July 1989.
5. Prior to filing an appeal with the Court of Appeals for the Ninth Circuit, Woodside had filed a motion for a new trial in the District Court, a necessary preliminary to taking the case to the appellate level.
6. Interview with Steven Woodside.
7. Interview with James Dawson.
8. Interview with David Rosenfeld.
9. There is no transcript of the oral argument at the circuit court stage, as there is at the trial and in the Supreme Court, since oral argument at this level has

no evidentiary value. The Ninth Circuit does record oral argument, but because of the large number of cases it hears each year, it only stores these tapes until there is a final disposition of the case. Once the Supreme Court handed down its decision, the Ninth Circuit librarian disposed of the tape. I wrote to each of the three members of the panel, and all responded, but none of them remembered any of the details about the oral argument, which is understandable considering the large number of cases they hear each year. The following account is based on interviews with Steven Woodside, James Dawson, and David Rosenfeld.

10. *Johnson* v. *Transportation Agency, Santa Clara County, California, and Service Employees International Union Local 715*, 748 F.2d 1308 (9th Cir. 1984).

11. When the circuits do act in this manner, different circuits will sometimes come to different rulings and interpretations of the law. When that happens, an appeal is usually taken to the Supreme Court to resolve differences among the circuits.

12. 682 F.2d 1275 (9th Cir. 1982).

13. *U.S. Postal Service Board of Governors* v. *Aikens*, 460 U.S. 711, 714 (1983). *Vel non* means "or not" and is used in situations where one must find that a certain condition did or did not exist.

14. Interview with Steven Woodside.

15. Wallace had claimed that Blackmun had said that *more* than an "arguable violation" of Title VII is required to support voluntary affirmative action, and Fletcher wrote that in fact Blackmun had endorsed the "arguable violation" standard as one narrower than that adopted by the plurality. 433 U.S. at 211.

16. The amended opinion is at 770 F.2d 752 (9th Cir. 1985).

17. While the district court decree had awarded Johnson his attorney's fees for the original suit and trial, he had to carry the cost of the appeal, while, as he put it, Diane Joyce had been getting a free ride with the county and the union arguing her case for her.

18. Interview with Paul Johnson, 15 April 1989.

19. See Louis J. Paper, *Brandeis* (Englewood Cliffs, N.J.: Prentice-Hall, 1983), Chapters 3–14, and Philippa Strum, *Louis D. Brandeis: Justice for the People* (Cambridge: Harvard University Press, 1984), Chapters 5–11.

20. See Mark V. Tushnet, *The NAACP's Legal Strategy against Segregated Education, 1925–1950* (Chapel Hill: University of North Carolina Press, 1987), 98*ff.*

21. *Wygant*; see pp. 108–110.

22. Interviews with Paul Johnson and James Dawson.

23. The "clock" starts to run when a court has had its final say in a case. Thus the thirty-day limit for appealing Judge Ingram's decision began not when he handed down his decree, but when he turned down the request for a new trial. The ninety-day period for appeal to the Supreme Court did not begin on December 4, 1984, when the panel issued its decision, but on September 5, 1985, when the Court of Appeals turned down the petition for a new hearing or a hearing *en banc*, and issued its revised opinion.

24. The best analysis of how cases are appealed and how the justices decide which cases to accept is David M. O'Brien, *Storm Center: The Supreme Court in American Politics* (New York: Norton, 1986), Chapter 4.

25. About 30 percent of the cases appealed to the Court come from state tribunals, and the rest come from federal courts.
26. For figures on the number of petitions received, certs granted, and cases argued for the 1986 through 1988 terms, see 58 L.W. 3144 (29 August 1989).
27. Each member of the Supreme Court also serves as circuit justice for one or more of the thirteen Courts of Appeals. This arrangement serves a number of purposes, both institutional and procedural. From an institutional point of view, the individual justice provides a two-way line of communication between the lower courts and the high bench. He or she will usually attend the annual conference of all the judges—both district and Court of Appeals—in a given circuit, hear the concerns they wish to relay up the line, and also pass down some information on certain matters. Procedurally, the circuit arrangement helps to funnel traffic for special appeals, such as requests for extensions of time in filing papers. (If an attorney cannot reach the appropriate justice, he or she may make the request of any other justice.) While the full court can override an individual justice, it is rare that it will do so in relatively trivial matters such as time extensions.
28. *Janowiak* v. *Corporate City of South Bend*, 750 F.2d 557 (7th Cir., 1984).
29. *Petition for Writ of Certiorari . . .* , 9–10.
30. Interview with Steven Woodside.
31. *Reply Brief for Respondent*, 3.
32. *Britton* v. *South Bend Community School Corp.*, 775 F.2d 794 (7th Cir. 1985).
33. *Petitioner's Reply Brief*.
34. Rodney A. Smolla, *Jerry Falwell v. Larry Flynt: The First Amendment on Trial* (New York: St. Martin's Press, 1988), 176.
35. 476 U.S. 267 (1986). The case had been argued on November 6, 1985, and a decision had been reached by the time the conference discussed Paul Johnson's case. The formal opinion, however, did not come down until May 19, 1986.

Notes to Chapter 6

1. Interview with Steven Woodside, 31 July 1989.
2. Provisions in the decree dealing specifically with the fire department paralleled a 1974 decree agreed to by the city in a broader employment suit filed by the Justice Department, and affecting all city employment.
3. *Firefighters Local Union No. 1784* v. *Stotts*, 467 U.S. 561 (1984). Justices O'Connor and Stevens concurred, while Blackmun, joined by Brennan and Marshall, dissented.
4. *New York Times*, 1 February 1985.
5. Charles Krauthammer, "In Defense of Quotas," *New Republic*, 16–23 September 1985.
6. *New York Times*, 13 June 1984.
7. *Id.*
8. Linda Greenhouse, "Bias Remedy vs. Seniority," *New York Times*, 14 June 1984.
9. Douglas F. Seaver, "Memphis Did Not Kill Affirmative Action," *New York Times*, 1 July 1984.

10. *New York Times*, 4 August 1984.
11. 14 June 1984.
12. "Assault on Affirmative Action," *Time*, 25 February 1985.
13. 478 U.S. 1014 (1986).
14. For an attack on the district court and Court of Appeals decisions that exposed serious logical inconsistencies, see Carl Cohen, "Naked Racial Preference," *Commentary*, March 1986.
15. *New York Times*, 21 and 26 May 1986. Reynolds's attack came as no surprise, since the Administration had been unsuccessfully trying to do away with the set-asides since it took office.
16. "High Court's Five-Way Verdict," *U.S. News & World Report*, 2 June 1986.
17. *New York Times*, 26 May 1986; *U.S. News & World Report*, 9 June 1986.
18. 478 U.S. 501 (1986).
19. *Local 28 Sheet Metal Workers* v. *EEOC*, 478 U.S. 421 (1986).
20. "A Solid Yes to Affirmative Action," *Time*, 14 July 1986.
21. "A 'Yes' for Affirmative Action," *Newsweek*, 14 July 1986. See also the comments in *Jet*, 21 July 1986.
22. "A Solid Yes . . . ," *Time*, 14 July 1986.
23. Stuart Taylor, Jr., "Mixed Opinions: The Supreme Court Works at Its Mandate," *New York Times*, 6 July 1986. In fact, the discrimination by the union had been so blatant that several Jewish groups, normally opposed to quotas, had joined civil rights groups in opposing the Reagan Administration in this case.
24. Daniel Seligman, "Dubious Distinctions," *Fortune*, 23 June 1986.
25. Although feminists wanted the Court to go further than it did in some of the sex discrimination cases, there is general agreement that the Burger Court, more so than any of its predecessors, took the question of gender equality seriously. See the article by Wendy M. Williams, "Sex Discrimination: Closing the Law's Gender Gap," in Herman Schwartz, ed., *The Burger Years: Rights and Wrongs in the Supreme Court, 1969–1986* (New York: Penguin, 1987).
26. *County of Washington* v. *Gunther*, 452 U.S. 161 (1981).
27. The issue here skirted dangerously close to the idea of "comparable worth," in which compensation would be based on the alleged "value" of the job, thus equalizing pay between jobs traditionally held by females and those similar in nature traditionally held by men. The Court avoided this hot potato, and made it clear it was deciding a much narrower procedural issue in this case.
28. Justice Rehnquist, joined by Burger, Stewart, and Powell, dissented on the grounds that Title VII clearly intended that there could be no claim of sex-based wage discrimination without proof of equal work.
29. 463 U.S. 1073 (1983). In the *per curiam* decision, Justices Marshall, Brennan, White, Stevens, and O'Connor agreed with all or part of the Court's main rulings. Justices Powell, Burger, Blackmun, and Rehnquist concurred in part and dissented in part.
30. *General Electric Co.* v. *Gilbert*, 429 U.S. 125 (1976).
31. *Newport News Shipbuilding & Dry Dock Company* v. *EEOC*, 462 U.S. 669 (1983); Justices Rehnquist and Powell dissented.
32. *Hishon* v. *King & Spalding*, 467 U.S. 69 (1984). The Court did not decide the

merits of Ms. Hishon's case, but only that she did have a right to sue a law firm under Title VII. Justice Powell entered a short concurrence emphasizing that the decision did not affect the management of a law firm by its partners, but only the relationship between the partnership and associates.

33. *Meritor Savings Bank* v. *Vinson*, 477 U.S. 57, 68 (1986).
34. "Closing the Law's Gender Gap," 115.

Notes to Chapter 7

1. Interview with Suzanne Wilson.
2. The case would eventually be argued the same day as *Johnson*, and the Court approved a quota program to add blacks to the Alabama Department of Public Safety in light of a record showing four decades of systematic racial exclusion. *United States* v. *Paradise*, 480 U.S. 149 (1987).
3. In fact, the county did keep trying to reach some agreement with Johnson right on up to the time the Supreme Court heard the case. By then, however, Johnson had received his monetary award, which the county did not try to recover after the Ninth Circuit decision, and after holding the job for a while, he had decided to retire. The county had very little it could offer to him to withdraw the appeal, and with Mountain States fighting the battle out of its pocket and not his, he had very little reason to back off.
4. Interview with Steven Woodside.
5. *Brown* v. *Board of Education*, 347 U.S. 483 (1954), overturning *Plessy* v. *Ferguson*, 163 U.S. 537 (1896).
6. *Gideon* v. *Wainwright*, 372 U.S. 335 (1963), reversing *Betts* v. *Brady*, 316 U.S. 455 (1942).
7. *Baker* v. *Carr*, 369 U.S. 186 (1962), and *Reynolds* v. *Sims*, 377 U.S. 533 (1964), departing from *Colgrove* v. *Green*, 328 U.S. 549 (1946).
8. The joint appendix for the *Johnson* case included docket entries for the district and appeals courts, the original complaint made by Johnson, the EEOC right-to-sue letter, the county's answer to the complaint, the joint pretrial statement, exhibits from the trial illustrating the county's notice of positions and its affirmative action plan, and an affidavit by Kristina Sermersheim.
9. The following section relies on the petitioner's brief submitted in Case No. 85–1129, *Johnson* v. *Transportation Agency, Santa Clara County California* and *Service Employees International Union, Local 715*. The brief lists Constance E. Brooks and Diane L. Vaksdal of Mountain States Legal Foundation, and James L. Dawson of Gruber & Dawson, with Brooks as counsel of record.
10. This section is based primarily on an interview with Constance E. Brooks, San Francisco, California, 2 August 1989.
11. *Brief of Respondent Transportation Agency* . . .
12. *Brief of Respondent Service Employees Union* . . .
13. A trial in which there is no jury, with the judge serving as the finder of fact.
14. In that case, *California Federal Savings & Loan* v. *Guerra*, 479 U.S. 272 (1987), the Court upheld a California law requiring employers to provide unpaid leave and then reinstatement to employees who became pregnant. The 6–3 majority ruled that Title VII did not preempt all state action, and that the states

remained free to go beyond the statute as well as the 1978 Pregnancy Discrimination Act to provide greater job protection to female workers.

15. Interviews with David Rosenfeld and Steven Woodside.
16. *Amicus* briefs cannot exceed thirty pages, and must be bound in green; they follow the same general format as those of the litigants.
17. David M. O'Brien, *Storm Center: The Supreme Court in American Politics* (New York: Norton, 1986), 207.
18. An excellent overview of the role and responsibilities of the solicitor general is Lincoln Caplan, *The Tenth Justice: The Solicitor General and the Rule of Law* (New York: Knopf, 1987).
19. O'Brien, *Storm Center*, 209.
20. This section, except where otherwise noted, is based on an interview with Charles Fried, Cambridge, Massachusetts, 12 May 1989.
21. Caplan, *The Tenth Justice*, 175–76.
22. See pp. 110–111.
23. Interview with Constance Brooks. Brooks also believed that it might help her case, and certainly would not hurt it, to have a woman argue Johnson's case, another reason to keep Fried out.
24. *Brief for the United States* . . . Neither Johnson (who had retired) nor Brooks wanted a new trial; they wanted to vindicate a principle. So did Fried, but after having been burned so badly the previous term, he would have settled for the implied victory of a remand.
25. Interviews with David Rosenfeld and Kristy Sermersheim.

Notes to Chapter 8

1. Interviews with Steven Woodside and Constance Brooks.
2. *Meritor Savings Bank* v. *Vinson*, 477 U.S. 57 (1986); see pp. 114–115.
3. O'Brien, *Storm Center*, 226.
4. See the discussion of oral argument in William H. Rehnquist, *The Supreme Court: How It Was, How It Is* (New York: Morrow, 1987), 271–85.
5. Bernard Schwartz, *Super Chief: Earl Warren and His Supreme Court* (New York: New York University Press, 1983), 306.
6. The following section is drawn almost entirely from the official transcript of the oral argument, deposited in the library of the U.S. Supreme Court. The transcript, however, does not identify the justices, other than the Chief Justice; identifications of the speakers, therefore, came from the oral tape made of the argument. I also had the benefit of discussing the oral argument in my interviews with Constance Brooks, Steven Woodside, and James Dawson.
7. The Court had held in previous cases that a particular employer could not use general societal bias as a basis for a preferential hiring plan, but had to show that it had discriminated against certain groups. Moreover, if a particular group believed, for whatever reason, that it would be foreclosed from certain types of work, even if no discriminatory barriers existed, an employer could not be held liable for such attitudes. Brooks's argument throughout was that while bias can account for statistical imbalances, there are other causes as well, and before an employer imposes a preferential plan based on imbalance,

the employer has to go through a process to determine if discrimination had been the villain, or other causes had been involved.

8. Interview with Kristy Sermersheim.
9. Interview with Suzanne Wilson.

Notes to Chapter 9

1. Rehnquist, *The Supreme Court*, 287–95.
2. The following material is based on Justice Brennan's file on the *Johnson* case, which he generously allowed me to examine.
3. Under *Wygant*, Brennan added, the burden of proving the constitutional invalidity of an affirmative action plan rests on the plaintiff, and that approach applied as well to Title VII cases.
4. Clerks have been almost as close-mouthed about their work as the justices. William Rehnquist talks, discreetly, about his experience as a clerk to Justice Robert H. Jackson in Chapter 10 of *The Supreme Court*. For a charming but equally discreet memoir of a year's clerkship in the Marble Palace, see J. Harvie Wilkinson III, *Serving Justice* (New York: Charterhouse, 1974).
5. Regan also had the responsibility for changes in all the subsequent drafts save one; Brennan did the final editing on the last iteration that then appeared as the Court's opinion.
6. *Hazelwood School District* v. *United States*, 433 U.S. 299 (1977).
7. Powell suggested the following paragraph be added:

Our decisions have made clear the method by which a "manifest imbalance" should be ascertained in order to justify the adoption of a voluntary affirmative action plan. A comparison of the percentage of minorities or women in the employer's work force with the percentage in the labor market—or in some circumstances even in the general population—may be appropriate to determine conspicuous underrepresentation in jobs that require no specialized training or experience. See *Weber, supra* (comparison between proportion of blacks working at plant and proportion of blacks in area labor force appropriate in calculating imbalance for purposes of establishing craft training programs); *Teamsters* v. *United States*, 431 U.S. 324 (1977) (comparison between percentage of blacks in employer's work force and in area general population proper in determining extent of imbalance in truck-driving positions). Where a job requires special expertise, however, the comparison should be with those in the labor force who possess the relevant qualifications. See *Hazelwood School District* v. *United States*, 433 U.S. 299 (1977) (must compare percentage of blacks in employer's work ranks with percentage of qualified black teachers in area labor force in determining underrepresentation in teaching positions). The requirement that the "manifest imbalance" relate to a "traditionally segregated job category" provides an additional assurance that the adoption of a voluntary affirmative action plan is based upon a bona fide remedial objective consistent with the purposes of Title VII.

8. This draft also had a few minor changes designed to support the argument that the county plan had responded to a real problem of discrimination, and had been narrowly tailored.
9. Kathleen M. Sullivan, "The Supreme Court—Comment, Sins of Discrimination: Last Term's Affirmative Action Cases," 100 *Harvard L.R.* 78, 96 (1986).
10. Stevens circulated a second draft, with minor changes, on December 23, 1986.

11. Four days later, on January 6, O'Connor circulated a second draft, incorporating stylistic changes only.

12. In the final, published iteration of his opinion, Brennan wrote (in footnote 7): "As one scholar has put it, 'When a court says to a legislature: "You (or your predecessor) meant X," it almost invites the legislature to answer: "We did not." ' G. Calabresi, A Common Law for the Age of Statutes 31–32 (1982). Any belief in the notion of a dialogue between the judiciary and the legislature must acknowledge that on occasion an invitation declined is as significant as one accepted."

13. *Mississippi University for Women* v. *Hogan*, 458 U.S. 718, 730 (1982).

14. Although both cases had been argued on November 12, work on the *Paradise* case had been completed earlier, and the decision handed down in mid-February.

15. White agreed with Parts I and II of Scalia's dissent, and while he did not join in Scalia's condemnation of the Court's previous affirmative action decisions, he indicated that he, too, would overrule *Weber*.

Notes to Chapter 10

1. *Washington Post*, 26 March 1987; "A Woman's Day in Court," *Newsweek*, 6 April 1987, 58; "Supreme Court Puts Mike in Diane Joyce's Hands," *People*, 13 April 1987, 53; interview with Diane Joyce.

2. Interview with Paul Johnson.

3. *Washington Post*, 26 March 1987; Paula Dwyer, "Affirmative Action: After the Debate, Opportunity," *Business Week*, 13 April 1987, 37. See also "Court Ruling Affirmative," *Black Enterprise*, July 1987, 20, for other comments from business officials.

4. *Washington Post*, 26 March 1987.

5. Articles in the law reviews tended to focus more on legal questions, but they essentially split along the lines of whether, under the law, one could legitimately favor a particular minority, or if Title VII forbade *all* discrimination. See G. Sidney Buchanan, "*Johnson* v. *Transportation Agency, Santa Clara County*: A Paradigm of Affirmative Action," 26 *Houston L.R.* 229 (1987), and Thomas J. Lonzo, "Note: *Johnson* v. *Transportation Agency*: Are We All Equal?" 21 *Creighton L.R.* 333 (1987).

6. Editorial, "Tribal Justice," *National Review*, 24 April 1987, 18; TRB, "Ladies' Day," *New Republic*, 20 April 1987, 4. See also Gerald F. Kreyche, "The New McCarthyism," *USA Today*, September 1987, 98.

7. Mary E. Becker, "Prince Charming: Abstract Equality, *1987 Supreme Court Review*, 201, 206.

8. Nancy Gertner, "*Bakke* on Affirmative Action for Women: Pedestal or Cage?" 14 *Harvard Civil Rights–Civil Liberties L.R.* 173 (1979).

9. Mary Ellen Gale, "Unfinished Women: The Supreme Court and the Incomplete Transformation of Women's Rights in the United States," 9 *Whittier L.R.* 445, 448 (1987).

10. See, for example, Kathryn A. Sampson, "Note: Negotiating a Slippery Slope: Voluntary Affirmative Action After *Johnson*," 14 *J. Corporate Law* 201 (1988).

11. These and other issues, are explored in Robert Belton, "Reflections on Af-

firmative Action After *Paradise* and *Johsnon*," 23 *Harvard Civil Rights—Civil Liberties L.R.* 115 (1988).
12. Interview with Paul Johnson.
13. *Watson* v. *Fort Worth Bank & Trust Co.*, 487 U.S. 977 (1988).
14. *Griggs* v. *Duke Power Company*, 401 U.S. 424 (1971).
15. *Wards Cove Packing Co.* v. *Antonio*, 109 S.Ct. 2115 (1989).
16. *Lorance* v. *AT&T Technologies, Inc.*, 109 S.Ct. 2261 (1989).
17. *Martin* v. *Wilks*, 109 S.Ct. 2180 (1989).
18. The ruling also reduced the effectiveness of class-action suits on behalf of minorities. Class actions were once a favorite weapon of civil rights activists, but the Court has narrowed their use, and as a result, the number of such suits has sunk from 1,174 in 1976 to less than 50 in 1988. Because many of these decisions involved statutory rather than constitutional interpretation, bills were introduced in Congress to overrule the Court. Both houses of Congress had passed versions of a 1990 Civil Rights Act as this book went to press.
19. 448 U.S. 448 (1980).
20. *Richmond, Va.* v. *J. A. Croson Co.*, 488 U.S. 469 (1989). For an evaluation of the case and its import, see Gary C. Leedes, "The Richmond Set-Aside Case: A Tougher Look at Affirmative Action," 36 *Wayne L.R.* 1 (1989).
21. *Time*, 6 February 1989. However, in *Metro Broadcasting Inc.* v. *FCC*, 58 U.S.L.W. 5053 (1990), a majority of the Court reaffirmed the federal government's power under the 5th and 14th Amendments to authorize minority set-aside programs.
22. *Time*, 26 June 1989.
23. *New York Times*, 5 June 1988.
24. *New York Times*, 20 March 1988.
25. Gerald David Jaynes and Robin M. Williams, Jr., eds., *A Common Destiny: Blacks and American Society* (Washington: National Research Council, 1989), quoted in *Time*, 7 August 1989.
26. Gary S. Becker, "Productivity Is the Best Affirmative Action Plan," *Business Week*, 27 April 1987, 18. Becker notes that where married women in the 1970s earned about 60 percent as much as men, single women earned 80 percent, because they stayed in jobs long enough to realize benefits of promotion and pay increases.
27. Susan Faludi, "Diane Joyce," *Ms.*, January 1988, 64; see also Sylvia A. Law, " 'Girls Can't Be Plumbers'—Affirmative Action for Women in Construction; Beyond Goals and Quotas," 24 *Harvard Civil Rights–Civil Liberties L.R.* 45 (1989).

Index

263

Currently professor of history and constitutional law at the Virginia Commonwealth University in Richmond, **Melvin I. Urofsky** has taught at Ohio State University, the State University of New York at Albany, and lectured abroad at the Hebrew University in Jerusalem and Tel-Aviv University. Dr. Urofsky holds his doctorate in history from Columbia University and his juris doctor from the University of Virginia. Over the years he has received grants and fellowships from the Mershon Foundation, the National Endowment for the Humanities and the American Council of Learned Societies, as well as other awards. Mr. Urofsky is also the author of, among other books, *A Mind of One's Own*, a biography of Justice Louis Brandeis.

He is married to Susan L. Urofsky and they have two sons, Philip and Robert.